MIDDLE TECH

PRINCETON STUDIES IN

CULTURE AND TECHNOLOGY

Princeton Studies in Culture and Technology

Tom Boellstorff and Bill Maurer, series editors

This series presents innovative work that extends classic ethnographic methods and questions into areas of pressing interest in technology and economics. It explores the varied ways new technologies combine with older technologies and cultural understandings to shape novel forms of subjectivity, embodiment, knowledge, place, and community. By doing so, the series demonstrates the relevance of anthropological inquiry to emerging forms of digital culture in the broadest sense.

For a full list of titles in the series, go to https://press.princeton.edu/series/princeton-studies-in-culture-and-technology.

Middle Tech

Software Work and the Culture of Good Enough

Paula Bialski

PRINCETON UNIVERSITY PRESS

PRINCETON AND OXFORD

Published by Princeton University Press
41 William Street, Princeton, New Jersey 08540
99 Banbury Road, Oxford OX2 6JX

press.princeton.edu

All Rights Reserved

ISBN 9780691257150
ISBN (pbk.) 9780691257167
ISBN (e-book) 9780691257174

British Library Cataloging-in-Publication Data is available

Editorial: Fred Appel and James Collier
Production Editorial: Jaden Young
Jacket/Cover Design: Benjamin Higgins
Production: Lauren Reese
Publicity: Paula Bialski
Copyeditor: Valerie Ahwee

This book has been composed in Adobe Text and Gotham

10 9 8 7 6 5 4 3 2 1

For Götz Bachmann

CONTENTS

ILLUSTRATIONS

ACKNOWLEDGMENTS

Stating that something is "good enough" is a by-product of straddling two or more worlds: negotiating care for one thing, one person, one practice, then pausing and shifting our care toward another. Not surprisingly, perhaps, this book is about one of the most intimate practices I experience in my life on a daily basis, a practice we can call "good enoughing." For the past fifteen years, I have been both a musician and author, living in two (or more) cities, and constantly having to say something is "good enough for now" in order to be able to leave it for a moment, switch hats, and shift into my other obligation. Now as a mother, I can safely say that every parent knows what I'm talking about: that moment when you say, "This will have to be good enough for now," because somebody needs you somewhere else. The following acknowledgments are dedicated to all the people who helped me negotiate good enoughness and who didn't mind all the compromises I made at one moment, knowing and believing I'd somehow care for them eventually down the line. Karol Strzemieczny and my other bandmates, in particular the band Paula & Karol, felt this while I was traveling to and from concerts from my university lectures in Poland and Germany or responding to e-mails during sound checks.

This project began with a friend named Ori. Although this book didn't turn out to be his life story (as we always joked it would), it's safe to say that without him, I wouldn't have made it to MiddleTech, and this book wouldn't have been written. Ori's humor, his care for communicating his technical experiences with me, and his general hunger for knowledge will always stay with me. At MiddleTech, my gratitude begins with Greg for letting me into his department the first year, as well as his entire front-end development team: Dariusz, Florentina, and Keith deserve thanks for all the hours drinking beers, playing cards, eating burgers, and practicing esoteric fortune-telling. I'd also like to thank Amira for her candidness, wisdom, and friendly nature, and Pedro for taking a chance on my weird ideas and blindly meeting me in a small English town to play strange experimental games. I would also like to express my gratitude to the team of Oleksei, Jelena, and Aseem for treating me as part of their development family. I would like to acknowledge Charlie for helping sort out my thoughts, joking with me, and being up for analyzing any situation with me, as well as Youssef for waking me up with his yerba maté breaks, algorithmic problems, and personal stories about his family. Moreover, I am grateful to Simon for all the hours and hours walking home with me, confiding in me, poking fun at me, laughing with me, and trusting me. This time was invaluable and helped me to gather and refine my thoughts. While much of the ethnographic energy that I spent on these developers spilled onto the pages of this book, the majority of my experiences, conversations, and realizations didn't actually fit here. As with most ethnographies, choosing what stories to put in and leave out became a very tough balancing act. Nevertheless, I'd like to thank everyone whom I spoke to, but whose experiences here were left unwritten.

Institutionally, the seeds of this work were already sown over ten years ago at Lancaster University, where I started to work in two research fields that greatly contributed to my thinking. There, I'd like to thank Monika Buscher, Lucy Suchman, and the late John Urry for impacting my work by building a kind and caring space for sharing and building my thoughts. Other colleagues-turned-friends (or vice versa) throughout the years whom I am indebted to include Dominik Batorski and Grzegorz Brzozowski at the University of Warsaw. I also spent a lot of time thinking with my Science and Technology Studies/History of Science crew, which include Thomas Turnbull and Jeremias Herberg, who also shaped my work with their feedback on a few versions of the manuscript, as well as our pandemic reading group Mace Ojala, Andreas Bischof and Jeremy Grosman. Jeremy, in particular, spent over one year reading my manuscript on a monthly basis, and his involvement was pivotal in finishing my first draft.

The majority of research for this book was financially and intellectually supported by my wonderful research community at the Digital Cultures Research Lab, the Center for Digital Cultures, and the Institute of Culture and Aesthetics of Digital Media at Leuphana University in Lüneburg, Germany. For more than seven years, over countless seminars, lectures, lunch hours, evening drinks, and train rides back to Hamburg, I received constructive and critical feedback from my dear colleagues Armin Beverungen, Lisa Conrad, Laura Hille, Mathias Denecke, Marcel Mars, Randi Heinrichs, Sascha Simons, Boris Traue, Florian Sprenger, Martina Leeker, Nishant Shah, Robert Rapoport, Timon Beyes, Jan Muggenburg, the late Wolfgang Hagen, and Goetz Bachmann. I am deeply grateful for their invaluable contributions to my work. Armin and Götz were particularly dedicated in reading manuscript drafts, helping me refine my ideas and approach. Wolfgang was an ally and sparring partner for years, and his sharp critique still somehow resonates throughout these pages.

I am also appreciative of Nina Wakeford, Joel McKim, Lilly Irani, Adam Fish, Ben Peters, Christopher Kelty, Fred Turner, and Gabriella Coleman for supporting me along the way, both during their fellowships at the Center for Digital Cultures in Lüneburg and beyond. Fred and Biella in particular helped me immensely during the publishing stage of this manuscript. I also would like to thank the Re-Configuring Anonymity research group, especially Michi Knecht at the Department of Anthropology and Cultural Research at the University of Bremen, for her methodological and moral support. Most of the initial fieldwork analysis was also done during my fellowship at the Kulturwissenschaftliches Kolleg at the University of Konstanz, for which I am also very grateful.

I would also like to acknowledge my closest colleagues at the University of St. Gallen, in particular Tanja Schneider, Veronica Barassi, and Insa Koch from the School of Humanities and Social Sciences; Johannes Schoening and Guido Salvaneschi from the School of Computer Science; and my research team, Julien McHardy and Daniela Weinmann, for rooting for me during the last phases of this process. My longtime friend Norah Franklin has also played a crucial role in professionally editing my drafts and motivating me until the end with her caring, thoughtful, and humorous approach to proofreading. The anonymous reviewers at Princeton University Press gave me overwhelmingly detailed editorial comments that had a tremendous effect on the past few drafts, and I'd like to thank them for going above and beyond their call of duty (wherever they are!). Although unusual in academic settings, my mother, Yaga Bialski, and my father, Alec Bialski, have also heard various versions of this book, and I'd like to thank them for their contributions and for listening to me, supporting me, and challenging my ideas. I'd finally like to thank my dear husband, Götz Bachmann, for all the wonderful ways he inspired me to think (which led to the concept of "good enough"), for motivating me to write and to keep writing, and for raising the bar of my understanding of what "good" and "enough" can be.

MIDDLE TECH

Introducing Good Enoughness

The notion of "good enough" is strange: often it means that we have given up on the desire to be great, or even excellent, and sorrowfully succumb to compromise. Even though the phrase "good enough" means that there is "enough goodness," and that things are generally fine, the phrase also evokes failure or giving up and embracing mediocrity. I bet you would quickly return this book to wherever it came from if on the back cover a reviewer wrote, "This book is not bad, not excellent, but just good enough." Or what if I told you that the software running in your car was good enough? Wouldn't that be slightly scary? Or what if a colleague or boss said that the job you were doing was good enough? "Good enoughness," a term I use throughout this book,[1] might have a pejorative ring to it. It connotes mediocrity, a failure to achieve more; it's something that we humans have learned *not* to desire. Yet this book offers another perspective on what "good enough" means by focusing on the regular, ordinary work of corporate software developers making regular, ordinary software, and on the complex decisions, everyday practices, hidden ethics, and implicit and explicit collective negotiations that make good-enough software possible. My point throughout this book is that achieving good enoughness is an incredibly complex and interesting endeavor.

---

1. I toyed with using the neologisms "good enoughing" or "good enoughness," yet chose the latter to stay consistent. Both are a bit awkward, but it was important for me to create a term that highlighted an unfolding and negotiated process. Throughout my book, "good enough" is less objective criteria, more a state, and for sure a practice. Both "good enoughing" and "good enoughness" could have worked.

The first moment I remember encountering good enoughness in my field was on a Friday afternoon during one of my first weeks of fieldwork at a company I call MiddleTech, a mapping and navigation software company in Berlin. It was getting close to 4 p.m., and happy hour was approaching. A few software developers were planning to meet up for beers across the street, and Marek (a front-end developer working on the Android navigation app) had not yet finished his code review. Much like any peer review, software developers have to review each other's code before submitting it to the main code base. It was getting late, and the other developers called to Marek: "Are you joining? Just give a +2 and come on!" They started laughing. Giving a +2 during code review meant giving the code a green light and integrating it into the working software system. A web developer on Marek's team later confessed that when he feels like leaving work and running off for a beer, he quickly goes through the code review system and just adds +2, +2, +2 to all the tickets waiting to be reviewed. Marek followed suit, and fifteen minutes later we were all sitting and sipping craft beer, enjoying the warm autumn Berlin weather.

The gesture of giving fellow developers a +2 in order to leave work was not done out of sloppiness, laziness, resistance, or protest, or at least not mainly so. Engineers care about the software they work on, and Marek was no exception. Marek was also not prone to political resistance against the demands of his labor process. Marek clicked on +2 that Friday afternoon because he knew his colleague's code was good enough. By clicking +2, he expressed an understanding that the code was good enough for now. Moreover, he knew that if anything went wrong, he would have the ability to come back and fix it later. Knowing when to stop and say something was good enough was not about not caring but about understanding the balance between care and compromise.

As my first encounter with good enough software culture unfolded before my eyes, it seemed counterintuitive, shattering my own stereotypes about what software production looked like. Weren't software developers supposed to be aiming for seamlessness and efficiency? It stood in stark contrast to the narratives I encountered earlier that summer, interviewing various technologists from the San Francisco Bay area—people at Facebook, the Wikimedia Organization, Mozilla, the Electronic Frontier Foundation, and a slew of entrepreneurs.

The Silicon Valley techies I encountered seemed to believe that technology had to be great, and that work on technology had to be hard and sweaty. I spoke with Eric, an older investor and entrepreneur in San Francisco whose long career was based on liaising between venture capitalists and programmers. During my discussion with him in San Francisco, he explained, "Coders do it just for their *art*. They want to sit and perfect their little babies. Coders sit over their laptops and want to develop until it's done. The harder the project, the better. If they code something that's outta this world, they will get recognized for it. And it's that recognition they're after. Like, 'Hey man, you did it, you're the shit.'"

While Eric might have been an extreme stereotype of somebody with Silicon Valley tech fever, many engineers I met that summer in Silicon Valley fit his description: They were driven by a similar narrative to change something in the world with technology, to do something difficult, and to strive for a sort of aesthetic excellence. What I found striking was the repetitive narrative that software developers were dedicated to working into the late hours perfecting something "outta this world." Software was not just patched together to run, occasionally break down, and be maintained; it was meant to run, disrupt, and innovate all in one go. Within this cloud of Silicon Valley hype, I never could have imagined that a software developer somewhere, on a Friday afternoon, would give another software developer a +2 in order to go out for beers with their friends.

My long-term fieldwork at MiddleTech helped me understand that the discourse and practice of making excellent software under a hyped work ethic are at odds with regular, run-of-the-mill corporate tech offices, where software and software work practices are about being good enough rather than excellent. The corporate tech office—both in Berlin and, as I will discuss, in Silicon Valley and beyond—propagates and maintains a state of good enoughness, despite discourses stating the contrary.

I spent an intensive six months (with additional field visits and interviews spanning two years) observing and at times participating in the work of software developers at a Berlin-based corporate software company that makes mapping, routing, and navigation software. This research focused on the software developers and their managers in both the front-end and back-end routing and navigation teams. During my fieldwork there, I worked among hundreds of people.[2] On a daily basis, I would discover new people, new conversations, new departments, and new projects, all of which would send me down another interesting research path. I recorded these stories in

---

2. In this book you'll notice that I often describe the field by directly quoting various interlocutors. It is worth noting that the conversations I reference from MiddleTech were not audio recorded but taken from my field notes in which I paraphrased the discussions with my interlocutors.

my field diaries, both on paper and digitally, during my fieldwork and after I left the office. The latter helped me blend in with the people I sat next to: while hunched over typing away on my laptop, I was at times mistaken for a new programmer on the team. I concluded that at MiddleTech, software is an ephemeral object that needs to be only good enough to function until the next update. The people working on it are well aware of this fact and often don't feel too pressured to perform perfectly during the first, second, or even third iterations. As a consequence, software can never be great but is instead just, well, good enough.

Drawn directly from my observations in the field, this book joins recent efforts to complicate the discourse that software is seamless and awesome (and not just good enough), and that the corporate software worker needs to be driven to achieve excellence. As we have witnessed throughout the past, technology breaks: staff cutbacks cause media platforms to break,[3] in-car GPS systems cause catastrophic incidents (Lin et al. 2017), and chatbots "tell lies and act weird."[4] The stories we hear in popular media shape our understanding of digital technology as either a technosolutionist savior, a mediocre disaster, or a robot-apocalyptic nightmare. As many ethnographies hope to do, this book provides a more complicated, less sensationalist, empirical story of why software can't be perfect. My time at MiddleTech helped me highlight how the ethics of practice prevalent in corporate software cultures encourages a state of being good enough, where something (like software) or someone (like a software developer) needs to be only sufficiently competent to operate. As I will show throughout this book, good enoughness is an inevitable part of software culture that contrasts with the popular understandings of how software is built and what software is. Defining good enough is collectively negotiated in resistance to managerial ideology while fluctuating between care and compromise for what, with, and for whom one is building software. It is an aspect of German software culture but is also present in larger, aging corporate software companies globally, and it might be inherent in all software development.

3. Ryan Mac, Mike Isaac, and Kate Conger, "'Sometimes Things Break': Twitter Outages Are on the Rise," *New York Times*, Feb. 28, 2023, https://www.nytimes.com/2023/02/28/technology /twitter-outages-elon-musk.html.

4. Cade Metz, "Why Do A.I. Chatbots Tell Lies and Act Weird? Look in the Mirror," *New York Times*, Feb. 26, 2023, https://www.nytimes.com/2023/02/26/technology/ai-chatbot-information -truth.html.

Studying Software Developers

Before I dive into this book's central argument, I'd like to explain the origin of the thinking behind my book. My exploration of the culture of good enoughness first began as a quest to understand the fluctuating relationship between the production of technology and society. My research started by asking how "the society we live in affects the kind of technology we produce" (MacKenzie and Wajcman 1985, 2) and turned to the producers, designers, and programmers of technology and those who managed them. Focusing on the producers of technology, rather than the users, was not as self-evident as it might seem. Following a tradition of science and technology studies scholars, I ethnographically focused on an overlooked group of engineers rather than on the simplistic narrative of the lone-wolf innovator (Haigh and Priestley 2015).

MiddleTech was always meant to be an ethnography about how a collective group of people collaborate, communicate, care, and compromise in order to make software work. By getting to know their work hierarchies, their forms of interaction, and the micropolitics of their profession, I encountered the programmers' social world. As I will illustrate throughout the next chapters, good-enough software is achieved through collective software practices, where programmers learn the process of programming something in a good-enough way, which is part of their sense of belonging and engagement in their sociotechnical worlds. Negotiating what is good enough or not—through discussions, jokes, fights, and other practices—is an important part of the collective practice of corporate programming.

My research resonated with maintenance and repair research, which focuses on the programmer and those conducting the maintenance and repair. As Lee Vinsel and Andrew L. Russell (2018) reminded us, life with technology is usually far removed from the cutting edges of invention and innovation and is instead devoted to keeping things the same. Drawing on these researchers and their tropes, *MiddleTech* starts with an interest in the programmer: interest in the human condition of being engaged with the craft of programming, their relationship to their machine, and the way their work and their profession are negotiated within their community.

MiddleTech also became an empirical description of the material constraints of software work, where software cannot be perfect in practice due to certain forms of complexity in software production. Throughout the following chapters, I describe how old code, software's constant cycle of being updated, its architecture, and how it is designed and by whom all contribute to the material complexity of software. As Marisa Leavitt Cohn (2016) has highlighted, our software and our software companies are aging. As our software ages, our software projects become more and more complex, evolving into multilayered beasts, "polluted" by programs, reports, files, or data that lose their purpose over time (Visaggio 2001). Much of the software we use today is built on years and years of effort by software developers who have managed to patch together a project to make it work. As our societies continue to strive for smarter systems (Halpern and Mitchell 2023) and better solutions to our problems, it is crucial to understand the faults in the technologies we so trust. Software's increasing complexity and age also challenge the relations between programmers, managers and their programmers, programmers and their code, and various other actors involved in the entire process. The moments when these actors have to negotiate care and compromise are also a crucial part of the story of our technological societies, and understanding this can help us as users, customers, and creators grasp the tricky materiality of software: that the tools we use are sometimes based on forgotten updates, lost pieces of code, and scrapped software projects, which, among other issues and mishaps, contribute to merely good-enough software.

Lastly, this book looks at the environment in which these material software practices unfold. In particular, I became interested in how corporate culture is shaped and reinvented (Kunda 1992) in the tech sector, both top-down through managerial discourse and bottom-up via the practices of engineers. My analysis zooms out to the corporate, organizational level, where understanding the power dynamics, work processes, and management dynamics within a corporate setting becomes central to understanding the culture of good enoughness—both how it is counterintuitive to various corporate narratives and rituals, and how it becomes negotiated on a day-to-day basis. We will witness the contrasting and chaotic priorities and understandings between designers, managers, and programmers working on the same product, which has been also observed in other ethnographies of software cultures.

While these other ethnographies look at how race and class are negotiated in corporate software settings (Amrute 2016) and how programmer work is organized (O'Donnell 2014), this book's specificity lies in its ethnographic account of the work cultures within older, aging companies. In the past decade, increasingly digitized Western societies have had an abundant need for programming work. Additionally, as tech companies grow bigger and become more established and embedded within our society, they are here to stay—meaning they are growing older, adding a level of complexity to the code being worked on and produced. Taking into account that software is an "object subject to continuous change and lived with over time as it evolves" (Leavitt Cohn 2019, 423), one that does not sit still "long enough to be easily assigned to conventional explanatory categories" (Mackenzie 2006, 18), *MiddleTech* zooms in on a work culture within a growing and aging software industry and aims to give a more nuanced understanding of digital media as inherently made up of these mishaps and compromises, bugs and breakdowns, and wonky, half-baked, good-enough work and good-enough software. Thus, to understand good-enough culture, understanding the material agency of software is important, specifically in relation to how corporate software is still produced, repaired, and maintained.

Not Bad, Not Excellent

The notion of "good enough" in this book contradicts and complicates the discourses and normative orders of excellence and improvement that permeate the tech world and shows that there is a distinction between discourse (which includes metrics and management methods) and the everyday practices of software developers. Throughout the following chapters, we will witness how workers reject notions of excellence *in practice*, but I'd like to highlight that a hegemonic excellence discourse does exist *in theory*. Corporate software companies, like many corporate environments, propagate an ideology of excellence and improvement, both in relation to the software product they are building and regarding the type of work that goes into building a software product. But where do these normative discourses of excellence originate?

One of the best places to search for the roots of the narratives of excellence, perfection, and 100 percent–ness is management literature. Written for managers, usually by more successful managers or management scholars, these books and journals show what types of narratives permeate corporate culture. At MiddleTech, it was quite common to find this sort of management literature lying on a desk or tucked away on a bookshelf in the company library. For example, the *Harvard Business Review*, a key publication for managers and management scholars, is full of case studies in which clear "performance expectations" are set by managers and team members, "performance measures" are delineated by said managers, and finally, the goal of achieving "performance excellence" is (hopefully) met by the given team. The *Harvard Business Review* and other similar industry journals are full of tips on how to foster or scale up a "culture of excellence" in the fastest way possible.[5] This type of rhetoric can also be found throughout management handbooks, one of the most prominent being Thomas J. Peters and Robert H. Waterman's *In Search of Excellence: Lessons from America's Best Run-Companies*, which despite having been written in the early 1980s, is still used today to help managers achieve "productivity through people" in order to become a "learning organization" (1982, 111) that experiments with and tries new things while striving to be the best.

More recently, Robert Sutton and Hayagreeva Rao (Stanford professors of Management Science and Organizational Behavior and Human Resources, respectively) promised to show managers "what it takes to build and uncover pockets of exemplary performance, spread those splendid deeds, and as an organization grows bigger and older—rather than slipping toward mediocrity or worse—recharge it with better ways of doing the work at hand" (2014, 20). In their book *Scaling Up Excellence: Getting to More Without Settling for Less*, "driving towards mediocrity" is seen as the first step to downfall, and Sutton and Rao are here to help companies foster a "relentless restlessness" that helps them constantly innovate (20).

As Paul du Gay explained, "Excellence in management theory is an attempt to redefine and reconstruct the economic and cultural terrain, and to win social subjects to a new conception of themselves—to 'turn them into winners,' 'champions,' and 'everyday heroes'" (1991, 53–54). This is done through a new form of management that emphasizes good corporate culture that can foster these "winners" and "heroes." Corporate culturalism, in its central argument, strives for an expanded practical autonomy of the worker. Yet as Hugh Willmott has pointed out, it aspires to "extend management control by colonizing the affective domain. It does this by promoting employee commitment to a monolithic structure of feeling and thought, a development that is seen to be incipiently totalitarian" (1993, 517). As I will show in the following chapters, engaging in good enoughness can thus be the software workers' way of regaining power over their "affective domain,"

---

5. See, for example, Tony Gambill, "A Leader's Challenge: Developing Teams That Have Strong Relationships and Excellent Results," *Forbes*, Sept. 14, 2022, https://www.forbes.com/sites /tonygambill/2022/09/14/a-leaders-challenge-developing-teams-that-have-strong-relationships -and-excellent-results/?sh=37d953766bb5, or Jeanine Murphy and Michael Sioufas, "How Agile Teams Can Pursue Technical Excellence," *McKinsey Quarterly*, Feb. 2, 2022, https://www .mckinsey.com/capabilities/mckinsey-digital/our-insights/tech-forward/how-agile-teams-can -pursue-technical-excellence.

rejecting the notion of excellence and settling for a software product and a way of working that's just good enough.

In my specific field at MiddleTech, I first noticed that when building critical software like routing and navigation infrastructure, corporate software developers work under the orders of managers who strive to build software that meets particular requirements and safety standards in order to gain certain levels of certification. These standards and certifications help order the world of software developers, their manager, and their customer (Bowker and Star 2000): it communicates to customers that the product (in this case software) they are using is seamless. At MiddleTech, software product managers gained certification from the International Organization for Standardization (ISO), a nongovernmental standards board that sets out various types of standards certificates for corporate software companies, including "quality management standards" and "IT security standards" among many others. In order to gain these certifications, products had to meet certain safety criteria or achieve certain metrics. Managers would meet these metrics by incorporating discourses and methods of working that would strive for perfection, particularly during the months leading up to a certification audit. Thus, to achieve seamlessness or these "great metrics," the office had to have a work discourse of excellence. In practice, developers negotiate what is good-enough work in order to meet these standards and metrics (or get away with not meeting them), but excellence is something managers still push as the overarching narrative to legitimize their own position and the ways of working around the office.

An Ideology of Improvement

Beyond the notion of excellence, another normative discourse that circulates around the corporate software office is the concept of improvement. If we accept that the update is a defining characteristic of software work culture, then we can also imagine that the notion of continuous improvement is essential to how programmers work. Each update carries the implication that developers can and should continuously iterate and improve on their product. That said, the ideology of improvement can be found everywhere in software work, materialized in the tools and methods that managers use to make software teams work better together and individual programmers code better. With hundreds of moving parts and dozens of teams of software developers carrying out work that their managers often do not understand, corporate software development processes have fostered cultures, rituals, and forms of organization that get a product delivered, create accountability, and stabilize continuous improvement. One particular method is called "Agile", one iteration of which is called "Scrum," where software developers are meant to work in "sprints," two-week stretches devoted to particular tasks, which are broken down on Post-it notes on a whiteboard. In this method, the head of the development team reports on progress using software that includes a dashboard indicating the state of every project. "The manager could also show a graph of the team's 'velocity,' the rate at which the developers finished their tasks, complete with historical comparisons and projections" (Posner 2022). Developers also engage in a daily ritual called the stand-up, where they all stand around in a circle and take turns explaining how their work is progressing or how they are improving on each task.

This methodology emphasizes a culture of improvement, where discussions in team meetings, company meetings, and one-on-one manager-to-programmer and programmer-to-programmer meetings are often focused on how to improve something: how to improve a work process, how to improve communication, how to improve a piece of software, or how to optimize (improve!) an algorithm. The notion of improvement is woven through everything.

Additionally, in a company like MiddleTech, the velocity of improvement is quantified and measured using something called a KPI or key performance indicator. This performance indicator is not specific to software companies in particular (those who have worked in any other corporate environment have probably come across the term). As the metric is quite broad, a KPI has to be defined within each industry, based on something that a management team can track. In the past decades of software production, managers have attempted to track certain practices of the software developer's work, such as the number of lines of code a developer committed or entered into the system, or the number of features completed on a certain day (the more, of course, the better). Managers have also turned to software itself to measure KPIs by looking at the number of bugs in a software system or the code simplicity, meaning the number of independent paths code must take to run a piece of software (the fewer the better).

Progress is thus characterized by a distinct normativity of numbers (Anders 2015), meaning the use of numbers as norms for measuring a company's progress in fixing bugs, implementing innovative solutions, and introducing systems like the KPI or various company software tools to collect and process numbers in a standardized fashion. Numbers like KPIs are essentially about projecting power and coordinating activity (Porter 1995, 44). In bureaucratic business corporations like MiddleTech, "quantification is simultaneously a means of planning and of prediction" (43), and there is great pressure for workers and their managers to conform to ever-increasing demands for "greater workplace productivity and enhanced efficiency modulated by computational systems that manage KPIs" (Rossiter 2016, 18). In other words, developers are being increasingly pushed into productivity by software-driven metrics, where KPIs and the real-time measurement of labor imply a constant acceleration described in terms of improved productivity. More specifically, the belief in the neutrality of certain metrics and measurements helps to enforce the corporate ideology that the software team and the software product can continuously improve and actually achieve excellence.

Excellence and Improvement and Reality

I discovered throughout my fieldwork that while these metrics, methods, and modes of excellence and improvement are present in the MiddleTech office culture, the reality is different. On a discursive level, corporate software environments can be understood as factories of so-called technological acceleration (Wajcman 2014, 16), where technology is constantly updated to improve and strive for excellence. Yet in the everyday, often mundane reality, software developers are more informed by good-enough principles and practices.

   Good enoughness implies settling for the here and now, as opposed to accelerating forward to achieve something better. While in theory, an old software version is always being updated and improved, a software developer's practical tasks at the workplace don't necessarily have to be oriented toward improvement or some form of innovation. For example, a piece of navigation software that is shipped today might be full of bugs that slow down users. But the good-enough developer's tasks are often self-defined. One update might fix just two bugs instead of the imagined fifty. While cleaning up these few bugs might give users a more seamless experience, it can also cause other bugs to appear and other slowdowns to occur. Thus, while on a discursive level, managers and software workers may speak of accelerated improvement and innovation, in practice their relationship to this innovation and constant improvement can be quite ambivalent. Improvement doesn't always mean peak innovation and can instead be just good enough. This example also shows us that what is good-enough work is also a matter of subjective estimation, normally arrived at by the developers who hold a more intimate knowledge of the code than their managers or the customers they work for.

The normative orders of excellence and the ideology of continuous improvement are strong forces driving the software industry and its socio-technical culture. This company ideology is something that is reproduced in day-to-day, face-to-face discussions, in meetings, conferences, and coffee breaks (Wittel 1997). Yet these ideologies are not necessarily something that everyone in the corporate software office believes in (Wittel 1997). While excellence and continuous improvement may permeate the office discourse, I observed that often neither software workers nor their managers really believe in the importance of excellence nor in the ability to continuously improve. For a particular ideology to survive, it is not essential that people actively support or believe in it. As Renata Salecl stated, "the crucial thing is that people do not express their disbelief. For them to abide by the majority opinion, all that matters is that they believe it to be true that most of the people around them believe. Ideologies thus thrive on 'belief in the belief of others'" (Salecl 2011, 10). What she means here is that people often do not believe in something but pretend to in order to avoid offending those who might believe in it.

Something similar in our context of software development is described in Frederick Brooks's *The Mythical Man-Month*. In his seminal text on software production methodology, Brooks (1975) explained that software development teams, particularly their managers, repeatedly plan for software projects to go well and be finished on schedule, when in reality projects are full of bugs and are always delayed. Brooks says that programmers hold beliefs or assumptions that "all will go well" or "that each task will take only as long as it 'ought' to take" (14), while in reality they often settle for good enough. As you will see in this book, when you candidly ask a manager or a developer if they really believe that a project will be finished on time, or if a piece of software will work seamlessly, they will emphatically say "no."

At MiddleTech, most developers and managers would openly (in meetings or job interviews, for example) express their belief in excellence, technological innovation, or the efficiency of production, while in reality, they practiced the opposite, meaning the work ethic and software ethic of good enough. Good enoughness, therefore, becomes an emergent cultural practice that happens in practice, juxtaposed to its more dominant other. These "others," which will reappear throughout this book, are excellence, technological innovation, and the efficiency of production.

Good Enoughness

The concept of good-enough software production is not one I coined myself but rather found in the field during conversations among developers at MiddleTech, in online hacker forums, or in software engineering literature. In their article "How Good Is Enough: An Ethical Analysis of Software Construction and Use," W. Robert Collins and his coauthors suggest that the software industry should "encourage reasonable expectations about software capabilities and limitations" (1994, 89), both among users and producers of software. This call to be "reasonable," as Collins and his colleagues explain, is about understanding "how good is good enough," a responsibility of the software provider or the programmers and their team. The term "good-enough software" highlights that perfect software for a complex system cannot be guaranteed in practice (Collins et al. 1994); thus, releasing software to the public will always be done under a good-enough principle, and will include some level of failure (Pelizza and Hoppe 2018). Good-enough software is, as Collins and colleagues explain, a principle that understands that every piece of new software can be assumed to contain errors, even after thousands or millions of executions.

In the mid-1990s, the concept of good-enough software was "getting a lot of attention" (Yourdon 1995, 78) in order to counteract the "we'll deliver high-quality, bug-free software on time" battle cry (78) that was sweeping the industry. In his short article in *IEEE Software* magazine, Yourdon explained that software engineers were shifting from working on proprietary, one-of-a-kind systems, developed according to schedules measured in years and funded by budgets measured in millions to software as a cheap commodity that can be made and reproduced relatively quickly. In other words, instead of making software for a shrink-wrapped CD to slip into our PC, the dawn of the internet brought programmers cloud computing and the ability to iteratively change the software in our fridges, phones, and desktops. Instead of perfecting and preserving a piece of software for eternity, the update became like a lifeboat or an eraser, enabling developers to fix their work at any time. In essence, the update gave the software developer the ability to settle for something good enough for now, only to be fixed later, which, as Yourdon explained, began "to challenge some of our basic assumptions about software development" (78).

Aside from software development, the good-enough principle has been used in psychoanalysis, pediatrics, urban studies, design, philosophy, biology, economics, and more popular self-help books. For example, using the concept of the "good enough mother," the British psychoanalyst Donald Winnicott describes the caregiver who settles for "good enough parenting": recognizing the fragility of a baby but failing at meeting all of the infant's demands and one's own standards of the perfect mother. Through this failure, mothers allow their babies to find their own way of doing things (see Winnicott 1987 or Doane and Hodges 1992). The concept has also been taken up in medicine (Ratnapalan and Batty 2009), where practitioners argue that excellence in medicine can be achieved by ensuring results that are good enough rather than by aiming for perfection, or in psychological research methods, where researchers set standards that indicate what kinds of experimental outcomes are good enough (Serlin and Lapsley 1985).

In economics and organization theory, Herbert Simon coined the term "satisficing" to describe the decision-making process whereby individuals or organizations seek a satisfactory solution rather than an optimal one. Similar to good enough, satisficing is when people choose the first option that meets their minimum criteria for acceptability, rather than continuing to search for the best possible option. Simon argued that satisficing is a practical and efficient approach to decision-making as it allows individuals and organizations to conserve resources and make decisions quickly. He contrasted this approach with the idea of optimizing, which maximizes the benefits of a decision but can be time-consuming and requires extensive information and analysis: "Evidently, organisms adapt well enough to 'satisfice'; they do not, in general, 'optimize'" (Simon 1956, 136).

This approach also resonates with wider discussions around the prevalence of good enough in both biology and culture, where the evolution of many species on Earth was not optimal as Darwin believed, but they survived anyway in a good-enough state (Milo 2019). Other scholars called for society to embrace the "good-enough life" as a state that understands what "goodness" and "enoughness" mean (Alpert 2022). Alpert in particular links good enough to the human need to change our relationship with nature and ecology. He calls for a reduction in our production and consumption in order to live more in harmony with nature, building our "good-enough life within these good-enough conditions" (5). This plea for restraint and reduction goes hand-in-hand with notions around the "good enough job" (Stolzoff 2023), or the "smart enough city" (Green 2020), where "enough" means rolling back our need for acceleration and overproduction in our optimization-centric jobs or urban planning endeavors and "limiting growth" (Meadows et al. 1972). Here, being good enough can also be connoted with mediocrity, which, as Groth (2019a, 2019b, 2020a, 2020 b) highlighted, is increasingly becoming a positive point of reference in different fields of practice. Keeping up with the midfield, earning a middle-range income, or being part of the middle class are powerful models for socioeconomic behavior and lifeworld interpretations (Groth 2019a).

Two Good Enoughs

As we can see, the notion of good enough has been used in various fields, including in organization studies and computer science (where this book is situated more closely). Rather than merely demonstrating that good enoughness exists, what I hope to highlight throughout these next chapters are the cultural aspects of good enoughness in practice. Over the course of my ethnographic observations, I noticed that two specific kinds of "good enoughs" emerged from my field, somewhat related but different at the same time. The first type of good enoughness addressed in this book relates to software itself. Software is a material product destined to be just good enough. Contrary to the seamless save-the-world technology promised in YouTube clips from product demos touted by CEOs like Elon Musk, Steve Jobs, or Mark Zuckerberg, software isn't all that it's cut out to be. When we look into software's constitution and how it's built and maintained, we see that at its core, it will always be merely good enough. Software is complex and made up of hundreds of lines of code that are constantly changing, constantly in flux. Due to this complexity, the people who work on software can never understand it in its entirety, which also makes these projects hard to manage, and as Brooks (1995) explained, they are hard to estimate in terms of scope and duration of completion. As I will describe in later chapters, managers refrain from micromanaging a project on a technical level but still implement various strategies to maintain control of a project's completion time. Developers also often give up on achieving what they promised and settle for a good-enough project in a good-enough time frame.

Another issue with software, as Brooks explains, is that it functions on a logic of constant improvement: nobody gets it right the first time, and often "one has to build a system to throw away, for even the best planning is not so omniscient as to get it right the first time" (1975, 116). In programming, for example, programmers iterate a project by building one version, only to improve upon it in a second version, only to improve upon this in a third version, and so on. This means that no software project is ever complete, with each version being just good enough for the time being, to be improved upon in the following version.

The second type of good enough is good enoughness in corporate software work. After a few years of studying how corporate software developers build a seemingly boring everyday software product, I noticed that contrary to corporate discourses of efficiency, productivity, and meritocracy that permeate the corporate office, workers, most of the time, are doing work that's good enough and are happy with jobs that are good enough.

The two types of good enoughs do not function separately but co-inform each other: the good-enough worker in good-enough work conditions makes good-enough software. We can also flip this relationship around: if software has limitations to what it can do (be merely good enough), then a worker will settle for doing a good-enough job and come to work with a good-enough work ethic.

While good enoughness might superficially function in the excellence and efficiency discourse as something subpar or even as a failure, it can be embraced and accepted as something "okay." Good enoughness is about being pragmatic or realistic about the amount of work developers want to put into their projects and about the limitations of what a piece of software can do.

That said, good enoughness—particularly in terms of a good-enough work practice—can often be achieved only from a position of worker and company privilege. The worker who gets away with doing a good-enough job is a privileged worker. Good-enough jobs are sought after and coveted and often flourish in a culture that provides safe working environments. Not many software developers in an outsourced coding farm in Krakow or Bangalore, working to meet deadlines and concerned about their job security, would be able to work in a good-enough job (see Amrute 2016, 103). The same can be said for software. Only companies that were successful at building a software asset—meaning a product that continuously makes money—can settle into being good enough. Large old tech companies like Google or Facebook or even MiddleTech have certain assets (the search algorithm, the advertising infrastructure, the mapping engine) that they created years ago but still generate profit. Because they were eager, driven, and efficient years ago, these companies now have assets that give them the financial stability to be good enough in the present. A small start-up wanting to burst out into the tech scene and get noticed can't hire good enough workers and expect to financially survive. I'll discuss this dynamic in more detail in the next chapter but mention it briefly now to illustrate the "privilege of good enough." Being a good-enough company like MiddleTech means also supporting an inequality in work speeds and demands, allowing some people to sit back and opt out of hyperproductivity while cruising on the unrecognized labor of other software developers and service workers.

This book is about a specific type of software worker in a certain kind of software company. MiddleTech is a specific type of company—one that sits on a certain software asset that allows it to be continuously relevant in a global software market. The company has a decades-old technology that is still embedded in various networks of software devices. Both the age and scope of MiddleTech are important for understanding how good enoughness emerges and becomes stabilized in such a company's culture.

Book Structure

This book's specific case study at MiddleTech brings to the fore a central mechanism in all software engineering, whether in Bangalore, Berlin, or Silicon Valley: that software is always merely good enough, in particular in companies sitting on older, still-valuable software assets. Like software's different layers of abstraction, this book is also structured in layers. Each chapter brings the reader into a different layer of abstraction that contributes to the larger picture of how good-enough software is made and good-enough work cultures are constituted. I begin with how programmers relate to their software, then move on to those who build software, and finally to the levels of management and organization that influence them.

Each of the following chapters addresses good enoughness in its own way and is structured around stories from my field. I take ethnographic storytelling seriously as I believe "stories display, juxtapose, figure, guide, and enliven in ways that philosophical concepts or abstract procedures cannot" (Kelty 2019, 4). While stories are too often dismissed as "'illustration" or 'evocation,' as if they lacked the (masculine) rigor of the 'concept' or the 'procedure'; stories . . . are the space of emotion and affect—too often demoted in power as something incidental, soft, solipsistic, not academic, or inadequately precise for thinking" (4). The first chapters will be largely based on the stories I encountered in my field, and the final chapter will be mainly analytical, focusing on the practices and figurations we encountered at MiddleTech.

In chapter 1, "Welcome to MiddleTech," I introduce the company, what makes it distinct but also similar to other "Medium Tech" software companies, and how this particular corporate software environment is the ideal site where good enoughness takes root and flourishes. I situate MiddleTech within the global software industry and show how its workers self-consciously define themselves in opposition to Silicon Valley discourses, particularly through how they work. I highlight the many similarities between what I call Medium Tech and Big Tech companies, particularly in how programming work is defined, how management is organized, and how various management methodologies are implemented. I also explain how good enoughness flourishes in older companies (both Medium Tech and Big Tech) because their software is still embedded in various social and technical infrastructures currently in use—and making money—today. This dependency on an older asset turns the focus of a Medium Tech company to maintenance and repair rather than "disruptive" innovation.

Once we get a picture of the way in which MiddleTech is situated in the software industry, I'll focus on the software developers and their relationship with their community and technical objects. In chapter 2, "Software's Sociality," we get to know Ori, the Java developer-turned-lead software engineer, who helps readers imagine the type of care and compromise that programmers must constantly negotiate when building software. This is where the reader first encounters good enough at work. I explore the craft of working on software, showing how it requires the knowledge of the inner workings of a software system, experiencing moments of "closeness to the machine" (Ullman 1997, 40) and zoning in to a software environment to find a sense of flow in one's work. These ideal forms of care are often disrupted by various social and technical factors, and developers are forced to compromise and settle for something that's merely good enough for a customer to use. Describing software's sociality from the get-go is important as it helps the reader understand what is at stake and what kind of care and compromise programmers have to negotiate with their managers and customers when building software.

Focusing on yet another layer of abstraction, I bring us deeper into the social and technical conflicts that arise when working on software. Chapter 3, "Where Stuff Goes Wrong" builds on the understanding that software is a social object and paints a picture of the chaos, conflict, and misunderstanding that software inherently holds. I will show how conflict and controversy are inherent and inescapable in the software development process and an important part of understanding software development culture. I also frame the software company as a sort of "organized anarchy" (Cohen, March, and Olsen 1972), where the company's purpose or what it's working on becomes unclear for those working within it. To connect us to my central concept of good enough, I show that when stuff goes wrong, software is shipped to its customers in a state of good enoughness. While it may seem that stuff goes wrong in any company, the difference with software lies in the rapid speed of change within the software industry, which is rooted in software update culture. The constant drive to update, fix, and innovate software means that it quickly becomes obsolete, and how it is programmed does too. This speed of change during software development challenges the stability of the knowledge of the people involved. These heterogeneous forms of knowledge result in processes of explanation and translation. Through explanation and translation between software developers, their code, managers, and customers, misunderstandings happen, and software development plans fall through the gaps between states of knowing and not knowing. Chapter 3 will also explain the different roles in programming, the nature of the customer-programmer relationship, as well as the role of management in organizing software work.

After describing how good enoughness is fostered through programming practices on an individual as well as collective level, I will introduce the processes of production and management in software development. Chapter 4, "Managing Good Enoughness," highlights how good enoughness in software work and the product results from the politics behind its development—both the macropolitics from the perspective of the software industry and the micropolitics from the perspective of the developer.

As Gideon Kunda showed, managerial ideology and managerial action designed to impose a role on individuals are normative demands that play out differently in action (1992, 21). To illustrate this, chapter 4 will outline the tensions among developers, their managers, and their machines, as well as how power and control are exerted, performed, and achieved when building software. While these forms of politics and power might be similar to those in other large corporations, my ethnographic descriptions underline the specificities of corporate software development, as well as the way in which power and politics influence how software is built, deployed, and how robust it becomes. Moreover, I also ethnographically show that software's materiality shapes the way in which programmers, managers, and customers interact with one another.

Chapter 4 also describes the deep tension between managers, who need to quantify their developers' work, and developers, whose goal is to build and fix their software, preferably with ample amounts of time. To highlight this tension, I describe the culture of speed and the drive for efficiency, velocity, or agility, which are all part of the office discourse at MiddleTech. I also describe the industry-wide software development management tools or methodologies that help drive this discourse (that is, the Scrum or Agile methodologies of organizing software work) and how good enoughness becomes a way of pushing back against the desired outcomes that such methodologies aim to foster.

While my ethnographic stories are often more focused on the social and cultural dimensions of building software, in Chapter 5, "Slowdown," I focus more specifically on the culture of speed and efficiency when building routing and navigation software. Mobility systems, and the development of software for them, are intrinsically dynamic processes encompassing various temporalities, which are shaped by the interaction of sociality and technology. Yet slowdown is often at the core of software work. The slowdowns do not happen because the programmer chooses to take time to think through a topic; instead, slowdowns are imposed on programmers and their teams through various social and technical constraints. Once faced with these constraints, programmers need to compromise on what they are creating and releasing to the public. These slowdowns lead developers to create good-enough code. In chapter 5, I show how slowdown is the precursor to good enoughness, where part of a programmer's practice is halting the inertia of acceleration in the corporate software environment. Through various stories, we will witness good enoughness at work with constant stutters, blockages, breakdowns, moments of slowness, and deviations from the plan.

I conclude my journey through MiddleTech by theorizing the stories we encountered and placing them into a wider understanding of what good enoughness is and how it functions. To do so, I analytically explore good enoughness from a variety of angles, showing how different relational *constellations* inform good enoughness. Through this notion, we will start to understand the myriad of actors relating to one another and helping shape what "good for what" and "good enough for whom" can mean. When exploring the various stories of good enoughness in the previous chapters, we encountered different good enoughs for the programmer or good enoughs for MiddleTech's management or their customers. These parties have different concepts of what counts as good enough, which are often in conflict with each other and in need of negotiation. Of course this leads to compromise on what's good enough for the different parties involved. I will conclude by exploring the ways good enoughness is under threat, mainly by the forces of postindustrial capitalism that work against its logic, and how it is then kept alive.

This book is about the collective struggle to keep the software we all use alive, viable, and functioning. It is also a story about what is happening to our tech companies today, particularly the larger, older, aging software companies that built a good product sometime in the mid-2000s and are now trying to maintain the one or two software assets that keep their revenue flowing. I paint a picture of one specific "software world," bringing you closer to places where software is made and maintained, while introducing you to the people who build it. I hope that this approach will also help personalize your everyday digital objects, giving you an intimate picture of software's complexity. I hope it will be good enough.

1

Welcome to MiddleTech

In the center of Berlin's Mitte (middle) district, above tramway lines, coffee shops, drugstores, and Vietnamese restaurants, stands a big glass building housing MiddleTech. The office is large and quite generic, with a lightly air-conditioned interior, the breeze of which saved me from Berlin's scorching August heat during my fieldwork. Like many corporate offices, the entrance was guarded by a keycard gate and a receptionist's desk.

I loved the building's glass elevators, which would always contain an assortment of developers whom I slowly grew to know over my fieldwork, making my elevator conversations more meaningful and less awkward as the months went by. There were seven floors in the main building, and while each looked almost exactly the same, I prided myself on knowing the difference between the second-floor front-end developers and the fifth-floor HR department. There were two kitchens on each floor that had coffee machines with very strong coffee and microwaves where developers would occasionally warm up their morning oatmeal or soup cups at lunch.

The developers who witnessed my excitement at the smell of the corridors or the shape of the garbage cans in the meeting rooms would roll their eyes or shake their heads. After all, to them, this was just an average, uneventful tech company. Indeed, beyond my ethnographic excitement, MiddleTech's head-quarters was just a run-of-the-mill tech office. The building, the lunchroom, the elevator, and the receptionist were not that special. On the contrary, they were quite average and quite mundane, with developers who worked during the day and went home to their families or friends in the evenings.

It was the second summer of my fieldwork, and I came back after months of not being at MiddleTech. That day, I was invited to join a team of data science researchers (also working with the routing and navigation team) for lunch at an Italian restaurant around the corner from the office. While munching on white bread and olive oil, the six of them sat around me and started talking about their new bosses, who were all based in Chicago, and how they had recently been interacting with the teams in Chicago. Charlie, a product owner, chimed in with a look of confusion: "I was on a call with them today and they somehow always seem to be yelling. Why are they yelling? It's like they are constantly getting into a heated argument about something."

Ori, who was sitting next to Charlie, said, "Yeah, it's so awkward. I was once in Chicago, and two guys in our meeting said they had to step out and discuss something, so they went into a meeting room and started yelling at each other. It was very awkward. And embarrassing. And then they just came out and were like 'We sorted everything out.' But they didn't. Nothing seemed to be sorted out." The rest of the guys chuckled a bit and gave knowing nods.

The images of their American colleagues yelling made me picture Steve Ballmer, the former CEO of Microsoft, standing on stage in front of an audience of hundreds of software developers in the legendary meme known as "Steve Ballmer Monkey Dance," or merely "Developers." It's sometime in the year 2000, and Ballmer and his crowd have gathered together to celebrate Microsoft's twenty-fifth anniversary. His face is red, and his generic blue button-down shirt is dripping with sweat. Galvanized by excitement, he starts his speech by pacing the stage and yelling, "Developers, developers, developers!" nearly a dozen times until he can barely breathe and turns red in the face. The developers in the audience clap along to the rhythm of his yelling.

This moment embodies an emotional affect common to the Silicon Valley tech culture: a sweaty nerd shouting passionately for digital technology and those building it, making something nobody cares about sound like something astoundingly awesome. A software engineer like Ballmer shouldn't just like his work; he should love(!!!) his work. Showing passion for one's job, anger if something goes wrong, or excitement during a new release is often an integral part of tech culture. Kunda, explaining the rituals of product presentations in a tech company, wrote that the "intense, highly charged, and often conflictual interchanges" are "characteristic of the working stages of meetings" (2009, 139). Here, in engineering culture, emotional expression is "contrived and calculated" in order to "accomplish certain goals" (85).

As the data scientists around me at lunch snickered at their American colleagues' propensity for yelling, they also seemed to distance themselves from the expectation that engineers should get so emotionally caught up in their work, their company, and the products they are building. My interpretation during that lunch hour was that getting passionate about a software product—enough to get emotional and yell at others if things go right (or wrong)—was foreign to the developer culture at MiddleTech. This moment also helped position MiddleTech as a place where people don't yell, shout, or get overtly passionate about technology, and hinted at a different culture of expressing urgency, passion, and the importance of work at MiddleTech among managers and software workers. It wasn't as if the data scientists at lunch didn't care about what they were working on; they just didn't care *that* much. Not enough to yell at their colleagues in meetings. They didn't care too much, but they also didn't care too little. Their care was somewhere in the middle.

This middleness is what this chapter is about as I unpack the "middle" of MiddleTech, helping us position the company in the larger landscape of the tech industry. I will discuss what makes MiddleTech so "middle" in relation to its size, ambition, location, and the kind of product its workers were building.

This ethnographic focus on field sites of "average" quality is not new. In 1929, Robert S. Lynd and Helen Merryll Lynd published their seminal ethnographic study, *Middletown: A Study in Contemporary American Culture*, which focused on the forms of "human behavior" and "cultural conditions" in an "average" American town. The researchers had a list of criteria in finding their town: They looked for a town that had a population size that was neither small nor very big ("25,000–50,000"), was located in America's Midwest, and had a "middle-of-the-road quality" (Lynd and Lynd 1929, 9). While I did not originally search out MiddleTech for its "averageness," after years in the field, its middle-of-the-road-ness jumped out at me, making it hard to avoid addressing just how "middle" it was in relation to the Big Techs and small start-ups, as well as in relation to the hype that always buzzed around the latter two. Its geographical middleness also appealed to me. MiddleTech was located in Berlin, based not in the tech capital of Silicon Valley but also not in the outsourcing and innovation-hyped regions of India or East Asia.

I started to draw inspiration from Lynd and Lynd's decision to focus their attention on a middle-of-the-road town in order to highlight a part of society that is ignored or deemed uneventful. MiddleTech, while widely forgotten and not that exceptional, is a place worth studying as it represents hundreds of tech companies of its kind that are so often overlooked by researchers, and don't fit into the popular imagination of what tech companies should be.[1] Neither small nor very big and with technology that is largely invisible, what I call "Medium Tech" companies still play an important role in making up our digital infrastructures. This chapter sheds light on certain "average" features of MiddleTech in order to illustrate what these sorts of companies look like, how they position themselves in relation to Silicon Valley and Big Tech, how local laws help shape their company culture, and how these features become important for one specific version of good enoughness to flourish.

The notion of "average" here, as I iterated in my introduction, is positioned in relation to a tech industry discourse that values excellence and innovation. This can include a value for employee engagement, the drive to "scale up" as a software company and grow, positioning oneself in a location that fosters "innovation," or having the drive to make software technology that is "disruptive," "critical," or "important."

MiddleTech, our chapter's protagonist, fulfills none of these criteria. Or at least does so only sometimes. As a company, it is medium in size; its employees have a fluctuating, average amount of ambition; it's not located in a particularly exciting "tech hub" known for fostering after-hours work or go-getter work ambitions; the product its workers were building was largely invisible to users, and their ways of working were nor particularly well organized. MiddleTech was average: It was good enough.

This chapter will also provide you with a picture of how corporate software culture is structured, both on an external industry level and an internal, organizational micro level. Understanding some of the organizational structures behind MiddleTech will also help me highlight what can foster good-enough culture. In this chapter, a few structural dynamics at MiddleTech, including the company's age as well as the legal and corporate culture it is situated in, help good enoughness develop.

---

1. Beyond our popular stereotypes of digital media companies, averageness and middle-of-the-road companies have become an archetype in popular discourse, functioning mostly as comic relief in TV shows like *The Office* or *Superstore*. One can say that in the former American version of the series, the average paper company Dunder Mifflin is featured as a space of good-enough culture, constantly in negotiation with go-getter characters like Dwight Schrute, who represents an ambitious colleague striving to achieve excellence and top performance.

Medium Tech

Even without disguising the identity of MiddleTech with a pseudonym, most people wouldn't have heard of it. For most people, stories about tech companies often involve so-called "Big Tech" or the Tech Giants: Apple, Amazon, Facebook, Google/Alphabet, and Microsoft. These companies became more prominent over the past decade, becoming well known around 2013, when economists and journalists noticed that they were no longer disruptive start-ups emerging from the Dotcom boom but instead had acquired large numbers of tech users, large amounts of user data, and large shares of the market. Since then, Big Tech has been in the spotlight in our popular discourse. These companies are the protagonists in fiction and nonfiction books, feature regularly on the news, and are scrutinized by our governments. The wealth of the Big Five "total more than the entire economy of the United Kingdom" (O'Mara 2019, 17) or France (Foroohar 2021, 5). And if we expand our definition of Big Tech to encompass the global market, we can include companies like Samsung Electronics in South Korea, Tencent Holdings in China (the world's largest producer of games), Foxconn Technology Group (the world's largest provider of electronics manufacturing), or Taiwan Semiconductor Manufacturing Co., Ltd. (TSM) (the second-largest producer of semiconductors next to Intel). There is no denying that these companies matter—they influence the digital technology we use, and their technology influences us.

But beyond Big Tech, there are other companies that also employ many people, make lots of money, and create digital technology for countless users. They aren't big or flashy, and most people don't know who they are. These Medium Tech companies are other large organizations that go mostly unnoticed in the popular imagination. These are not small nor medium enterprises (a category that most start-ups fall into at first) but large companies of over a thousand employees. At the time of my research, MiddleTech housed about a thousand employees in its office in Berlin and had another seven thousand working around the globe. The company's objective was to make digital maps and to provide location data and other services to individuals (in the form of a navigation app on your phone or in your car) and other businesses (in the form of location data information needed for building certain software). Located in over twenty cities, with its largest offices in Berlin and Chicago, the company has a thirty-year history of growth, acquisition, and rebranding. In the mid-1980s, an American company called FastMap was building digital navigation technology, which focused on providing map data used in in-car navigation equipment. In the late 2000s, FastMap was acquired by a large mobile phone manufacturer, who, in 2012, rebranded its entire mapping and navigation services under the umbrella name of MiddleTech. In late 2015, six months before I arrived, MiddleTech was sold to a consortium of German car manufacturers, which, at the time of writing, held around 75 percent of the company's shares. Other hardware and semiconductor companies still held stakes in the firm. MiddleTech was, and still is, a company with years of history, a mix of programming styles, legal regulations, different work practices, and methods of conflict negotiation all coming together under one sleek, modern, community garden–covered roof.

The first "middleness" that defined MiddleTech was its number of employees. The company—with a multitude of locations and teams working on a large array of software products—was big enough for employees to get lost and for senior managers to lose track of who was working where. Yet the company was not too big—it was markedly different from powerful tech companies like Google or Microsoft who have scaled up to employ hundreds of thousands of people globally. It was also not a small start-up of a couple of dozen or a couple of hundred employees. Size mattered, as I observed that the number of employees at a corporate company was often tied to employee engagement, management style, and a sense of personal accountability. Charlie, a product owner, who also had experience working at a smaller start-up, explained that when companies have a handful of employees, it becomes easier for employees to feel they have "ownership": "You feel you have built something from the ground up . . . and it's small, and [the employees] are so driven by this. People feel they have a higher mission. They feel they can change how [the company] proceeds; they feel very accountable." The employee population size of a Medium Tech company gives employees the ability to hide and absolves them of feeling accountable to their company or software product. While there were other factors that contributed to this lack of accountability and the ability to be less noticeable at work, I felt that MiddleTech's size was a significant factor in keeping it in the middle—not scaling up, not striving for excellence, but establishing itself somewhere in the middle.

Apart from the number of employees, forms of employee organization also add to the averageness of the company. After years of conducting research on corporate software development—through short field visits to other companies, discussions with software developers who moved on from MiddleTech to other companies, and my field visit to San Francisco—I noticed that MiddleTech was a quite average representation of how any medium-size software company was structured, how the office was designed, and the type of job positions that made up a software company. For those of us who have briefly encountered a tech company, MiddleTech did seem like any other corporate software company, no matter the scale.

The office space oozed a mix of corporate anonymity and random camaraderie. Every day when I entered the office, I would take the desk of somebody who happened to be away on vacation, and I would sit down and start typing away on my keyboard, making the same "click click" sound that my developer neighbors were making. I would also check my e-mails, proudly hoping that a developer would walk behind me and peek over my shoulder to notice that I was just like them and used the same e-mail system they did (they never did notice). I would also log in to the chat system called "Spark," and much like the developers around me, I would read through the daily discussion threads. At 12 or 12:30, I would become part of the wave of developers standing up to go to lunch. I existed with them; I fused into their global tech ecosystem and felt that nobody really took notice of me—not because I wasn't the odd one out (I was) but because software developers have a social culture of not noticing one another and, moreover, corporations have the same culture of not noticing one another. When walking past somebody in the hallway—in the case of both the software developer and the corporate worker—not saying something is more socially acceptable than stopping to say hello. Developers work within their machines, and even when getting up to get a coffee in the kitchen, they are often still absorbed in their task at hand. For example, at the MiddleTech Christmas party, I was surprised to find a few developers laughing and joking with me after having, on their own, initiated a conversation. I asked Dimitri, one of the most introverted developers at the office, why he was so outgoing when he was usually so shy and avoided me, and he said, "Paula, you don't get it. When you see me in the office, I'm still inside my problem; I am talking to the computer, in constant conversation with it. I don't have the mental capacity to just change gears and notice you, let alone start talking to you." Silence at MiddleTech is a virtue.

As in most software companies, software developers were divided into teams based on what software product they were working on. During the first summer of my fieldwork, I was placed in a team of one hundred front-end developers building a map-based app similar to any navigation app in your phone. My second year was spent with the routing and navigation team, which was made up of around one hundred developers. In computer-speak, this group was known as the back-end team, meaning the group working "closer to the machine" on parts that the regular user of the navigation app doesn't see at all, such as the map-operating system, the cartographic data, the routing algorithm, etc. Aside from front-end and back-end developers (or full-stack developers who were jacks-of-all-trades and could do both), others I met called themselves data scientists. The data scientists' task was to conduct research experiments on large data sets and turn these experiments into working prototypes. They would take a large amount of data collected by the MiddleTech in-car navigation system about, for example, the number of mis-maneuvers on a route, and then use machine-learning algorithms to find patterns on the route that might cause these mis-maneuvers (such as the number of left-hand turns). There were also privacy officers, whose task was to comply with legal regulations and make sure the data they collected were encrypted and minimized and, as much as possible, destroyed. These diverse employees came together to build software, their roles resembling those in any other generic software company.

The word "software" suggests that there is "a single entity, separate from the computer's hardware, that works with the hardware to solve a problem. In fact, there is no such single entity. A computer system is like an onion, with many distinct layers of software over a hardware core" (Ceruzzi 2003, 80). These layers are built and maintained by different developers with different skill sets. A programmer working on the top layer of this hypothetical onion might not know how to work on another layer closer to the onion's core.

More specifically, at MiddleTech the front-end developers worked on the company's navigation app, and the back-end developers created and maintained the map-operating software that was built into cars for large German car companies (although throughout my few years coming in and out of the company, various software projects and products changed and grew). The front-end engineers making the navigation app performed the so-called "easy" tasks. They worked on problems that had clear solutions. Place a button here. Add a feature there. Debug or fix another error. This type of work was done by thousands of other developers in other companies around the globe, often regardless of whether they were building a map or a fitness app.

The back-end division, on the other hand, was made up of developers who worked on the part of the app you couldn't really see, such as the data and algorithms. These developers were also split into two types of engineers: those who worked on cleaning up data, fixing bugs, or updating old code, and a small number of programmers and PhD student interns who conducted experiments using the database and technical infrastructure in the company. Their task was to break new ground, invent, and be creative. As in many research environments, their goal was to develop a hypothesis and test it. As they tested their hypotheses, they often came up with prototypes that would (but often would not) be made into a working technology that the company used.

There were those programmers who conduct the headwork, or the research and creative work, and others who just do the manual labor of fixing bugs, testing code, or reviewing it for mistakes. The headwork is valued more (literally in terms of salary but also in terms of status) than the handwork, which in this case was characterized by repetitive copy-and-paste Googling, bug-fixing, or perhaps even testing.[2]

Throughout my work, I became accustomed to interchanging terms like "software developer," "software engineer," and "programmer." These terms were (and are) frequently used and interchanged by programmers themselves, who admit to having slippery job titles that evolve all the time. As the profession is rapidly shifting, a programmer can go from being a "lead developer" to "head programmer" to "lead software engineer" when switching jobs, but their tasks remain nearly the same. Aside from the front-end and back-end developers, there is also the data scientist, who is more of a researcher and who doesn't necessarily work on any software that will be of direct applicable use to anyone.

---

2. This division dates back to the beginning of work with computers. In one of the first pamphlets on computing published in the United States, called "Planning and Coding of Problems for an Electronic Computing Instrument," Herman Goldstine and John von Neumann (1947) outlined a division of labor in computing that clearly distinguished a symbolic hierarchy in the type of work involved in building a computer. The headwork was conducted by the (largely male) scientists or "planners" (Ensmenger 2010, 15). On the other hand, the handwork was conducted by the "coder," who was mainly female at the time. The planner did the intellectual work of analysis, and the coder merely translated this work into a form that a computer could understand. Coding was a "static" process—one that could be performed by a low-level clerical worker (Ensmenger 2010, 15). While the type of work that goes into building software and hardware has largely changed since the time of Goldstine and von Neumann, there are a few divisions that remain in place today, including the division between the headwork and the handwork. The latter today has moved from just typing or inputting data to a more subtle type of physical labor, such as copying and pasting code found on the internet or fixing bugs. While computers have drastically changed since Goldstine and von Neumann wrote their pamphlet, the division between the headworkers and handworkers still permeates the programmer's culture, with the headworkers holding more status, skill, and authority. These divisions are a bit more nuanced and could be divided into the creative research workers, the maintenance workers, and the cleaners or bug-fixers.

While front-end and back-end developers make a software product run for a specific customer or user, other software workers make software for other software developers (this division of labor also appears in many software companies). While this may sound confusing, this team is known at MiddleTech and other software companies as the DevOps team, short for "development operations." These workers create the software infrastructure that helps software developers deliver their code to the main project, test the code, and detect bugs in the code.

Another important division among software workers is between those developers working in-house and those developers working in an external outsourcing company hired to complete a part of the software project. Outsourcing companies are chosen based on cost, meaning that managers search for an outsourcing team that gives them the most productivity for the least amount of money. The teams I worked with at MiddleTech outsourced certain parts of their software production to companies in Poland, Ukraine, and Russia. The type of work done by these outsourcing teams is considered the boring, annoying, repetitive, less-skilled type of labor, or "monkey coding," as many developers called it. This included tasks like bug-squashing, in which developers had a long list of bugs/errors in their software and had to fix the issue in a given amount of time. Outsourcing teams made periodic visits (every few months) to their headquarters in Berlin, but most of their collaboration with Berlin-based developers was done via conference calls or online software collaboration platforms.

Outsourcing is part of the global software industry and also fosters inequalities among workers. Unlike Amrute, whose research partially looked at the ways in which Indian tech workers experience difference and inequality at the office, I observed less inequality between workers who did the same type of work (for example, the DevOps engineers) than between engineers with different software development skills (for example, code reviewers versus researchers), or those located in Berlin and externally in outsourcing teams. For example, a team of DevOps engineers at the MiddleTech office, made up of Ukrainian, Indian, German, and American engineers, would generally be treated the same way within their team—they would receive the same tasks and work on similar projects, and their peers would all judge each other's work based on its technical proficiency, rather than on who wrote the code. People from outsourcing teams were, from the get-go, othered. They received different types of more mechanical tasks than the teams working in Berlin; their work was more scrutinized and reviewed; and because of how the outsourcing contracts were structured, they were more disposable than the workers in Berlin. I witnessed a number of occasions when managers dropped a team in Wrocław, for example, because they found another team that was cheaper and more reliable in Kyiv. While this book does not directly address the forms of inequality and tension that arise between different classes of coding work, and the regional inequalities in labor distribution, these forms of difference are nevertheless a prevalent part of corporate computing culture and exist throughout the industry beyond the offices of MiddleTech.

There are others who make up the corporate software world, including managers of all levels (middle managers, senior managers, CEOs, and team managers); the legal team, which deals with lawsuits or copyright; the privacy team, which focuses on data privacy; designers; user experience teams who conduct research on how the software is being used "in the wild"; and cleaning staff, support staff, and the human resources department. There are many others whom I don't focus on within this book, but I would like to acknowledge that their work is indeed a part of the way software is made and maintained.

This characteristic rather than exceptional way of organizing a software company at MiddleTech also made my study typical and helped my observations, with a bit of caution, become relatable to other digital media production environments.

The Sometimes-Invisible Middle

Another way we can characterize the middleness of MiddleTech is the way its technology was invisible both to users and the programmers building it. Software, much like any infrastructure, is "by definition invisible," taken for granted, and becomes "visible [only] on breakdown" (Star 1999 380). Here, these authors are referring to the actual seamlessness of a software system—how we, as users, don't really see or interact with the code operating our everyday systems until these systems break down. I would argue a bit further and say that certain software gains a status of visibility (think of the iOS operating system in your Apple phone) or complete invisibility (a traffic-control system), both in the sheer number of users using the product and also in the way in which an average user notices it. There are also some companies that function between this space, with their product being somewhat noticeable only to a smaller group of people. This has a lot to do with the back-end or front-end focus of a software company. While Google might be working on new machine learning technology, Facebook/Meta might be building its next Second Life, and Apple will be working on yet another new interface design for their new phone. In these examples, users don't actually see their technology run, yet the front-end experience—or the part of the software and hardware that users see, touch, and engage with—is quite explicit and becomes meaningful to the users.

This ability for a sensory engagement with software gives users the feeling that software and the software company are somehow impactful or socially relevant. What Medium Tech companies are making—products like medical software, transport software, systems that help us navigate, or smart home software—are much more invisible (yet, one can argue, they impact us in ways that might be hard to quantify but are still salient). MiddleTech didn't particularly focus on their front end. After my first year of fieldwork observing the front-end team build the user experience mapping/navigation app for iOS and Android, the whole project was drastically downsized, turning the company into building mapping infrastructure for other businesses, cars, and other systems. While the front-end app was still there, running on the phones in some of the pockets of some users, the company didn't particularly focus on it, making the MiddleTech name, as well as the software they produced, less visible. For German car manufacturers, delivery services, logistics teams, or companies in need of a mapping and navigation app, MiddleTech was important. Yet, as you can see, it was not a very popular app that was generally recognizable. It was not completely irrelevant but also not highly relevant to the general population.

Middle-Aged Tech

Another way of characterizing the middleness of MiddleTech was its age and the older software assets the company held. While older companies in any industry are often replaced by new ones that build better or more innovative products, I would argue that because of the way in which software is embedded into a variety of other systems, many software companies survive for years, "living alongside new technologies" (Pinch 2010, 409) MiddleTech was no exception. It morphed out of a company that was founded in the late 1980s, and their mapping system, which is still in use today, was built in the late 1990s. While MiddleTech wasn't one of the oldest companies in the software industry (see my example of CAE in the next paragraph), it certainly wasn't the youngest.

Throughout my fieldwork, I noticed that the age of the company is highly relevant to how software developers work and how a company functions in relation to its industry competitors. Both Medium Tech and Big Tech have aged and survived because they created a software asset that is still in use today. Here, we can understand the aging of a software company not as a failure but as a privilege. Most software companies don't pass their start-up phase, and the software they create is briefly used and then forgotten. If a company ages and stays around for ten, twenty, or thirty or more years, it usually means that they have created a software asset that is successfully embedded in a social and technical infrastructure. Once embedded in such an infrastructure, it becomes harder over the years (and often impossible) for the infrastructure to retract this particular technology. One example of another Medium Tech is CAE (formerly Canadian Aviation Electronics), a Canadian manufacturer of, among other things, simulation and modeling software for airlines, aircraft manufacturers, health-care specialists, and the military. CAE was founded in 1947, and its software, while changing and adapting over the company's seventy-five years of existence, also features very old products that are still embedded and locked within certain aviation infrastructures, both generating revenue for the company and making their software irreplaceable.

At MiddleTech, this digital asset is mapping and navigation software, called the map engine, which they sold and continue to sell to third-party businesses in need of maps in their products (such as a car or another app that needs a map feature). Due to this prolific embeddedness of the company's software, the company is able to coast on its revenues from its asset, which was built years ago, not necessarily needing new innovative ideas to pay its employees.

As Marisa Leavitt Cohn explained in her ethnographic study of engineers operating a large-scale, multidecade technological infrastructure, systems (like software systems) age at different rates and are entangled with each other. Additionally, "what decays or ages are the relations across multiple parts of the infrastructure and among people, the organization, and its technologies" (Leavitt Cohn 2016, 1519).

Such processes of aging and infrastructural embeddedness are common but not limited to Medium Tech companies. A Big Tech example of this phenomenon is Google's PageRank. Has it been reinvented since its introduction in 1998? There have been some variations since then, but the essential asset, the PageRank algorithm, has existed ever since its inception. Despite being built years ago, this digital product continues to make the company a large amount of money as it has been embedded in a large network of systems. The difference here is the scale: Big Tech companies created a more prolific software asset that is able to age, while at the same time making such huge revenues for them that they are able to reinvest some of that revenue into more innovative products and services. Medium Tech companies do not make as much revenue as their Big Tech counterparts, and their scope for reinvestment in research or innovation is quite limited.

With this limitation, the software work at MiddleTech was dedicated mostly to maintenance and repair. All infrastructural systems, including software, are "prone to error and neglect and breakage and failure" (Graham and Thrift 2007, 5), and those working with such systems accept decay, errors, and failure as normal. Software becomes more complex over time: the number of components making up a software system has been "proliferating, becoming more complex and becoming composed from an ever-greater range of materials, thus requiring ever more maintenance and repair" (Graham and Thrift, 2007, 3). As I aim to show in the following chapters, working on maintaining software at MiddleTech was not simply about tending to the material software infrastructure but was also about "maintaining relationships among people, organizations and technologies" (Bietz et al. 2012, 904).

My focus on MiddleTech's maintenance work was part of accepting erosion, breakdown, and decay, rather than novelty, growth, and progress, as my "starting points in thinking through the nature, use, and effects of information technology and new media" (Jackson 2014, 221). I started to notice that programmers working in maintenance and repair require a certain specialized skill. They are the ones who have to keep systems stable, which is not easily achieved mainly because those software developers who maintain and repair their own system are faced with a large corporate software legacy: an "old and layered (software) world, making history but not in the circumstances of its choosing" (223). In most cases, successful software is not built from scratch over and over again and then sold to customers like any other consumer object. Despite seeming new and "updated," software is dependent on and encased in years of code that constitute the very structure of its existence. As Vinsel and Russell (2018) reminded us, life with technology is usually far removed from the cutting edges of invention and innovation. It is crucial to distinguish certain forms of work that are devoted to keeping things the same—to highlight maintenance (the work that preserves technical and physical orders) over innovation (Vinsel and Russell 2018). David Edgerton sees these activities as part of a broader concept that he calls technology-in-use, through which "a radically different picture of technology, and indeed of invention and innovation, becomes possible" (2008, xi).

During my research at MiddleTech, I noticed that only a very small number of engineers were dedicated to research or building new products, whether that was in the Routing and Navigation team or elsewhere. On the other side of the spectrum, at Google, the 20 percent rule is encouraged, where at least 20 percent is spent on "exploring or working on projects that show no promise of paying immediate dividends but that might reveal big opportunities down the road."[3] As we shall see in the following chapters, the practice of "keeping software present" (Leavitt Cohn 2019, 432) is much more part of the practice at MiddleTech. Here, making good-enough software or judging what is good enough for now is deeply entangled in the continuous work of maintenance and repair but might seem quite out of place among workers striving for innovation and big opportunities.

In the introduction, I highlighted how excellence and continuous improvement have become ingrained in the discourse and work culture of any tech company whether it is Big Tech or Medium Tech. Yet at MiddleTech, discourses around excellence and improvement are not actually at the center of what it does on a day-to-day basis. Its focus is rather on not-so-exceptional maintenance work.

MiddleTech: Not the Global Tech Hub

One afternoon, I met an American security developer through some MiddleTech colleagues. Tyler had long hair and was completely dressed in black, perhaps the visual epitome of a security hacker. He had been living in Berlin for only a few months after having worked for a German company in Munich. In the United States, he worked in various cities, including San Francisco. He saw a drastic difference between the two countries.

"I mean generally in Berlin—it's slower here. In San Francisco, the idea is mainly to get involved in any hot start-up you can, work eighty hours a week, and then become a billionaire. That's the general mentality . . . In San Francisco you can't have a conversation that isn't about money. It's a million miles a minute. Dog eat dog. When I came to Berlin, I was in shock. People can say, 'No, I'm not going to do that.' They just say it. Not because they don't know how, but just because they don't want to get their hands messy, or because they want to do something more interesting . . . So they just work—but they aren't about delivery. They care about everything else but the results. I have a feeling people in Berlin just love being right, but

3. Bill Murphy Jr., "Google Says It Still Uses the '20-Percent Rule,' and You Should Totally Copy It," *Inc.*, Nov. 1, 2020, https://www.inc.com/bill-murphy-jr/google-says-it-still-uses-20-percent-rule-you-should-totally-copy-it.html.

they do a lot of time-wasting. In San Francisco, all that matters is 'Did it make you money and what is the result?' Here everyone plays the lazy game. Nobody can fire you. Sometimes they say they can't do something for an honorable reason like picking up their kids from work, but a lot of the time I've seen them just make some stuff up. Or they just say 'Umm, yeah, I'm not doing that.'"

Here, Tyler contrasts two software worlds: San Francisco, where software developers overwork, work fast, and express their ambition, and Berlin, where employees engage in "time-wasting" and are able to say, "I'm not doing that." While Berlin and Silicon Valley might have more similar work cultures than we may think, Tyler described how MiddleTech workers position themselves as "other" in contrast to a region that carries with it a "model" (Pfotenhauer and Jasanoff 2017b) of innovation, performing efficiently, holding the utmost expertise, and working passionately to build awesome software around the clock.

Over the past fifty years, Silicon Valley has become a key site where imaginaries in computing and digital cultures are not only created but enforced and reproduced. What I mean by "imaginaries" is the way that those behind building technology collectively enact their hopes and expectations through technological innovation. These imaginaries are reproduced over and over again through discourse, which instills an ideology in human agents and institutions (see Jasanoff and Kim 2015, 17), and companies like MiddleTech were no exception. Over the years, Silicon Valley had become not "merely a place in Northern California" but "a global network, a business sensibility" and "a cultural shorthand" (O'Mara 2019, 20).

MiddleTech was situated outside Silicon Valley, while also somehow relating to it or constructing its identity as "other" to Silicon Valley. Berlin, of all places, was situated geographically and symbolically also somewhere in the middle of Silicon Valley and the Indian and East Asian tech giants. In the 2010s, Berlin began branding itself as the "Silicon Allee" (Schimroszik 2015) as the German start-up capital of Germany,[4] in an attempt to create a Silicon Valley in Europe (Casper 2007), although some industry discourses were skeptical of its ability to really be a "meaningful player" in the global software industry, with its ambitions fizzling in the past decade.[5]

---

4. Nik Afanasjew, "'Silicon Allee' in Berlin: Det nächste grosse Ding" ["Silicon Alle" in Berlin: The next big thing], Sept. 28, 2013, https://www.tagesspiegel.de/gesellschaft/medien-_-ki/det-nachste-grosse-ding-6343603.html.

5. Martin Kaelble, "Grenzen der 'Silicon Allee'" [The borders of "Silicon Allee"], May 24, 2013, https://www.capital.de/wirtschaft-politik/Grenzen-der-Silicon-Allee.

It was hard for MiddleTech to completely ignore Silicon Valley's way of working, its discourse, and its ambition. By "theorizing" itself as a specific "world model" of technological progress and innovation (Pfotenhauer and Jasanoff 2017b), Silicon Valley creates a common understanding of "otherness," which it expresses to the rest of the world (Hasse and Passarge 2015, 8). The region also imagines itself as a "center of a progressive force for global change" (Darrah 2001, 4) and thus situates itself in a way that attracts gigantic amounts of investment capital. Silicon Valley also exerts a passionate "master narrative" of "making the world a better place," repeated through venture capitalists, consultants, innovators, start-up owners, and social media.

More specifically, companies in Silicon Valley have a way of propagating ideas about ways of organizing a software company (who works on what and how), ways of speaking about company values (with slogans, company mottos, and principles), ways of hyping up the purpose of one's company (with technosolutionist excitement), and propagating the notion that new technology will save us from the problems of older technology (Morozov 2013). These ideas and discourses are expressed and spread to the rest of the global tech industry through a variety of channels.

Silicon Valley's ideology (Barbrook and Cameron 1996) has been so ingrained into the narratives of our tech imaginaries, particularly as business schools, consultancy firms, and other media of neoliberalism keep positioning Silicon Valley as a global world model. Drawing an example from a recent (2021) consultancy study about "Technology Innovation Hubs," KPMG surveyed eight hundred "global technology company leaders" (CEOs, COOs, etc.), who suggested a list of "leading technology innovation hubs over the next four years (in addition to Silicon Valley/San Francisco)." From the outset of the study, the San Francisco Bay area was positioned as the top model, or the standard of a leading technology innovation hub, further promoting the world model narrative I mentioned earlier. Among the top 10 rankings were Singapore, New York, Tel Aviv, Beijing, London, Shanghai, Tokyo, Bangalore, Hong Kong, Austin, and Seattle. According to this study, a "tech hub" is defined by "local factors" and "macro factors," which "can help position a country as an incubator of technology innovation."[6]

It is striking that the authors then provide a table of the countries that show the most "promise for developing disruptive technologies" and a comprehensive list of questions that "company leaders" should ask themselves

---

6. Alex Holt and Mark Gibson, "Technology Innovation Hubs," KPMG, https://www.kpmg .us/content/dam/global/pdfs/2021/tech-innovation-hubs-2021.pdf.

before acquiring a tech company, such as "Is the regulatory environment favorable to technology companies?" or "Is the prevalent culture of the new locale compatible with the overall company culture?" These questions are quite broad but seem to point toward two important axioms valued in the tech industry: tech companies need an environment to "innovate" and a governmental ecosystem that allows for "disruption." While these notions are quite vague, they also gesture toward an ecosystem that fosters speed and labor laws that also allow for a quick changeover in relation to whatever "disruptive" workforce is needed at the time (that is, absence of labor laws that allow for the quick hiring and firing of staff), building a local "culture . . . compatible with the overall company culture."

This study is part of a whole genre of reports that establish Silicon Valley as a "role model," helping "government and company delegations . . . report back on Silicon Valley's secret sauce" so that their company or organization "can use it as a seasoning" (Pfotenhauer and Jasanoff 2017b, 784).

MiddleTech, while situated in the capital of Germany, was not a "role model" for innovation and disruption in the eyes of developers like Tyler. The master narratives propagated by Silicon Valley and various industry discourses were also largely incongruent with software work itself, placing demands on software workers that they cannot and don't want to, in the end, fulfill. MiddleTech's focus on maintenance was already a factor in its non-innovation-driven work practices. Additionally, as I'll show, Germany's work culture at large protected its workers and fostered pushbacks against overwork.

The German Labor Laws

This discourse of American othering doesn't manifest itself only in lunchtime jokes about yelling. I met a handful of MiddleTech developers, like Tyler, who ran away from their jobs in Silicon Valley or vowed never to set foot in San Francisco again. These characters became legends around the office. Every developer I spoke to knew somebody who had worked in the Valley and who had stories to tell about the pressure, lack of work-life balance, or obsession that didn't fit their way of working.

One developer, who used to work in San Francisco, stated, "California is a 'work at will' state, which means that at any time somebody can come up to you and just fire you on the spot (which is supposed to also protect the worker who can 'leave at any time,' ha ha). But since you don't want to live under a bridge, you will do whatever your boss wants you to do."

German tech companies are also different on a legal level from American companies due to the makeup of German labor laws. To state that labor laws are more just and fair for workers in Germany compared to the United States would be an understatement. Germany is also situated in a European culture that takes into consideration that workers care about things other than their work. First of all, German labor law gives the employee more protection against unfair dismissal than in the United States, meaning that companies can fire their workers only under certain clearly defined circumstances. In most of the United States, employees can be fired from one day to the next. Germans typically receive unlimited work contracts, and working on Sundays and public holidays is generally prohibited. MiddleTech employees, like most German employees, also receive between twenty-five and thirty vacation days per calendar year (for more about German labor law, see Weiss and Schmidt 2008, or McGaughey 2016). All of this adds up to a quite relaxed work culture, where workers do not have to worry if they will be fired.

German labor laws make it possible to create good-enough software and do a job that's just good enough. Mediocrity is, de facto, written into the German Civil Code. The German Civil Code (BGB)'s law of obligations, which German employment laws draw upon, has a subsection (subsection 243, section 1) called the "Leistung mittlerer Art und Güte" (Right to average performance and quality). According to this subsection, workers have to deliver their labor or object only in "Mittlerer Art und Güte" (average type and quality). This means that an employee is not obliged to deliver the best possible performance but indeed only work of medium quality (subsection 243 BGB). It is difficult for an employer to fire somebody on the grounds that they are not reaching certain performance targets.

Thus, the feeling that one cannot be fired is possible only because German laws make it more difficult for an employer to fire someone simply because they are not good enough. Firing somebody is possible if a company downsizes, suffers huge losses, or in some other very specific circumstances. But if a permanent employee is just slow or doesn't really care that much about their job, German employers are not as quick as their counterparts in the United States to lay somebody off. For this reason, it is acceptable to be good enough in a German office. While it's not the responsibility of the German legal system to define company culture, a legal structure that makes layoffs more difficult can affect workers' approach to their work. One can imagine that German workers would not consider every mistake or setback they make, or even their permanent state of mediocrity, as a threat to their jobs.

Conclusions

This chapter situated MiddleTech in a discussion of the larger landscape of tech companies today to illustrate the significance and specificity of my field site. Here, I highlighted its middleness from a variety of angles. While not extremely profitable like the biggest companies in the world, nor highly exciting like some of the newest start-ups, MiddleTech can survive because it provides a product that people still need and have become dependent on over the years. This dependence on an older asset turns the focus of companies like MiddleTech to maintenance and repair rather than "disruptive" innovation. This focus means that both the work culture within companies like MiddleTech, as well as the software they produce, become inescapably good enough. I will turn to the reasons for this inescapability in my later chapters.

I also described MiddleTech's middleness through its size, invisibility, and average, run-of-the-mill employee work structures. Indeed, MiddleTech was the lesser known, less exciting version of the corporate tech office. It was just average, with regular office buildings, no baristas selling coffee, and programmers who don't get too emotional at work. While some parts of the MiddleTech office can resemble the offices of Big Tech—with whiteboards, a small gym, and the occasional beanbag chair lying around—these office perks and add-ons, as well as the company culture, seemed more restrained, more toned down, somehow more repressed at MiddleTech. More broadly, we also learned about the structure of a tech company and the jobs that go into building software, focusing on MiddleTech while also highlighting its similarities with other global software companies.

Through describing MiddleTech's middleness, I tried to hint at some of the structural causes that help foster a good-enough culture. While we will get into more detail about how good enoughness emerges in later chapters, I showed how Medium Tech companies are characterized by their age and older software assets they hold. These companies still make money on a unique software product that is embedded within a large, wider network of software and hardware systems, making other companies dependent on their product. This dependency absolves Medium Tech companies from the need to keep innovating, as this asset keeps earning revenue for them. These companies then structure their workdays around maintenance and repair, rather than around innovation.

While MiddleTech might seem like a very ordinary, generic office, the company fosters a a particular culture, and the workers within it are a particular class of people, characteristics that need to be understood in a larger global software landscape. I started this ethnographic journey by focusing on MiddleTech as my main character precisely because as a company, it is part of other similar middle-of-the-road companies that are often forgotten yet important pieces of our digital media discourses. We are so often confronted with stories from the Silicon Valley Big Tech that we forget that most of our digital infrastructure isn't actually made by these companies. For those interested in the political, economic, or social implications of digital media technologies, our understanding of the tech industry should expand to encompass the stories of such Medium Tech companies. In the next pages, I will zoom in on another level of abstraction by explaining the relationship between the programmers, their programming community, and their programming practice, in order to provide a better understanding of life within MiddleTech, and how the programmer's practice both supports and clashes with the corporate culture of good enoughness in which it is situated.

2

Software's Sociality

"We are surrounded by machines . . . we are suspicious of the new 'psychological machines' and fear the hacker's intimate relationship with his object."

—*TURKLE*, THE SECOND SELF

Many of us have a techie friend in our lives. The go-to person whom we like to turn to when our laptop crashes or our smartphone doesn't turn on. The friend who can explain to us what machine learning or AI chatbots are all about, or why our smartphone map gives us the wrong directions. Ori was that friend of mine.

He was extremely thin, with curly hair that fell over his expressive eyes, and he managed to be both shy and outgoing at the same time. He was a wonderful storyteller, the type of storyteller who made you feel as if you were there with him during his adventures. My favorite stories were the ones of his years in the army, of his escape in the middle of the night and running in his uniform through the desert to get to a music festival, or getting an extra blanket from his supervisor he was in love with and cuddling it while he went to sleep. I was surprised that somebody so soft-spoken could ever be in the army in the first place.

His grandparents on both his mother's and father's sides were Yemenite Jews, who arrived in Israel in 1949 on the bizarrely titled "Operation Magic Carpet," an Israeli-led rescue operation that airlifted nearly fifty thousand Jews from Yemen to Israel. Ori moved to Germany around the same time

I did, in October 2012. His reasons for moving were a bit of a cliché: He met his German girlfriend in Israel when she was working in a kibbutz, they fell in love, and after about a year of traveling back and forth, he got on a plane and flew to Berlin for good. His father, who ran a lucrative flower farm, had always hoped that Ori would take over the business when he retired. His mother, who had Ori's older sister when she was only nineteen, thought that her world-wandering son had abandoned the family on the day he left for Germany. His stories about his family were always laced with a tiny drop of guilt, knowing that his mother and father were disappointed that he wasn't around in Israel to support the family as a good Jewish boy should.

Before discovering his gift for programming, Ori was a writer. One of his first jobs at the age of fifteen was working as a betting bookkeeper in a smoky bar in his hometown near Tel Aviv. The bar featured a small betting shop at the back, where local men would come to place their bets on various games and events around town. His task was to sit in front of a small computer and input the customers' bets. The computer wasn't that powerful and featured only a text-input program and a bookkeeping software. The pub was very seldom frequented, and his section of the bar even less so. Ori, therefore, had a lot of time on his hands. This time became precious as it opened the door to his talent for writing. Every day at work, he would fire up his very slow computer, and instead of recording bets (nobody was betting at that time anyway), he would open up a text document and start typing. He would describe everything around him: the men smoking their cigarettes, the conversations they would have sitting around the bar. He would also treat his afternoon as a time to dig deep into his inner, magical world, and talk about the discoveries of a teenage boy: the young women he was fantasizing about, the emotions he was experiencing, the things he was angry about. His boss never found out. His typing just made him look like he was working. Little did Ori's manager know that he had written hundreds of pages of personal and pseudo-ethnographic discoveries over the years under his manager's employment.

One day, the job came to an end as Ori had to prepare for his military service. At the time, he didn't have any way of backing up the data of his diary files, so he left the pub and his small computer, thinking that he would come back a few months later to find it. One afternoon on his way home from military service, he checked in at the bar to find out what had happened with his database of locked-up memories. Much to his disappointment, he discovered that his boss had thrown out the old computer and replaced it with a new one. Ori's heart sank, feeling frustrated at himself for not saving his data.

While he didn't say so explicitly, I wondered if his time at the betting shop, and the fateful way it ended, somehow shaped his relationship with computers. His process of writing was very similar to the practice of programming: writing locked him into a machine where his imagination was able to run wild, building and inventing a world filled with all sorts of interactions and descriptions of people and places. Software developers, at their most engaged moment, become "close to the machine" (Ullman 1997) and, using their imagination, focus on building another world. The teenage Ori also experienced something all programmers encounter: sitting behind a machine can help disguise their actions, giving them a sense of power, secrecy, or even partial anonymity. Ori's boss at the betting shop thought Ori was working on his betting statistics, not realizing that Ori was really pouring his heart out into a very personal diary. Ori also did not possess the skills nor the tools to save his material. Perhaps if he did, he would have saved his files before leaving his job.

This first encounter between Ori and his betting-bar computer touched upon two of the deep driving forces that entice young people into learning how to program: (1) a computer provides the programmer with a private space, a sense of connection between the programmer and the machine that nobody else can enter, and (2) knowing how to program becomes a way of solving a problem that the programmer would not know how to solve without the knowledge of programming.

Ori never stopped writing. When he wasn't writing code, he was writing in his diary. He would take vacations to write in his diary. He once rented a remote cabin in the farthest reaches of Norway just to write for two weeks straight, uninterrupted. He had a knack for reflection about his own practice, which, I assumed, came from his years of introspection.

Over the few months leading up to my fieldwork, I would take the train to Berlin and sit down with him over a bowl of our favorite warm chickpea dish, called Massabaha, and discuss the philosophy of technology. I came alive when speaking to Ori, who helped me imagine what happened within our laptops or smartphones. Through his stories about where and how he worked, Ori taught me to care about all the people behind that smartphone or laptop screen—their frustrations, the tests they were doing on us, the conversations they were having about one feature or other. Each button, each tiny object suddenly had a back story. My chat app had certain swipe features, certain colors, certain moments of flashing on and off, and ways of behaving that no longer seemed arbitrary. Who decided that my thumb would swipe left and not right? When my phone collects my GPS data when

I run, where does that data go, and who are the people making the decision that my data will trigger another feature that allows me to listen to music at the speed of my running pace? Ori made me want to meet all those people. To talk to them and see what they looked like, what food they ate for lunch, or what music they listened to while coding. Through Ori, digital media technology became social: close to me, personal, human. Despite not being a programmer, I started to understand software as being nonstatic, viscose, and constantly shifting like a ball of modeling clay that a group of people was collectively pushing and pulling, reshaping its size, purpose, and scope.

Sociality, Care, Creativity

Software workers like Ori, beyond just making software, experience moments of creativity, conflict, frustration, humor, silliness, laziness, awkwardness, and various other forms of social and antisocial behavior while working with code. Indeed, software is a social process (Mackenzie 2006). Understanding technical artifacts as social artifacts is nothing new and is perhaps one of the central claims of science and technology studies. In the research program set forth by Wiebe Bijker, Thomas Hughes, and Trevor Pinch, they aimed to contribute "to a greater understanding of the social processes involved in technological development" (1989, 10). Specifically, they underlined how the social environment shapes the technical characteristics of an artifact, meaning that technological artifacts are first and foremost social constructs. What they meant is that during the development of an artifact (such as software, for example), innovation is not at all linear but involves many stages of variation and selection of the right path to take, which includes much negotiation on behalf of the artifact developers (in this case, the programmers).

So, while we might know quite generally that technical systems are social systems, how does this sociality play out in software production? Through Ori's stories and the stories of his colleagues, this chapter explores how programmers relate to their practice of programming and the software they create. It does so through the notion of sociality, which in this chapter is an umbrella term that encompasses the interactions among programmers and between the programmers and their software. In uncovering the sociality of software production, I will also describe the care and creativity that result.

In doing so, this chapter shows the intricacies of a software developer's work. I use the term "software's sociality" to mean: (1) an interaction between the programmer and the material object of the computer, a "closeness to the machine" (Ullman 1997); and (2) a sociality between software developers, defined by closeness and care for one another's work. We will see that, in the best of times, software development is about care, craft, and closeness to one's programming work (for example, finding a solution to a problem, building something that works, etc.), harnessing certain social relations among developers and working as a collective, and using one's skill to engage with, manipulate, or hack into various digital infrastructures.

Describing software's sociality is crucial to understanding my broader argument about good enoughness as it shows how the programmer's work practice and the social interactions that come along with it clash with the corporate software culture's narrative of production. More specifically, multifaceted forms of sociality are part of software work, including moments of slowness, care, and creativity. This sociality often conflicts with the narratives and logics of corporate software production, including discourses of excellence, speed, and agility, which I mention in the previous and following chapters. This forms a tension between care (for one's own work) and compromise (for the sake of the production process or customer demands). In addition, I will show how the craft of working on software through specific software development tools (yes, software for software developers!) also informs the developer's care and creativity and often shapes how good-enough software and good-enough work practices emerge.

In this vein, we will see that delivering good-enough software doesn't always mean that software developers are sloppy and do not care about their projects. Rather, programmers are often forced to disrupt their care for and engagement or interaction with the project they are working on in order to compromise and settle for something that's merely good enough for now, good enough for a customer to use. As this chapter reveals, understanding the depth and dimensions of software's sociality will help us grasp the type of compromises that software developers have to deal with when working on a software project.

Material and Human Sociality

Throughout my research, I understood sociality as "interactive practices" (Law and Mol 1995), studying how groups of entities (both human and nonhuman) are gathered into specific forms of collective association, enabling interaction between the entities concerned (Latour 2005). As John Law and Annemarie Mol highlighted, "when we look at the social, we are also looking at the production of materiality. And when we look at materials, we are witnessing the production of the social" (1995, 274). In this sense, my work looks at the interactive practices of software, the programmers and their teams, and the users and customers for whom they are building their software.

This approach is an expanded conception of sociality that includes (but is not limited to) material objects, which Karin Knorr-Cetina termed "object-centered sociality." This concept "attempts to break open such notions as that of an expert, of technical competence, of an expert system or of scientific-technical work" (Knorr-Cetina 1997, 9). These notions often presuppose but do not unfold or interrogate the object relations on which expertise depends. In contrast, the concept of an object-centered sociality takes its lead from these relationships. But it also serves as a "convenient gloss on the entire range of social forms that are governed or mediated by objects" (Knorr-Cetina 1997, 9).

Sociality is thus a familiarity between humans and objects composed of "affect, knowledge, mutual action, and norms" (Forstie 2017, 1). In addition, this chapter focuses on sociality as a form of closely knowing and closely interacting: the close knowing of the people, spaces, and/or tools one engages with, which allows for an easy familiarity with them.

This definition of object-oriented sociality can thus be a form of "professional vision" (Goodwin 1994), meaning a set of skills, tools, and practices that enables a programmer like Ori to use this collection of knowledge to engage with, infiltrate, or hack the world around him. While a profession such as archaeology, for example, gives the professional archaeologist the ability to see a map or excavation differently than nonarchaeologists, the specific adaptability of software makes Ori's professional vision more far-reaching. What I mean here is that a Web site for a train ticket system, a city hall's Web site, or an app for a university can be programmed in the JavaScript language, making Ori's close knowledge of the digital under-belly of the world around him more far-reaching. As an expert, Ori has a multitude of object relations (Knorr-Cetina 1997), where objects (like an app or a Web site) serve as centering and integrating devices for regimes of expertise. One can theorize that software gives Ori a huge range of "embedding environments" in which his similar type of "expert work is carried out, thus constituting something like an emotional home for expert selves" (Knorr-Cetina 1997, 9).

Expanding our understanding of sociality to include our form of closeness not only to a person or animal but also to an object or a sociotechnical system (like, for example, a piece of software, a human body, a train line network, etc.) can be useful when trying to understand how tacit knowledge is constituted. Specifically, it can help us to understand how craftspeople or skilled workers connect to the inner workings (or inner self) of physical objects or the technical systems they are working on. Closeness here is thus the depth of experience, like knowing and caring about somebody or something closely (this can be an object, one's space, etc.). Researching this form of sociality, therefore, involves acquiring an understanding of how closeness and distance are constructed. The following paragraphs will return to Ori but will also introduce other interlocutors I encountered in the field who helped me to develop my account of software's sociality.

Close to the Machine and Craft

As I mentioned earlier, Ori began writing before he started writing code. He began to code later in his teenage years, slowly teaching himself, and then again while studying computer science at university. I would argue that his writing introduced him to zoning into something or deeply focusing on a craft. Writing is an intimate endeavor as it involves mirroring our own thoughts back to ourselves. This is a state of mental inwardness that many craftspeople, artists, and writers experience. During this process, the person creating something is locked within a nonmaterial, imaginary world, which then manifests itself through a material medium—whether through a paintbrush or paint, code, a processor, a server, or some other medium.

Ori's desk was on the fifth floor of the MiddleTech building in an open-concept office space. His desk was simple. He kept it uncluttered for the sake of convenience: The senior managers at MiddleTech liked to shuffle the workspaces every few months in order to keep the teams dynamic and the programmers "agile" (the term, meaning dynamic and quick to react, is one that I will return to in a later chapter). While the desk space lacked photos, personal trinkets, or gadgets, Ori did have two computer monitors that were adjusted to his body: they were ergonomic, fitted just high enough to suit his gaze and back comfort. He had two screens: One was turned vertically on its side, and the other, sitting to the right of it, was horizontal. Programmers like turning their screens vertically in order to fit more lines of code onto the screen, much like the way you turn your camera vertically in order to capture the entire height of a skyscraper. When the skyscraper screen was filled with the project Ori was working on, the other screen was open to all sorts of other work tools, such as a chat system, which connected Ori to his other colleagues, and a code review system (which I'll get into later).

After a few years of working in the front-end team, Ori moved up the software development ladder into a more prestigious researcher role as a data scientist, where he worked among PhD dropouts and supersmart brains applying, among other things, machine learning models for various car- and navigation-related problems and a variety of experiments to help improve the products that MiddleTech was selling to other businesses. MiddleTech has a number of software products that they sell to customers, and in such large companies, software developers are assigned the task of building just a tiny component of a piece of software, which then fits into a larger piece of software, sort of like a Russian doll. Ori, as a researcher, usually builds little programs, which then become part of larger research projects that do not necessarily ever have any practical application. These programs attempt to improve the navigation software, allowing it to work with new hardware, like a self-driving car or in-car cameras, and helping it detect lane data more precisely.

When Ori becomes "zoned in" or immersed in coding, he fills both screens with a "programming environment," a set of processes and programming tools used to create the program or software product. Part of this programming environment is something called an IDE or an integrative development environment, which can contain a code editor, as well as a compiler or an interpreter. I find it quite suitable to call this tool an "environment." As *Miriam-Webster* defines it, an environment is literally "the circumstances, objects, or conditions by which one is surrounded." When it comes to a programming environment, I will emphasize the word "surrounded." The programming environment surrounds Ori in his work and envelops him from all sides. After fifteen years of working in this profession, he has come to find this environment very cozy, familiar, and even intimate. He speaks the language (Python, usually) of this environment and generally understands what he is working on and where he can find the tools to build his program.

During a typical work week, he is assigned a small task and then zones into it, working at it for a few weeks or even months. While he is not always alone, of course, a large part of his work is about his relationship with what he is building or fixing.

In the late 1990s, Ellen Ullman was one of the first software engineers to write a firsthand account of computer engineering and its social and personal implications. While not directly ethnographic, *Close to the Machine: Technophilia and Its Discontents* (1997) gave its readers a detailed understanding of what programming entails. "Closeness" here was partially about "retreat into some private interior space, closer to the machine, where things can be accomplished," where "the machine begins to seem friendlier than the analysts, the users, the managers" whom programmers encounter in their daily work (Ullman 1997, 23). By working alone to build something on a computer, Ori is able to build a private world between himself and his computational system, a practice that often involves high levels of concentration and craft.

In Richard Sennett's *The Craftsman*, he highlights how a craftsman's work (like a programmer's work, which Sennett also studied) involves a whole culture of material interaction, what he terms "material consciousness" (2008, 120). Here, the craftsman becomes particularly focused and interested in the things they can change (Sennett 2008, 121), which in Ori's case can be a bug fix, a line of code, or a new feature. Through his own material consciousness, Ori also discovers and understands his own capabilities.

Much like a carpenter sets up a workshop, how programmers set up their IDE is significant to their level of material consciousness, as it's the space that their creativity inhabits. We can also imagine an environment in programming as a space that one figuratively enters. Christian, another programmer working on a research team that finds ways of improving a routing algorithm, told me that he can close his eyes, look inward, and imagine the entire architecture of a system like his own home. He knows where everything is. His colleagues often ask him to solve a problem, and he can close his eyes, visualize the space where the problem might lie, and sit down and write code. The sense of familiarity and comfort Christian experiences comes with knowing the software infrastructure and how to build it. Programming, as Sherry Turkle describes, requires an "intimate understanding of the logic of the machine" (2005, 175), meaning a knowledge of how a piece of software works, what libraries and components it takes to run the software, and, more importantly, where to go to fix a problem. In order to understand this logic, one has to understand intimately the programming environment or space.

Flow

Some programmers at MiddleTech have termed this process of zoning in, or inwardness, as "flow." One programmer explained, "We have this thing . . . It's basically an agreement with a team. Whenever I have my headphones on, don't disturb me. It's these times where we agree to allow ourselves to work without distraction and interruption . . . It's disruptive to call somebody out. To disrupt the flow."

This rule was easily agreed upon within the team because most programmers understand this state of being in flow and have experienced the necessary pains of being taken out of this state. A signal to other programmers that one is in the state of flow is achieved by wearing headphones. Bigger headphones are more effective at repelling others (as opposed to earbuds, which can easily be hidden by a hoodie) as they are more visible and signal "Leave me alone, I'm coding." For many programmers, sound is also an important component of the programming environment, and many programmers like to listen to certain playlists or genres (I noticed that mostly metal and electronic music were preferred). Finding flow has nothing to do with skill, writes psychologist Mihaly Csikszentmihalyi: It is a sort of "mystical, intuitive understanding" of one's work and work environment and a "gradual focusing of attention" (1997, 151). Csikszentmihalyi, who pioneered the academic study of creativity, wrote about how labor practices achieve flow by drawing on an example of a team of Italian psychologists who studied a rural inhabitant of the Italian Alps. One inhabitant, Serafina, who was in her seventies at the time of this study, woke up every day at 5 a.m. to milk her cows. Through this daily routine, she knew "every tree, every boulder, every feature of the mountains as if they were old friends" (1997, 145). By connecting to the environment around her, she worked with joy and contentment. Much like Serafina, software developers are in a privileged position to work in a job that becomes part of their lives and that most of them deeply enjoy. And when zoning into their work for hours, they are also connected to the environment they are working in. They know the software space they are working with much like Serafina, who knew every tree, every boulder, and every feature of the mountains as if they were old friends.

A Serbian developer named Marko once stopped me in the hallway to explain his frustration whenever he was taken out of his state of flow: "Meetings are slow. I feel sleepy. But you know why, Paula? Because we are in a different mental mode when we are working. It's faster. The speed of coding just pushes you forward. And you work and work and go quickly, and then you are in a meeting. And somebody is late, and then you have to go find an adapter, and then this and that. It's slow. I just see the time clicking away, click click click. I feel so sleepy. I just want to sleep. And I just think it's because I've been interrupted from this deep state of concentration. I am also like this at home, when I'm working. My wife has to call my name or shake me to get my attention. It's not like I don't care—I am just deep into concentration."

Here, Marko is much like Serafina when he is in a deep state of flow. We can also see that software development for Marko is more than just the practice of typing in commands on a keyboard. While the relationship of programmers to their machines has been conceptualized in programming textbooks and historical accounts of the programming profession as a command-and-control practice, this same relationship can be understood in another language, the language of sociality. Through Marko, Ori, and others, we can see that the practice of programming is achieving a form of sociality with the machine. Software gives programmers a relationship with the computer because it allows them to see as well as influence what happens inside of a machine and between machines. It gives them access to a huge complexity that is playing out in the electrical circuits of a computer.

Therefore, it's no wonder that when programmers talk about their work, they talk about their "closeness to the machine" (Ullman 1997). To clarify what this "closeness" means, Ullman doesn't simply mean that a programmer is close to an inner core of a machine. She means closeness to a form of abstraction. Software is always an abstraction and thus brings us close to the machine by providing layers of abstractions that hide much more than they make visible and accessible. An abstraction can be the Graphical User Interfaces that we use on our laptops or smartphones, as well as programming languages that programmers use. Closeness is therefore a closeness to some form of abstraction. One could say that closeness with people works in a similar way: We can intimately know somebody without really knowing everything about them, or by knowing only one layer of their personality.

Yet what makes coding in a programming language, as opposed to just swiping your phone, so special? The knowledge of how to program the machine gives programmers like Ori much more power, providing them with a greater ability to shape the technical system they encounter. This power is an increased ability to shape the very abstractions that allow programmers to be close to the machine. It is also an engagement with the contradictory properties of written code, which is, on the one hand, fully understandable, consisting of a set of commands, and, on the other hand, so increasingly complex that no human being can understand it in its entirety. It is an engagement with software that is constantly moldable and changing, that consists of many layers of older legacy code that still exists within the system. These layers of code were created at earlier phases when the software was written and could not be taken out of the system anymore. (I will address legacy code in a later chapter.) It is an engagement with a dizzying plurality of libraries and languages and multiple translations and interfacing moments that make the overall system work.

Collective Sociality

By this point, I have explained that software development is a relational endeavor as it requires knowledge of the inner workings of a software system and also involves moments of closeness to the machine, craft, and zoning in to a software environment and finding a sense of flow in work. In our quest to grasp the sociality inherent in software development, another element worth uncovering is the collective sociality among members of the group building a software project and the level of interpersonal understanding and communication that comes with it. As we have learned through Ori and his colleagues, software development is a highly social endeavor, analogous to dozens of people writing an ongoing Google document at the same time. Code is written by a collective of people. Much like any profession in which people work collectively and passionately on a particular project, software work is also, in this way, intimate. While building something together, developers share a common understanding—they use the same language and the same forms of participation—and through this understanding, they become close to other developers around them. Software developers told me that after working together for a while, they can identify who wrote a certain line or section of code because those particular individuals write in that specific style. As I will explain later in this chapter, a team of programmers develops common coding standards, but individual styles of coding are still discernible to those who intimately know the team and those coding within it.

Collective Coordination

Throughout my months at MiddleTech, I learned that software is a strong team effort, and coordination is very important. Software is made up of lines and lines of code written by a multitude of people, and these lines have to make sense as a whole. Without close coordination, software would become a large mess much like a group of dancers performing to music without knowing their exact choreography. In order to coordinate their code, developers have planning meetings during which they discuss what they need to work on, and how they will go about doing it.

I would crash these planning meetings, sitting in the corner of the small ten-person meeting room and take notes. At one particular meeting between the algorithm research team, a group of six developers were discussing how to solve a problem. The decisions about how to solve the problem had to be made collectively so the changes could be individually implemented into each team member's own subtasks. The nature of software development requires these types of meetings as developers working in large software companies like MiddleTech cannot build something solo, in a corner, cut off from the rest of the development team.

One of the only female developers in the back-end development team was Jelena, who worked in the Electric Vehicle routing team. She was a Serbian in her mid-thirties. She liked ordering lots of Amazon packages for her nephews back in Serbia and loved explaining things in metaphors. Jelena explained the fragmentation of a software project using the metaphor of a house: "It's like the house metaphor. When building a house, the plumber works on something, and then the carpenter. Often this doesn't happen at the same time because they would get in the way of each other . . . but we are all doing it at the same time." What she means is that a team of developers has to know what to build and make sure it fits with what the rest of the team is also building (much like a carpenter has to speak to the architect to make sure the door is the right size to fit into the house). Jelena also drew attention to the temporal dimension of software work, where development is done at the same time—for example, carpenters do not wait for the floor to be laid down before the door is built (in keeping with the house metaphor). Software developers merge their code into the main code base at the same time, which sometimes causes bugs in the system, as a piece of Jelena's software is often deeply intertwined and dependent on what her other teammate has built. She added, "We are constantly breaking each other's stuff. What you are creating communicates with other code others are building."

One way to synchronize this work, which is done simultaneously, is to "align the coding style . . . to keep code easy to understand," as Christian, the team lead or manager, told the other team members. As coding style is a subjective matter, aligning coding style means being closely acquainted with the style itself and with how other developers code. As Christian explained, developers constantly review one another's code after it is written: "This is done to maintain a coding style. There might be sixteen ways to do something, but you want to have everyone writing something in a similar way." This similarity helps define the boundaries of the coding collective. If this style is broken, and somebody writes in a different style or builds something that disrupts another section of the code through a rough hack (meaning a careless way of writing code), one can say that the closeness is somehow broken, and conflict or frustration arises, or certain components of the software system won't work altogether.

In the first front-end team I joined, the team of Dev-Ops programmers made up an automated system to test their code. It was a verification bot they wrote in order to make "the system flow quite smoothly." Marco, one of the Dev-Ops programmers, explained, "so we write code now that has to fit the standards of this bot. We send what we wrote out to the bot. The robot runs some tests and analyzes it."

Jan, his teammate, added, "It's very socialist. Everything has to be equal and clear."

This so-called "socialism" that Jan referred to is, again, about creating a common coding collective that writes code in a similar style. Rather than having an each-programmer-for-themselves mindset, programmers are forced to think about the system as a whole, in collective coordination.

Code Review Style

Developers also explained to me that there is even a "style" of code review. At MiddleTech, developers use code review software that requires developers to review one another on a scale of +2, +1, −1, or −2. A front-end developer named Dariusz explained this process to me:

> DARIUSZ: The ratings depend on the reviewer's style. My style was 'I can give you +2 even if something is a bit wrong, as long as I can highlight it, and you will fix it in the future' because my main goal with code review was to make the other person a better programmer for the future.
>
> PAULA: Oh wow! How interesting! What are some other styles?
>
> DARIUSZ: "I know some asshole reviewers who would see a very small bad piece of code . . . for instance, a variable name they didn't agree with because it wasn't descriptive enough, and they would give the committer −1 and tell them to fix it. I would in that case give them +2 and say, 'Make the variable more descriptive in the future.'"
>
> PAULA: Wow! So you're a kind of 'benefit-of-the-doubt, let's-give-you-a-chance-to-learn' type of code reviewer? And then there are assholes?
>
> DARIUSZ: That's how I'd put it.

In this example, the code review process provides another layer of closely knowing the other developers: Dariusz knows who the "asshole" reviewers are, and others in his team know that Dariusz is a relaxed and forgiving reviewer.

A year prior to my conversation with Dariusz, in the summer of 2016, Ori came down to my office area to ask me to lunch. As it turned out, a lot of the developers in my new team work area used to work with Ori. I asked the team if anyone wanted to come. Three guys nodded and said "yes." (It's a small fieldwork victory if I convinced any new developer to come to lunch with me. Three at once made me feel like I was getting bonus points.) We decided to go for lunch at a generic Vietnamese restaurant frequented by business lunch-goers in that particular district of Berlin. We sat down and ended up having a long and intense conversation about a number of topics. At one point, I asked them if they ever see a line of code and can identify who wrote it:

Jan joked, "Sure, but I never saw Ori's code ever. I don't even know if he ever wrote a piece of code in his life." The other guys laughed. "Whenever we touch something, we say 'What a crap line of code' or 'Who the fuck wrote this? Oh, it's *that* person!!'" The guys continued to chuckle at Jan's joke. "But we are really trying to eliminate the personal factor in the way in which we write code at this company."

The guys then explained to me that there are a few ways of noting down how people write code. One is that you can actually turn on a feature to see who wrote this section of code. But the other way is just through the style people use.

I couldn't imagine how one piece of code has a style.

Jan said, "It just sort of has the same syntax or lines somehow." Here, the guys were quite vague, and I didn't really understand or fully grasp what they meant by "different style." I thought of something I learned previously about the difference between tabs and space bars. "Is that like a particular style?" I asked.

"Yes, exactly. So [the computer] reads your code much faster if the style is the same. Like, for example, tabs and not space bars. Right now we don't use tabs at all. You can make mistakes with a tab because it would just slow down the process," Jan explained.

Nishant added, "But I worked in a start-up before coming to this job and there they just wanted to do things very quickly. Just get out their products quickly and get on with it."

Jan explained that there "is an advantage of writing 'slow code.' You gather more knowledge about what is happening in order to prevent things from breaking in the future. That's what slow code is all about."

Automating Closeness

I found our conversation striking as it pointed to how software development is about building a collectively fostered sociality among developers that adheres to a certain style of expression. On the surface level, we can take Jan's point about eliminating the "personal factor" of writing code and assume that it eliminates the "humanness" in the code, stripping away the style and character of each developer, thus taking away the personal closeness developers have with one another. Yet if we look more closely, knowing how to eliminate the "personal factor" means being in tune with the entirety of the code and understanding what the rules, forms, and modes of syntax are in order to camouflage one's code and blend in. I learned that eliminating the "personal factor" in coding is about collectively understanding or intimately knowing the collective coding style. At one point, Ori sat down with me to explain how this collective style is enforced, particularly through the software platform that he and his colleagues use to write their code, called an integrated development environment (IDE):

"Many IDEs style your code. For example, [the IDE] automatically puts in indents instead of tabs, or it puts braces in one line instead of the next line, or does not put a space after a bracket. But a coding style is something you agree on with a team. Many teams take a reference from Google or other places online. The IDE also gives you guidelines that are written in text, like the Google JavaScript coding style, which is like a list of rules. An IDE just helps to enforce this rule. If we forgot a space somewhere, an IDE will reformat based on the coding style. You can also define your own coding style and change the definitions or parameters in the IDE."

Programming requires a great deal of collective understanding in order to build slow code, gathering more "knowledge of what is happening," as Jan explained. During this conversation, the developers hinted that start-ups do things quickly, hastily, without care for the style of how software is written. During my fieldwork, I heard countless stories from software developers about their quick-and-dirty start-up times, when software development was about "hacking together" ideas and getting them out quickly, rather than slowing down to maintain a cohesive system. Slowing down and creating cohesion is often favored—not simply to make code beautiful but rather to maintain the long-term stability of their system, to reduce the chance of potential bugs, and to help those who will maintain the code in the future. As Sennett also explained in relation to a craftsman's work, "slowness serves as a source of satisfaction; practice beds in, making the skill one's own."

Here, slow craft time also "enables the work of reflection and imagination—which the push for quick results cannot" (Sennett 2008, 295).

This "knowledge of what is happening" that Jan mentioned is also key in collective coordination: a close knowledge of the style of the collective, involving a level of care for one's software environment. Ori's code was invisible to people like Jan, not because he was sloppy and careless but because he had a close knowledge of the system and knew how to blend in with others. Developers become aligned with one another through the IDE, as well as from other forms of automated systems, like bots, which help check the code for bugs or inconsistencies.

The bot I mentioned earlier also tests the code for inconsistencies. The more intimately acquainted one becomes with the actual parameters that the bot is looking for, the more one can write code that is standardized with the rest of one's team. Additionally, this "socialist" and "equal" approach Jan mentioned is about creating a collective sociality; it involves shifting the individual coder's desire to work alone to a deeper knowledge of how to work in coordination with others.

During many team meetings and moments when I observed how developers code, I noticed that there are a number of other tools that instigate coordination between developers. For code review, which I mentioned earlier, programmers at MiddleTech use a software called Gerrit, a free, open-source, Web-based code-collaboration tool (see www.gerritcodereview .com), which has become a code review standard in many software development teams. The tool allows developers to review each other's modifications to their source code and approve or reject these changes. Gerrit displayed a list of merges, meaning updates or additions to the code base. This list included the type of update, who updated it, and the status of the update (whether it passed or failed).

Developers also use something called "Confluence," a team collaboration software that keeps all projects and ideas surrounding a given project in one place. All developers at MiddleTech also use something called GIT, an open-source version control system run on a piece of software that tracks changes to code and works alongside the developer environment or IDE. (There are other forms of version control systems, but GIT is the most popular.) When a developer writes code, each line has their name written beside it.

When a developer sees a bug or is unhappy with the code that was written, they type a command into GIT called "git blame," which reveals who wrote the last line of code. When a developer becomes frustrated or confused with a line of code, they use "git blame" in order to reveal that it was

Jan or Ori who wrote that piece of code, and they can then confront the author in person or via the GIT system. "Git blame" gives the developer an intimate knowledge of all the software developers and their mistakes, which becomes an inherent part of the software development process. One can read this as a form of sociomaterial sociality where the infrastructure itself, or the software system, knows the software developers by tracking their movements. Here, GIT also introduces an element of control through employee monitoring or direct surveillance. In this case, the GIT system not only provides management with more methods of employee surveillance but "today it is 'the team' of co-workers that bear witness to everyday work efforts" (Gregg 2011, 74), where software developers as a community track each other's frequency and quality of code performance. This type of mutual surveillance does not necessarily have to lead to competition, with workers attempting to outperform one another. Rather, it can lead to the opposite: One developer sees that another developer is still struggling with a piece of software, not "committing" anything, or even taking their time to fix a few lines of code, which can lead to a justification for good-enough work. More specifically, employee mutual surveillance through systems like Confluence or GIT can also help developers compare their code with one another, leading to developers justifying their decision to push or finish a project and commit it into the main code base in a good-enough state. While this may seem counterintuitive, watching others commit good-enough code may lead programmers to think, "Oh, their code isn't that good/isn't finished yet/ needs more adjustment so why can't mine be the same?" In this case, programmer cosurveillance can consequently create a form of sociality where developers align their programming practices with one another, fostering a culture of good enoughness rather than excellence.

After gaining a greater understanding of how a developer interacts with other developers through these various tools, we can start to imagine how different forms of sociality in software development arise from a deep understanding of (1) the software system (or the architecture), meaning the pieces that make up the software project, the software elements, the relationships between these elements, etc.; (2) a familiarity with the style of the code, meaning a deep understanding of not only the language in which the software is written but also the style in which it is written; (3) the ability to differentiate between software that is messy and wrong and software that is done well or beautifully; and (4) a familiarity with the developers writing the code with you—knowing how to identify who wrote which line of code and whom to turn to if something looks strange, as well as that person's wider work practices and the way in which they work on code. All of these forms of knowing and watching over one another's work using GIT are part of fostering a culture of good enoughness. GIT becomes yet another tool to individually and collectively negotiate a standard or limitation of what is good-enough work or not.

Conclusions

In this chapter, I touched upon a variety of examples from my field that highlighted how sociality arises during software development. The concept of sociality helps us understand the programmer's multifaceted ways of creating "closeness to the machine" (Ullman 1997). But what does this closeness actually look like in practice? What does it look like at a software company that has its own logics, agendas, methods of management, and various types of programmers all working together?

As I showed in this chapter, the concept of sociality helps us to understand the nuanced ways in which programmers relate to their software and to the community of people building software. In framing these various modes of closeness, I have shown that programmer sociality takes place in a distributed sociotechnical system that the programmer learns to navigate through practice.

But why is studying software's sociality important? For one, it can explain what is at stake in programming through the eyes of programmers themselves. In this chapter, I hoped to shed light on the care and craft that programmers put into programming. Computational objects are interaction partners to their users, more like thought prosthetics than simple tools (Turkle 2005, 3). The computer is evocative in an even more profound way for those who know it well, who interact with it directly, and who are in a position to experience its second nature (Turkle 2005, 19). For many programmers, programming is not a job but a creative endeavor that brings them closer to software and to the people around them.

Yet it is important to note that this chapter introduced the best-case scenario in a programmer's work. At times, programmers are not that closely connected with their work, and they don't care, don't focus, don't understand exactly what is required of them, or don't understand the complicated, mangled code base they are working with. Programmers can also care a lot, and despite their meticulous planning, there will still be incongruities between these carefully laid-out plans and the fundamental limitations of the machine in action (Suchman 1987, 2007). Furthermore, as we shall see in the following chapters, the temporality of work in a corporate software office as well as various customer requirements do not allow for the constant care and craft that I described in this chapter.

Moreover, while some programmers occupy positions in which they can constantly strive to achieve this level of care, craft, and flow in their software project, others are measured against those who achieve this level of closeness to the machine and become frustrated when they are not given enough time to do the same and are thus left behind. Acquiring this level of object-oriented sociality and being assigned (by one's managers or project leads) time to focus on these moments, to zone in and just build software, is regarded as a privilege.

Those like Ori, who work in more research-oriented and development positions, are considered the privileged ones because of the time they are given to devote to their projects. These privileges are still granted in various tech offices, at Medium Tech companies like MiddleTech, but even more so at Big Tech companies. These jobs are created to provide workers with "cushy flexible hours" and "creative workspaces," giving them time to think (Turner 2009), which becomes a way of trying to maximize these moments of intense flow and intimate engagement with the programmer's software project. This is a way in which some companies, such as Google, Facebook, or MiddleTech, construct status and privilege. Such companies often boast that their workers are the best of the best and must be given time to be creative and zone into their inspired software projects.

Software is also about maintenance and dirty work, often requiring so-called "code-monkeys" to punch away at fixing bugs, leaving little time for the levels of sociality and closeness I described in this chapter. These types of jobs are unequally distributed geographically, with outsourcing offices in Eastern Europe, in cities like Krakow or Kyiv, or in the Global South, in cities like Bangalore. This places programming work in the same category as other jobs in the labor hierarchy debate; workers from the rich North are hired for "elite" jobs and those in the Global South are given the noncreative "click-work."

That said, studying the sociality inherent in programming can help us in various ways. Firstly, it can help us understand the collective subjectivity and social interaction that goes into the practice of writing code. As I will keep highlighting throughout this book, programmers do not work alone. Their computers are networked to an entire software development ecosystem. This ecosystem requires that they merge their code into the code base by closely understanding the work of others around them, writing in the same language and style as others, and collaborating with others if something goes wrong.

A large part of programmers' work is devoted to rating and reviewing one another's code according to collective standards. These standards are enforced by a variety of factors: (1) by bots, small programs that monitor the work of the programmers and constrain the style in which the code is written to fit a general norm; (2) by the collective culture of how code should be written; and (3) by the infrastructural constraints of the software project (sometimes a component can't be built because another existing software component is standing in its way). The computer programmer is thus not a "creator of universes for which he alone is the lawgiver" (Weizenbaum 1976, 115) but rather a member of a large working collective. In order to do their job well, programmers must be intuitively attuned to the collective. This collective practice thus influences their subjectivity as it sets boundaries on their sense of agency and on their desires to code in a certain way or maintain a certain personal style. It forces them to constantly make subjective jumps between creatively coding on their own and monitoring their own code to adapt to the rest of the team.

Secondly, studying software's sociality helps to complicate the picture of programming as something rational and logical. Software is not only a set of algorithms but a sentient experience. Programming is not a command-and-control practice but a creative process, with programmers proud of what they have created. Software development involves a multitude of stories of creativity, personal struggle, power and powerlessness, meaning and meaninglessness, hierarchy, cultural norms, humor, and playfulness. These moments are messy and full of negotiation and force programmers to feel connected to the code they write, to argue with their team members who see things differently, to sense what's right and what's wrong, or what should be done correctly or not. Programming is thus a practice that is far from rational and calculated. This sociality, like the care and creativity around the craft of programming, clashes with the narratives and logics of corporate software production, including discourses of excellence, speed, and agility. This forms a tension between care (for one's own work) and compromise (for the sake of the production process or customer demands). Delivering good-enough software doesn't always mean that a software developer is being careless about work or a project. On the contrary, programmers are often forced to disrupt their care or engagement with a project they are working on, or a programmer they are working with, in order to compromise and settle for something that's good enough for now.

In that vein, studying software's sociality can give us a new temporal understanding of how software is produced and maintained, which I will return to in a later chapter dedicated to speed and temporality. We are accustomed to understanding software as fast, smart, and seamless. But when we insert forms of sentiment and emotion into our understanding of how software is built, we can see that these relationships take time and create resistance to the Silicon Valley "move fast and break things" motto that dominates our digital economy.

Lastly, understanding software development through the notion of sociality can help us understand that certain software tools, especially those that programmers use, negotiate closeness. As in the example of GIT software, software developers also use digital tools that mediate and shape forms of sociality. This is a sociality that is deeply entangled in software, displaying a human-machine interaction on a multitude of levels, including the connection between programmers and the software they create, a connection that is collectively being built or was built over the years and still exists in the system, as well as a relationship between software developers and the tools that shape and constrain their behavior in relation to the software product they are building and those building it around them. As software becomes an actor in negotiating forms of sociality between programmers and their collaborators, it also helps order the norms of what is good enough and what isn't.

The purpose of this chapter was to frame sociality as a direct characteristic of programming software, which becomes a key tension between programmers and their corporate work environments, with programmers constantly having to decide between more care (which leads to missed deadlines) and compromise (which leads to good-enough-for-now software projects). Various forms of sociality can generate explicit and open conflicts, and I could observe them playing out in my field: for example, between one developer who feels deeply connected to their personal style and others who beg to differ. Or it can trigger potential, simmering conflicts, such as when a programmer like Christian is always worried about being interrupted and taken out of his close connection with his machine. This can be the very source of the conflict, or it can further fuel other conflicts that are typical of any industrial workplace.

Now that I've introduced you to software's sociality, let's move to another level of abstraction in corporate software development by zooming out to the dynamics of the software development team and looking at how this collective experiences software's complexity, how they create misunderstandings, disharmony, and conflict, and how things simply go awry.

3

Where Stuff Goes Wrong

"Code is layered like lasagna. It's lasagna code. But it's more like an onion. Because when you cut it, it makes you cry."
—ASEEM, SOFTWARE DEVELOPER, AUGUST 2017

Every few weeks Aseem attended a photography meet-up in Berlin. The group was made up of a random collection of ex-pats and Berlin locals who got together a few times a month to share their love of photography. The small group would wander the streets or take day-trips to explore the land-scape around the city. Aseem absolutely loved nature photography. One afternoon in the office, I commented on the picture he used as his desk-top background. He smiled proudly and told me it was his photo. He then invited me to sit down with him to browse through his online portfolio. I was surprised. His photos were really good. He understood shape and light and the emotions of the people he was shooting. Landscapes in particular came to life in his photos. One of my favorites was a wide-angle view of a forest on a small hill, with a soft yellow meadow framing it from below. The autumn colored each tree differently, and the light from the sky was hitting only a small collection of trees at the front of the patch, giving the entire landscape a deeper texture. Aseem looked proud of his photos. Nature pho-tography helped him melt into the landscape, becoming one with the beauty he encountered. Photography seemed to be about precision and control for Aseem—many of his photos were deftly captured, with trees, clouds, and fog delicately placed in the frame. Nothing seemed out of order in any of his photographs. For Aseem, this sense of precision and control was hard to come by when building software. Not because he was a poor programmer (on the contrary) but because software is often unstable and uncontrollable.

Aseem was young. He was maybe twenty-four or twenty-five when we first met. He had joined MiddleTech as a working student, meaning he was just finishing up his master's degree in computer science at the Technical University of Berlin and was on probation at the company. He arrived in Europe a few years before getting his job at MiddleTech, first studying in Holland as an exchange student, and then transferring to Berlin. He grew up around New Delhi and was always very technically inclined. He enjoyed his studies because they provided an alternative to the practical side of programming. Studying was theoretical, about building and optimizing certain algorithms, and he liked that. He told me that his mind often races when he thinks about "good software architecture." He was also always interested in mathematics and engineering, and was drawn to the profession of programming more for building systems himself rather than copying and pasting from some open-source piece of code he found on the internet (which is the common practice of many programmers). He wanted to continue his graduate studies and do a doctoral degree, but he decided to take the opportunity to stay and work in Germany. In his opinion, Germany offered much more creativity for a programmer. He explained that India is seen as the outsourcing giant of the tech world: Software companies in Europe or North America will often hire an Indian outsourcing company to do the work that the programmers in the rich Global North do not feel like doing. This work can include bug-squashing or cleaning up old code, the maintenance work that is incredibly necessary when building software. He was grateful that he didn't have to work in an Indian outsourcing company but could instead work creatively on building new software and new features at MiddleTech. He explained that he yearned to live a "creative and challenging life," something that programming in India wouldn't offer him.

Aseem's biggest hobby outside of work was taking photos. He didn't need the motivation of the group meet-up to get out with his camera, but he explained that he did it mainly to make friends. We became friends throughout the second summer of my fieldwork. I felt a bit sisterly toward him. He would call me out for coffee or tea every few days, and we would sit together on the fourth-floor MiddleTech balcony, where I would listen to his stories and worries. His life in Berlin was, at times, painfully lonely. He would come to work and go home alone, often spending the weekends by himself. I was upset that a young kid with a friendly smile and bright eyes, full of ideas and burning creativity, would have a problem finding friends. The Polish mother in me wanted to walk through Berlin and help him find people to socialize with. I didn't mind listening to him, although I was painfully aware that I wouldn't be able to be there for him in a month or two when I would leave the field. I really hoped that by the time he read this book, he would be surrounded by people who cared for him.

It was useful to have a newbie on the team. I found that the people who were new to a team really highlighted the problems within a software project. At times it was because they were still learning and making mistakes. At other times it was because they didn't feel confident owning up to things going wrong, and I, as the ethnographer, was the only neutral outlet to complain to. Aseem was very open to explaining his struggles. He didn't hide if something went wrong. And because he was new at his job, he often didn't understand why something he was building was going wrong. So he would try to figure it out, and I would follow him during his journey. It was through Aseem's eyes that I started to understand the challenges and controversies that happened when building software. In the last chapter, I explained the way in which building software is a social endeavor—an act of sociality between programmers, their social world, and the sociotechnical system that is computational software. But when reading the previous chapter, you, the reader, might have been misled into thinking that software production is about finding a sense of creative craft, and that software developers work in friendly teams in a homogeneous, transparent system.

This chapter will look through the eyes of Aseem and his colleagues to show us that conflict and controversy are an inherent and inescapable part of the software development process and an important part of understanding software development culture. I will in particular focus on the role software's materiality plays in creating this chaos and controversy. As Bruno Latour highlighted, "it is with controversies that the heterogeneity of technological systems appears most clearly. An accident, a breakdown, an incident of pollution, and suddenly the 'system,' by dint of polemics, trials, media campaigns, becomes as unsystematic as possible, multiplying the unforeseen branchings that delight sociologists of technology" (2013, 218).

Organization scholars, particularly in anthropology and sociology, have looked at how decisions are made, how resistance and conflicts at work emerge, or how various forms of knowledge are employed and ignored in corporate cultures (see, for example, Burawoy 1982; Allaire and Firsirotu 1984; Courpasson et al. 2012; Paulsen 2015; or Beverungen 2019). Yet, software is a particular beast, shaping corporate work culture in a particular way.

Theoretically, it might help to frame the software company as an "organized anarchy" (Cohen, March, and Olsen 1972). According to the authors who coined the term, organized anarchies have three properties:

1. The first property refers to the purpose of the company itself, where it becomes not so clear what the purpose of the company is or what it's working on. Here, "the organization operates on the basis of a variety of inconsistent and ill-defined preferences . . . it discovers preferences through action more than it acts on the basis of preferences" (Cohen, March, and Olsen 1972, 1). While MiddleTech is clearly a mapping company and has customers and products that seem straightforward, deciding on how and when to finish a software project, or the scope of the project itself, is tricky as it is "difficult to impute a set of preferences to the decision situation" (Cohen, March, and Olsen 1972, 1). As we shall see, there are a variety of ways to solve a software problem, with no clear preference for how to tackle it.

2. The second property of an anarchic organization is what the authors term "unclear technology." Here, although the organization manages to survive and even produce a product (like software), its "own processes are not understood by its members" (Cohen, March, and Olsen 1972, 2). As I will illustrate in the following chapters, often managers don't understand how software development works, and software developers don't understand the logics and customer demand requirements or the methodologies of production. "Figuring out stuff" is also symptomatic of various forms of obscurity encountered in production.

3. The third property of an anarchic organization is so-called "fluid participation." Here, "participants vary in the amount of time and effort they devote to different domains; involvement varies from one time to another. As a result, the boundaries of the organization are uncertain and changing; the audiences and decision makers for any particular kind of choice change capriciously" (Cohen, March, and Olsen 1972, 2). In the following chapter, I will also highlight how developers devote their time to a project, but then get discouraged and give up for a variety of reasons.

While this list is not exhaustive, it helps us place MiddleTech, and software companies at large, within a larger discussion about the labor practices and work cultures of contemporary corporations, particularly those in which chaos and conflict are an integral and inescapable part of everyday work.

This chapter will illustrate software's role in an organized anarchy: how it becomes a medium that helps create and stabilize the existence of chaos and conflict in software organizations. Working with software means that different heterogeneous forms of knowledge are in constant competition with one another, and the code base often expands but is not always deleted, building convoluted, codependent legacy systems that are also challenging to figure out. These two factors lead to a particular work culture of "figuring out stuff," compromise, and confusion.

As we shall also see, this inevitable chaos and conflict help create a culture of good enoughness, as compromise and confusion become the status quo in order to move forward and complete a project. More widely, this chapter slowly paints the various structural, infrastructural, and communicative norms that shape the programmer's work culture.

Push the Update

It would be worth providing some background on why the software system is so prone to stuff going wrong all the time. In order to understand this, one must first understand the crucial role of the update within software development. The story of the update goes hand in hand with the role of the internet in software development. The internet revolutionized the temporal order of building software, allowing software developers to make mistakes and fix them at no cost to the customer. While software used to arrive at our doorsteps or computer store shelves ready to use, never to be changed, in a shiny new box, the 2000s brought us high-speed internet, which allowed for something called software-as-a-service. This software was (and is) brought to our devices through the internet. In the past, shrink-wrapped software, as it was called, had to be purchased, installed, and configured on a personal computer (PC), and updated regularly by the users themselves. Today, however, it suffices to log on to a single platform and install a service to easily access Dropbox, Facebook, Google, etc., and updates of this software are normally automated by somebody within the software team (Kaldrack and Leeker 2015, 10). In short, the team building this software has, with the owner's permission, the ability to change or update a feature in the software. In software development lingo, this is called "pushing an update." Because of internet connectivity, one software team, or even one developer, can push a new update to hundreds, thousands, or millions of devices with just one click.

The ability to push an update creates an important distinction between software and other types of engineered technologies. In the case of software, mistakes are, in essence, easy to fix and quite forgivable. When it comes to engineering and physical objects like a car or a plane, it's quite the opposite. A large company can sell millions of a particular model of their car, but if the car was engineered poorly, and something goes wrong with it, updating it is not so simple. If a car has faulty emissions meters (as we saw with the Volkswagen diesel emissions scandal in 2015), the VW team cannot just fix it with one click but has to go through a large and arduous process of recalling the physical goods.

Ori explained that "there are so many 'dammit' moments . . . like oh no people are suffering under my code, undo decision! It's quite paradoxical. That it's cheaper to fail with our kind of work. You aren't building something out of hugely expensive metal or something, that you have to get everything right. You are just using your brain . . . what we are creating is just lines of code. We don't have to carve out a new piece of metal. It's just stuff that comes out of our heads. I have all the tools in my hands. Creating bad code is cheap."

Not only does the ability to update software make it easy to undo decisions but moments of failure during software development are relatively cheap. Software is not heavy, expensive, or hard to handle. It's . . . well . . . soft. And it's precisely this "softness of software" that makes failure so cheap and easy to fix. Mark Zuckerberg's "move fast and break things" motto doesn't come out of nowhere. "Breaking things"—which, for Zuckerberg, can be interpreted as innovating, changing, testing, and rearranging—is relatively cheap and easy when working with lightweight, seemingly ethereal software that is stored within the cloud, with seemingly endless storage capabilities. Additionally, there is an out-of-sight, out-of-mind principle that cloud storage has given the programmer. When programmers write code, it is no longer stored on the central processing unit under their desk but in the cloud. MiddleTech (like most large software companies) rents server storage from the world's biggest cloud provider, Amazon Web Services (yes, it's that Amazon).

The move to the cloud in a certain sense created more stability, freeing software from being locked in a bunch of computers sitting around in a basement. But the move to the cloud also "seems to suggest that a qualitative shift towards a kind of hyper-instability is taking place: instead of a stable program nothing but a temporary relationship of queries across interfaces and devices, rendering something that was immaterial even more airy and vaporous" (Kelty and Erickson 2015, 41). This airiness not only makes it cheaper to fail but also easier to store old software projects and forget about them.

Software-as-a-service, cloud storage, and the update culture that have resulted from these changes write failure and iteration into the programmers' work culture. This can cause stuff to go wrong in a software system, and putting stuff back together when it does go wrong also takes a lot of energy, various forms of knowledge, and time. In order to understand the full picture behind the practice of software development, we have to understand programmers' obsession with breakdown, chaos, and bugs, as well as their almost mythical belief in the immateriality of software—that it can be constantly updated, shifted, and reinvented at (seemingly) little to no physical or financial cost. This, of course, is a myth. Updating a bug costs the software company money, as the programmers' salaries are high, and their work time is highly valued. Data centers use an estimated two hundred terawatt hours (TWh) each year, which is more than the national energy consumption of some countries, including Iran. Although I hate lumping them together, both Ori and Zuckerberg (sorry Ori!), like the majority of programmers, live within the myth that breaking things, undoing decisions, and making mistakes is cheap and easy. The truth is a little darker.

Types of Knowing

Now that we understand the wider principle defining the programmer's work, I'd like to describe the type of work a programmer actually engages in. Software work is knowledge work. Knowledge workers are "defined broadly as white-collar workers, including teachers, lawyers, politicians, scientists, social workers, accountants and computer programmers" (Darr and Warhurst 2008, 31). This knowledge work is quite often, but not always, technical work. As I hinted at before, "sociologists of work and occupations have paid scant attention to technical work" and this includes "computer occupations" (Barley 2005, 377). The building block—"knowledge *work*—upon which theory should be grounded remains an unopened black box" (Darr and Warhurst 2008, 34), inviting analysis of these occupations' work practices.

So what does the *knowledge* in "knowledge work" look like for a programmer? Like many technical systems, a software system is made up of heterogeneous parts that require the collective work of a team of people who specialize in knowing a lot about these various respective parts. Software developers as well as their managers and designers do not, and cannot, understand everything about the software they are building. Consequently, knowledge of how a software project is developed and maintained is heterogeneous, with the members of a software development team possessing various forms of knowledge about the system they are building.

This underlying differentiation of knowledge regarding how to get stuff done in a software company vibrates through the interactions between developers, developers and their managers, and managers and their customers. Software workers, therefore, have a few different forms of *knowing*.

It was July 2017, the first day of my second summer of fieldwork at MiddleTech, and I was about to be introduced to Aseem and his team of developers. Simon, Aseem's manager who ran the entire navigation and routing team, met me at the elevators of the seven-floor building and led me up to the fourth floor to meet a new team of one hundred developers. I loved being back at the office. It smelled like a mix of my grandmother's perfume and cleaning detergent. It must have been the stuff they used to clean the wooden floors or the bathroom tiles. It was slightly sweet, something resembling flowers with a hint of lemon. There were large windows on both sides of the office that stretched from floor to ceiling. Software developers filled the large rooms, which were designed with an open-office concept. The developers were clustered around two rows of desks, and they sat facing each other, separated by a large number of computer screens. I looked around, and they were either staring at their screens or meeting in teams to discuss their projects. Simon led me through the hallways, stopping to greet developers as we walked by them. There were Post-it Notes and whiteboards everywhere, as well as small photos of team members cut out and glued onto the walls and the odd funny poster of a meme or a joke posted up between the work-related scribbles. I was home.

Simon placed me at a desk with the Electric Vehicle team (called the EV team for short). There were two women sitting next to me—a Serbian developer and an Australian product owner—and three developers on the opposite sides of the desks—one Ukrainian, one older Spanish guy, and Aseem (whom you've already met). This was a stereotypical team of six programmers: a mix of cultural backgrounds, mostly men with one female developer. Huge black monitors (two per desk) were blocking my view of the Ukrainian developer Oleksiy, who was sitting across from me.

The EV team was making a new product: a navigation system for a new electric car that was supposed to come out on the market the following year. As I quickly found out, the electric vehicle presents engineering challenges to the navigation system that are different than those of gas-powered cars. Liz, the product owner sitting next to me, explained that the navigation system in an electric vehicle has to be different from the ones in other cars. "Was it about the type of fuel consumption that the app itself required?" I asked Liz. She said that it was not only that. It was generally about the type of fuel consumption and the refueling capabilities of electric cars. An electric car does not have that many options to refuel when driving down a highway, so it's a different "use case" than other cars. Liz explained that while the network of recharging stations is growing, it's not that prolific. So her team has to calculate the reachability of the vehicle, meaning whether the driver will reach their destination. (Fun fact: The official industry term for the driver's "worry" that their car will run out of battery power is called "range anxiety.") An electric car also consumes fuel differently when driving up a hill and recharges when going down a hill. "So we care about slope, about elevation, about altitude," Oleksiy, the team leader, chimed in to explain.

That morning, like every morning, the EV team started their daily five-minute stand-up meeting. This somewhat compulsory ritual provided the team with an opportunity to explain to one another exactly what they were working on that day. (I will explain more about the stand-up in the following chapter.)

The stand-up was very ritualistic, almost religious. The team members stood up near their desks facing a large whiteboard that had a list of tasks on it labeled "to do/in progress/completed." The meeting started with Jelena. She explained that she was working on "scaling the battery state." Everyone around her nodded as if they knew exactly what she was talking about. The attention then switched to Liz. She talked about the workshops with their clients that would take place in the following weeks, and she explained that she was getting ready to "set things up for them." Then Oleksiy started discussing the "dev drop" procedure that he would have to do with the client. Liz didn't know how that procedure worked, so she asked him, "What happens during the dev drop? How long does that take?" Oleksiy explained that it normally takes around twenty minutes but didn't give much more detail. (I assumed that a dev drop is a way of implementing a new piece of software nonlocally, on another computer in another system, such as the car manufacturer's system.) Aseem started talking about a "bad scaling parameter" that he needed to fix. Everyone else nodded. The meeting ended shortly afterward with Liz awkwardly saying, "Okay, let's start," as if she ran out of things to say and didn't really know how to break up the group.

This type of meeting provides insight into the entire software development process. A group of people with varying skill sets and forms of knowledge about their collective software project comes together to perform knowledge exchange. I use the word "perform" because knowledge is not always fully processed by each team member, and it is not a given that each team member really learns something from the others. When Oleksiy is nodding along to Jelena's report on her project of "scaling the battery state," he might be just superficially noting down that his own project relates to what she is doing. When Liz is nodding, she is perhaps just expressing copresence, without any real knowledge of what Jelena is doing. When Aseem is nodding to Jelena, he might not even know what she is working on, but he pretends to know in order to mask his freshman status within the team. Nodding is also about communicating acceptance and a way of performing phatic communication, where the maintenance of a relationship rather than the communication of actual information is at the center of an exchange. When Aseem nods for Liz's daily comments, for example, he doesn't necessarily have to understand what she is planning to do that day, but rather, through nodding, he communicates, "I trust that what you are doing is good for our common goal, and I care." Additionally, the misunderstanding or lack of knowledge is not one-directional, with the less technically inclined not understanding the more technically inclined. For example, we cannot assume that the inexperienced developers like Aseem or nontechnical employees like Liz don't understand the more technical programmers like Oleksiy, while Oleksiy understands everything that Liz and Aseem are doing. When Liz explained that she was "setting things up" for her meeting with the customer, most of the group had no idea what really goes into "setting up a meeting."

Knowledge is thus diverse, and as in most social settings, forms of understanding can be ingrained and embodied or strictly performative gestures. When team members ask one another what they are doing—especially if these team members hold completely different forms of knowledge, like Jelena and Liz—they do so rather to perform a sense of camaraderie and become one with the prevalent culture of "figuring stuff out" that dominates the corporate corridors at MiddleTech. The stand-up meeting is just one of many performative rituals that are an inherent part of MiddleTech's work culture. Having a good company "culture," as it's called around the office, is all about explaining to others what you are working on and sharing knowledge. While this is a culture that underlines practices of explanation, understanding, knowledge acquisition, and transparency, I am not assuming that knowledge is truly acquired or that software processes are made less opaque.

Knowledge Silos

On another day, Aseem led me to something called a "fixathon," a focused workshop where a team of developers works on one larger software problem that affects a larger part of the code base. These fixathons can last from one day to one week. This particular event was organized by a few people on one of Simon's teams, and around ten programmers from various teams attended. In a small meeting room, computer screens were squished together on long tables to accommodate these ten developers, who sat tightly together, almost elbow touching elbow. Gabriel, a Spanish programmer, explained, "As you look around the room, you'll notice that it's mainly the young guys who are here. We want to know more about the system. We want to break down the 'knowledge silos.'"

This fixathon was just another ritual in the culture of knowledge transfer and transparency building, an attempt to simplify the complex parts of software development. The fact that "only young guys" like Aseem were sitting around the room also highlighted their eagerness to make sense of the software system they were working on and break down these knowledge silos. I noticed that older developers, perhaps due to their experience, seemed to lack any hope of breaking down these silos.

Knowledge silos exist in any complex organization, but what is specific about software is that it is highly interdependent. In this case, developers work on a narrow piece of a software project and have little time to understand what another team is building, and thus do not develop any knowledge about how to build another software component or what is being built in parallel. Alexei, another developer at the fixathon, explained that it's simply hard to know what other people are working on, a reality that sometimes leads to multiple teams working on the same thing without any knowledge of one another. At a recent team demonstration (called a demo), he found out that another team was building the "exact same thing that was implemented six years ago." Not only does this create redundant work projects that waste developers' time, but not knowing what is being worked on elsewhere can also create other bugs, breakdowns, or unforeseen problems due to the interdependency of various software components.

When relating this experience to me, Alexei asked, "But how should we know something already exists?" Returning to the definition of the "anarchic organization," one of Middletech's features is a lack of understanding about the technology being deployed in the company. Although

MiddleTech manages to survive and produce a product (like EV software), its "own processes are not understood by its members" (Cohen, March, and Olsen 1972, 2).

Alexei's experience further made clear to me that developers often sit within their silo of understanding and have little insight into the large, complex system in which they work. Again, I was skeptical that a collective meeting like the fixathon could actually break down these silos. The event was rather another symbolic ritual in the corporate programming culture of knowledge transfer—much like the stand-up meeting—where members participate in order to understand but also to perform care for understanding, neither gaining nor embodying knowledge.

Where Stuff Goes Wrong

After spending some time watching the EV team over the next few months, I noticed that there are a number of ways to solve a certain problem, which is one reason why stuff can go wrong in a software project. If one developer has an idea of how to build this navigation system—which points to emphasize and which to avoid—another developer might have a completely different idea. This is also symptomatic of an anarchic organization where deciding on how and when to finish a software project, or the scope of the project itself, is tricky as it is "difficult to impute a set of preferences to the decision situation" (Cohen, March, and Olsen 1972, 1). Not only do the developers have to negotiate whose idea will be implemented, but the idea that the team of developers votes on has to be explained to the other developers, who might not fully understand either the logic of the solution or how to implement and build it. A long process of explanation ensues.

I will give you an example. Aseem was just finishing his master's in computer science when he joined the EV team, and he was hired as a work student. Although he was more experienced than an intern, his contract was intern-like and temporary. About a month into my fieldwork, the EV team had to provide one of their clients (a luxury car company) with a new feature on the routing system called the multistop routing feature, through which a driver would be able to make various stops on a route and still make sure that fuel consumption was accounted for. While this might seem like a simple task, this new feature meant optimizing or tweaking the current routing algorithm to provide a good, smooth, working multistop route for the user. All week, Aseem paced around the office kitchen, nervously awaiting his team meeting where he was planning to pitch his multistop routing solution to the rest of the team. I noticed his nervousness as he shared his ideas with me and told me about his attempt to approach a senior developer (known as one of the company geniuses) for help and approval.

Hours after his team meeting, where he pitched his idea, I wrote him via our in-company chat system to see how he was doing. The following is pasted from the chat conversation we had that day:

PAULA: Hey Aseem! How are you doing? How's your plan for implementing your multistop routing idea going?

ASEEM: The team seems to have decided to take the path that requires "less effort," whatever that means. But I guess there is still some confusion as to how we plan to do it . . . We had a meeting and people voted on the possible solutions. Mine didn't make the cut. We now plan to stick with the same solution as we have now, not doing anything new.

P: What's that about? Isn't the "less effort" path the one that leads to more "hacky" solutions?

A: But in a lower level of the stack. Yes, I like to call it a stack-of-hacks.

P: Oh I'm sorry to hear that yours didn't make the cut! Why do you think that happened? That yours didn't make the cut? (hehe, stack of hacks sounds very funny.)

A: I still don't know actually if the team will consider my solution, realizing at some point that what we plan now is not good enough. At least we need to prototype the solution I had in mind . . . I'm still going to discuss this with Oleksiy [team leader]. He went on vacation right after our meeting. But some of the team members who voted and, in fact, were the deciders . . . they have no idea how the current solution, "the hacky one," works.

P: Ah! So you think that at one point the team will be like, "Oh, we should use Aseem's idea after all?" Strange. So you vote even though you have no clue about the method itself?

A: What they plan now is definitely below my expectations of a quality delivery, unless the prototype proves otherwise, and we will end up firefighting like the rest of the routing team does . . . and regarding your comment: "So you vote even though you have no clue about the method itself?" At least [the rest of the team] don't have as much of a clue as the people who designed and improved it (read Oleksiy and me). And yes, after the meeting they were still trying to understand how to go about it . . . even after voting

all 5 possible points to that hacky-solution . . . So yeah . . . I guess
it's still only partially decided, and I will pitch in my concerns to
Oleksiy as soon as he is back from vacation on Monday.

P: I don't want to take up too much of your time, but I am curious about
what your proposal was—and what theirs was. What's the difference?

A: Theirs rests on an assumption that the routes for EV and otherwise
shouldn't be that different. Theoretically, that's a bad move in my
understanding.

P: Routes for EV and otherwise? You mean EV and other cars?

A: Of course I can't say that with certainty as both methods should
ideally be prototyped and then decided. Yes, EV cars and other
normal fuel cars, even after adding requisite charging stations. But
the team has decided, at least so far, the one is "easier" to prototype.

We decided that it would be easier to explain the technical solutions to
the problem over a cup of tea. Both of us wandered to the kitchen and sat
down. I pulled out a piece of paper to take some notes.

PAULA: So can you explain the difference between your idea and the
other guys' idea?

ASEEM: So imagine you are going to Munich. You will get a message
(in your navigation system) that says, "not reachable in one charge."
So you have to then drive along to X, Y, and Z. Then new stations
come up. The navigation is dynamic, depending on the map data
that's fed back to us. And the way in which the guys want to build
this system depends on the expectation that it will be the same
route forever. And that's not the case.

I still didn't understand. I asked him to draw it out for me on a piece of
paper.

P: So you have a road to Munich. And there is one line and another
line. The usual tank station is located every twenty minutes . . .
but then . . . I don't get it. How could you build a system that isn't
dynamic? Of course, data is changing and stations are being built all
the time. So what?

ASEEM: [Takes the pen from my hands and draws the A9 highway
near Nuremberg and then another highway, the A6, to Stuttgart.]
So let's say the car is driving down the A9: Should it go into the
city to charge, which will use more of its battery? Or should it go a
bit off-course and charge at the A9? You can use an algorithm that

changes the basic ways that the system works—so an inbuilt system
that evolves on its own—or you can build various modules, where
humans are going to make the choices and define the actions in
such cases. So which would you choose?

P: And by "humans" you mean developers?

ASEEM: Yes. But that latter option is plan B—what the guys around
me proposed. And that's why it's a stack of hacks—because you just
patch and build modules on top of modules . . . I am a bit selfish;
I am in this company for the multistop routing. I set my eyes on
this. I would be shattered if they took it in a direction that would be
a hack. If it starts off as a hack, it will remain a hack . . . I can't work
as a team if nobody believes in what I am doing.

Aseem clearly seemed frustrated. But I understood what he meant.
His proposal was to optimize a certain algorithm that would respond to
"dynamic data" that would feed into the map, meaning data that would be
updated based on traffic data fed in through different regions, new charging
stations that were being built, and the users' behavior. The other system—the
one that was chosen—was one in which developers would preprogram the best
choices possible for the driver, and this program would remain the same
regardless of the driver's driving patterns.

My conversation with Aseem had a number of points that help illustrate
the moments when software development can go wrong. At the first level,
there is Aseem's frustration with his team. Programmers have expressed to
me that they enjoy working on their own, especially when conceptualizing
a large solution, because they do not have to do the "translation work" that
goes into working with other programmers who have their own design ideas.
Developers are forced to work in teams because of the company's method
of managing their software project. (I will get into more specifics about
software project management methods in chapter 4.) Much like any team,
a programming team is characterized by conflict and direct competition
between programmers. Any programmer's idea can be rejected by the rest
of the team. Because programming is quite subjective—and there is rarely
only one right way of building something—ideas often have to be negotiated
based on allegiances to others in the team (like Aseem and Oleksiy), or for
various reasons relating to power, status, educational background, gender
politics, racial politics, or a slew of other factors. While I didn't ever find
out why Aseem's idea was rejected, I know it had little to do with his idea
being objectively worse than the others.

These frustrations can create conflict. Negotiating takes time, learning something new takes time, and Aseem's frustration takes time. This frustration then translates into differing ideas, which can lead to faulty code or delays in implementing any changes. Although Aseem was not the type of engineer to sabotage the team's project, I have witnessed other instances when teams actually split up, and one developer started building a solution in order to prove to the rest of the team that their idea was worthwhile. While this is an extreme case, it illustrates the types of tensions that might arise when two or more programmers have different ideas. These tensions can cause delays in coding a project or result in frustrated developers subconsciously coding poorly in order to prove that their idea was best.

Myth of Knowing and Understanding

When speaking of his team, Aseem noted that "some of the team members voted, and in fact were the deciders. . . . but they had no idea how the current solution, the 'hacky one,' worked." In this case, a group of five developers voted on a solution without fully understanding the method of implementation or the consequences of the solution. So why did they pretend to understand?

The problem is it is difficult for any developer to understand the consequences of a solution before the piece of software is actually built. This issue is quite specific to software development and has to do with how code is intertwined with other code that exists either in the code base or is being built and added to the system in real time.

I'll lean on a metaphor to help illustrate my point. For example, let's imagine software work as a Google document with hundreds of people merging their ideas onto the document at the same time. This complexity grows, as one person likes to write their sentences one way, another the other way, and others imagine the document completely differently and delete what was done before them. Similarly, we can imagine that every line of code ever written makes up the system that the programmers are working on. A software project holds layers and layers of legacy code built throughout the history of the software company. The sheer scale of the system being built, the speed at which it is changed and updated, and the number of people, processes, and machines collaborating with one another make posing the "right" solution very hard. As engineering scholar Nancy Leveson explained, "The problem is that we are attempting to build systems that are beyond our ability to intellectually manage; increased complexity of all types makes it difficult for the designers to consider all the potential system states or for operators to handle all normal and abnormal situations and disturbances safely and effectively" (2016, 4). Here, Leveson defines complexity as intellectual unmanageability.

So, within a setting where a handful of developers have to vote on a solution, how are they supposed to make sense of this huge complexity and predict how their solution will fare in action? Aseem was trying to push through his idea, but it was impossible for him to fully understand how his idea would work in practice with other code, with the future requirements and complaints of the customer, or with code that currently exists. Perhaps the hacky solution of his colleagues would indeed be better. The paradox is that within such a complex system like a large-scale software project, teams are presented with a choice in coming up with a good solution. Developers are thus forced to vote on the unknown, to make a bet or an educated guess. Within this software development culture, they have to make a decision as if a particular proposal is an engineering solution that is better than another one presented. The idea that there is a solution implies that there is a means, an answer, a panacea to fix a given problem. In the process of choosing a solution, developers and their other team members have to pretend to know something (as in the case of Aseem's team vote) in order to keep their project developing. This is what we can call the "myth of knowing," which allows teams to work within such a complex system.

Pretending in order to keep up this myth of knowing happens not only between developers themselves but also between managers and their developers (and vice versa), product owners and their customers (and vice versa), designers and developers (and vice versa), and all combinations of roles in between. During one of my many lunches with Simon, who managed all teams building the MiddleTech navigation system, he lamented that, "It's not even about knowing or not knowing. It's about pretending to know. There is constantly a myth of knowing everything technical. Which is not possible. For example, there is a project lead or product owner. And their job is to translate what type of product the customer wants to the technical team. And this product owner would start talking to their customer about a certain algorithm. They don't really know what that algorithm does. So why are they talking to them about something so technical?"

Simon attributed this "pretending to know" to a pressure around the office, in particular for managers, to know something: "There is constantly a myth that we should know something. But we shouldn't. This is a subjective feeling. Instead of feeling comfortable with their job and going out to ask somebody else or referring the customer to somebody else, they pretend they know something they don't. Or there is another problem: they learn the details that they shouldn't know in the first place. They start solving something over there when they should just really slow down and focus on what's in front of them.

Simon underlined two things here: firstly, that managers also fall under the myth of knowing in being expected to know the technical side of software production, which often they do not. His software developers know he used to be a programmer, so they may assume he knows what they are talking about. Instead of confronting him, or instead of Simon admitting he doesn't know something, both the developers and Simon himself sustain the myth of knowing in order to push a project forward. This myth is sustained by pretending—managers pretending to know as much about a project as their developers do; developers pretending that their manager also speaks their language; product owners pretending to know how an algorithm works when interacting with their customer (and vice versa); and programmers pretending to know something about a newly proposed solution. Instead of owning up to their lack of knowledge, they often pretend to know something they do not.

Pretending to know also happens between the software team's product owner and the customer. The role of the product owner is to mediate between the customer's demands and the software team's capabilities. They are the ones making the phone calls or flying off to meetings with various representatives of car companies or other customers. During these meetings, product owners are asked to tell the customer that they know how their team will complete the given software product (hence using the name of a certain algorithm as Simon explained) or perhaps give their customer a certain time by which the software will be completed, which is also often an assumption or a clear act of pretending to know when the project will, in fact, be completed.

Subjective Estimation

Staying with the customer-to-product owner relationship, another reason a project can go wrong and get messy is the vague, highly subjective method of estimating the amount of time that a project will take to complete. As Liz, the product owner, explained, "It's really hard. When we meet with the customers, the developers just have to go like this [sticks thumb in the air and moves it up and down]." What Liz means is that she often has to explain to her developers what the customer requires, and the developers have to give her an estimate of how long this project will take. In some instances, a thumb estimate is enough. More commonly, developers give an estimate using T-shirt sizes. Aseem explained how this method worked in his team's previous meeting: "The product owner then [this time Aseem, who was standing in for Liz] would get the developers to "T-Shirt Size" the amount of work it would take to finish their product. S, M, or L." I learned that this basic T-shirt sizing is a software-industry standard and works as follows:

S = one week to finish
M = two weeks
L = four weeks
XL = sixteen weeks

These estimates require a larger or smaller group of people such as Aseem's team to collectively create a project deadline based on a large number of very subjective factors. One project might seem very hard to one team member, while another team member might find it quite easy, but they have to rely on one another to create this collective estimate. How to determine this collectively? Jelena addressed this problem when she asked, "How could I assess something I don't even know how to build yet?" Developers are forced, in their producer-client relationship, to create an estimate of the amount of time it will take them to complete a software project. In order to create this estimate, they need to have a methodology for how to build something before they start, which as Jelena pointed out, they cannot.

The method of building something often arises while building it and not beforehand. The process is messy and full of improvisation (Feyerabend 1993), a reality that is not accounted for in the producer-client relationship. As a result, a software development team can become frustrated with their customer after a few years of working with them and estimate that the completion of a project will take longer just to annoy the customer. The problem again arises out of the customer's belief in the myth that the developer knows exactly how to build a particular software project. The customer will often demand something that seems useful for their users, but this demand will be difficult or impossible for the programming team to fulfill. Returning to Aseem's example of building multistop routing for electric vehicles, Aseem explained his impressions after attending a meeting with representatives from a luxury sports car company that was building a new EV.

Now [the car company] thought, "We want our drivers to be able to drive madly like a [sports car] consumer," so they asked us to make an estimated time of arrival for that—so keeping the user experience as close to a non-EV car. They wanted this on top [of their other demands]. My reservation is that it neglects a lot of things we do under the hood. Like time awareness [certain roads are blocked at a certain time, speed limits done at certain times] that we calculate. They want to override our current ETA [estimated time of arrival] predictions. Their idea is that a fast [sports car] driver will think that they can reach their charging station in time. The problem is that time awareness is off. The problem is that we do a hell of a lot of calculations to assist the driver. I can do ten different computations with ten different modules, and then give them this. But this takes so much computation. If we make a hack, I will compromise quality. To build their feature we would have to change the whole foundation.

Returning to our framework of the anarchic organization here, a customer is making certain demands based on "inconsistent and ill-defined preferences" (Cohen, March, and Olsen 1972, 1). Liz's team "discovers preferences through action more than it acts on the basis of preferences" (Cohen, March, and Olsen 1972, 1). While the EV team might have customers and a seemingly straightforward product, deciding on how and when to finish a software project, or the scope of the project itself, is tricky. This is where the relationship between the myth of knowing and stuff going wrong really comes to the forefront. Aseem's customer in this case believes that Aseem and his colleagues can make the EV routing system behave in a similar way to the system in a regular petrol car. In this case, the customer is forgetting the complexity of a software system, that a software project is a messy creative project and is highly contingent on the software legacy—or the lines and lines of code that the new project is sitting and drawing on. Here, software's complexity makes it "difficult to impute a set of preferences to the decision situation" (Cohen, March, and Olsen 1972, 1). A customer's assumption that the software team can just figure it out and exercise control over these complex, highly fickle machines does create messy, problematic, hack-driven projects that are prone to crashing. This example shows that Cohen, March, and Olsen's metaphor of the "anarchic organization" extends beyond the walls of the organization itself and also into the relationships between customers that help further the chaos, anarchy, and stuff going wrong.

A Stack of Hacks

Up until now, we have discussed how programmer-to-programmer relationships—their knowledge gaps (nonknowledge or the need to pretend), need for explanations, misunderstandings, and frustrations—can create chaos and complexity in software projects, helping to define the software company as an anarchic organization. I also described how the customer-to-product owner relationship can cause software to be faulty and teams to be frustrated. The final and perhaps most significant element that leads to things going wrong is the material object of software itself: layers and layers of code.

One common term for a messy coding style is a "hack," as Aseem explained previously, meaning a rough way of building software. We can liken a hack to the way a house might be built by an inexperienced or sloppy builder: the foundation is shaky, the materials used are of poor quality, and perhaps the structure doesn't account for the electric wiring or plumbing. A hack in coding is when developers use various coding shortcuts, do not account for the larger architecture of a system, or overlook the style of code with which their code interacts. As Aseem explained after his meeting with his team members,

> I feel that the lack of hack-driven implementations and lack of architectural vision promotes incremental hacks. You can build a house and make it stable for some time. But I know that you go to the [meeting with a customer] and say, "Well we know our quality is bad; somebody decided to make a hack and decided to incrementally improve." Incremental improvements end up in spaghetti code . . . Today we are adding features on top of it, but it is a leaning tower of Pisa.

Here, Aseem describes something called "hack-driven implementation." Hacks are often done out of a lack of time or are the result of a messy, creative, improvisational state of coding, but they can lead to interesting design ideas. In Aseem's world, where software development follows a methodology and software developers have an "architectural vision" before they build something, software should last for generations to come, and hacks make maintaining the software much harder for the people who will work on the project in the future.

With or without a vision, programmers cannot predict how a system will run before they actually build it. This is quite specific to software development: What a software developer makes today can react poorly with other pieces of code being built in real time or built years before. If a system is built quickly, sloppily, and messily, then something called "spaghetti code" arises—an entangled mess of source code that has a complex and tangled control structure. Spaghetti code is especially common in systems using many "goto" statements (used to jump or link one line of code to another). As computer programmer Bill Blunden writes, "Like a mound of spaghetti, when you try to pick up a few strands of pasta with your fork, you end up having to lift everything" (2003, 23). A lot of spaghetti code means that any change (imagine pulling out one strand of spaghetti) will affect the rest of the stack of code (the mound of spaghetti). If a developer tries to build a new feature when working in a complex system of spaghetti code, they will either have to take longer to build the feature, find other ways of building it, or not build it at all. This type of code can deeply impact the design process of a system: slowing down bug fixes, limiting how features are built, or creating more bugs in a system. In order to solve this problem, developers need to have a vision and create modules that are not that codependent.

Legacy Monsters

Another (and perhaps the main) code-based reason for misunderstandings and mix-ups during software development is legacy code. As you are likely starting to see by now, developers don't simply write new code every time a customer wants new software. They build on top of the foundations of other software that came before it, much like building a house. When constructing a house, one can build a new construction from scratch, renovate an existing house, or just use parts of the foundation and add on top. A software project is much the same. Code is often built on top of older code, much like adding new floors to the foundation of a building (Brooks 1995). Legacy code is also constantly being added to and patched, like new additions to the house. Patching is also an inherent part of legacy code as it denotes that legacy code is constantly in the making, neither new nor old but part of the entire software system.

The term "legacy code" has a wide range of definitions: It sometimes refers to code acquired from another company, and at other times it refers to code that was left behind by people on the original development team, who moved on to other projects, or found other jobs in different companies. Some developers define legacy code as a form of inheritance, meaning that they inherit code or a project to work with. For example, one developer used this sense of the term to explain a problem with a feature: "We realize this is a design defect that we inherited from others." Here, a problem with their software was inherited, not something of their own making. Inheritance implies that the developer can absolve the system of problems: Somebody else screwed up, and the developer's job is to clean up the mess. It also absolves the developer of any responsibility, placing the blame on other anonymous developers who came before them and left them with code that doesn't work or is causing problems by infecting other code, making their software more complex, full of bugs, etc. Legacy is also something to deal with, to be managed, and to be acted upon. A programmer can't just ignore legacy code. As another developer wrote to his team to explain the cause of a certain bug, "the problem is the script that does this—it was never refactored [rewritten] and [it was just] inherited." In this case, legacy code has to be updated or "refactored," and if left alone, it can mess up the rest of the system.

The turn to cloud storage was a big catalyst in the growth of legacy code. As computer engineer Bill Blunden explains, "Engineers in the days of yore had to meticulously balance memory usage with the need to minimize the number of CPU cycles consumed. . . . Engineers today are not faced with the same pressures to squeeze every ounce of performance out of their programs" (2003, xvii). What Blunden means is that due to improvements in cloud storage infrastructures, computing memory is now limitless. Today, companies like MiddleTech do not have to save their code on their company's hard drive or in their office basement, but instead, they send it to "rented" storage spaces provided by huge tech companies, Amazon Web Services (AWS) being the biggest global player (others include IBM Cloud, Google Cloud, and Microsoft Azure). As you can imagine, software developers do not have to worry about having too many lines of code. As long as their software works and the performance of their software is up to speed, a lot of legacy code can be lying around in Amazon's server farm in Iceland. Fernando, a developer in the front-end team, said, "It's very tempting to just forget about a project if it fails you. You don't delete from the source code." Here, legacy code is just like old objects stored in a basement—you can keep piling up the junk, and nobody will really notice.

An additional reason for leaving code lying around is, as another developer explained, a lack of trust in your new system: "Well, you are not sure your new way will work. So you just keep it. Because you might want to switch back to your old version at another time. It's like a safety net." As we know from previous chapters, software projects often fail or get scrapped, and software developers make mistakes or wrong design decisions, so keeping the code is a safety net.

Developers also have different relationships with legacy code. In his industry-specific text *Working Effectively with Legacy Code* (2004), computer scientist Michael Feathers wrote,

> If you are at all like me, you think of tangled, unintelligible structure, code that you have to change but don't really understand. You think of sleepless nights trying to add in features that should be easy to add, and you think of demoralization, the sense that everyone on the team is so sick of a code base that it seems beyond care, the sort of code that you just wish would die. Part of you feels bad for even thinking about making it better. It seems unworthy of your efforts. (Feathers 2004, xvi)

Some developers, like Feathers, think of legacy code as a monster, like Frankenstein's stitched-together creature, that needs to be tamed. Legacy code haunts some software developers as it has either been written in an older programming language a developer does not understand, or it has been fixed or patched so much that it has now become too complicated and messy. Initially, a given code might be well written, but then it might undergo a number of modifications based on the premise of customer demand, causing what was originally well written to evolve into a complex beast.

On the other hand, others think of legacy code as a wise elder, an important, tried-and-true, and robust part of one's software ecosystem. Dima, a senior software developer in the back-end team, told me that he has respect for legacy code: "If you don't need to change the functionality, why touch it? It's working ages in production, probably free of crashes and bugs, proven by years of running devices. Any new code is a risk." So perhaps it would help if we think of legacy code as an old, wise grandmother. In some instances, her grandchildren would treat her as a source of wisdom and knowledge with years of valuable experience. In other cases, she would be treated like a slow, annoying burden, speaking at snail speed, ranting about the "good old days," perhaps occasionally blurting out awkward, prejudiced comments.

Dima suggests this impatient approach to legacy code is the go-to strategy of inexperienced developers: "In my personal opinion this is 'juniorish,' a mindset to rewrite everything since the system is complex and you don't understand it and it looks to you like a spaghetti monster. After years you get used to that and know all the tentacles of this monster and the big picture of the system now in your head." Interestingly enough, while Dima wants to move away from the junior developers' perception of legacy code as a scary monster, he still imagines it in similar terms. For Dima, it is a friendly monster, but it's still a monster.

So, to summarize, legacy code is code written by somebody else, and because it is written by somebody else and inherited, it is something to be managed, explained, and clarified to the other developer. As Leavitt Cohn explained, "Working with code involves working across time and building legacies and inheritances that serve as connections not only between practice and the functions of a tool but between different ways of working with systems over time" (2019, 439).

Legacy code creates another level of complexity because not only is a programmer's code dependent on the team they are currently working with, as well as the other teams working on other pieces of the software, but it is also dependent on layers of code that came before (like the foundations of a house), which are often hard to challenge, remove, or rework. During one of my many group lunches, I was sitting with Ori's team at an Indian restaurant, and they started to explain how conflict arises when dealing with legacy code, as well as the deep entanglements of code:

> "You see," Jan explained, "the system is sensitive and it easily breaks. But it's also because some systems have been running for so long that you hardly challenge [the system]," he said. "Take somebody who is building a wooden toy. Let's say they want to change the color of the toy or add something to it. This wouldn't really change the basics of the wooden toy. The toy would stay the same. It wouldn't break. But in software there is this difference that there are so many entanglements . . . There are so many dependencies you can't see. You start building something and you can't really foresee what will happen . . . But you can't undo it sometimes."

The "many dependencies you can't see" makes it very hard to address certain issues that might make the current project problematic. For example, if one programmer finds that a piece of legacy code is complicating the rest of the system, and if the programmer who wrote the code is still in the company, the programmer dealing with the legacy code can just approach the programmer and ask them what their programming logic was when writing such a monster of a mess. But most of the time this is not possible. One of the developers at MiddleTech made me a chart showing how much of the code base at MiddleTech is legacy code by writing down each year since the software project started in 2005 and the percentage of code that is still being used in the main map-operating system.

At MiddleTech, a small percentage of the code base (15 percent) is being used from legacy code written in 2005. This example of the various ways of

FIG. 3.1 Legacy code at MiddleTech

both understanding and working with legacy code inherently "[troubles] the valuations that we place on current software development" (Leavitt Cohn 2019, 439) and helps illustrate yet another reason why stuff goes wrong.

During this lunch hour, I began to understand that the code base is both quite confusing and incomprehensible for the developers building it, which makes it mythical and full of blind spots; it is very interdependent and inter-twined (making certain changes difficult), and often it's also a really large mess that needs to be cleaned up or refactored, which becomes especially difficult if the code is quite old.

Both Leavitt Cohn and Nathan Ensmenger wisely pointed out that software is a tangible record. Within this record, one can discern not only the intentions of the original designer but the social, technological, and organizational context in which it was developed (Ensmenger 2010), and legacy code exists as a kind of record or organizational memory of "various pain points, like scars from wounds that have mostly healed over" (Leavitt Cohn 2019, 430).

Through this example of legacy code, we can see that software possesses "a secondary agency" that supports or extends "the agency of some primary agent: the programmer, the corporation, the hacker, the artist, the government, or user" (Mackenzie 2006, 8). This understanding of what software is highlights that stuff doesn't go wrong only in software development because manager-to-customer or programmer-to-programmer interactions involve conflict and misunderstandings. Rather, code has to interact with other code. This interaction happens between code written now, or written days, months, or years ago. This complex temporality complicates the relations between various layers and lines of code, causing stuff to go wrong.

The Culture of Good Enough

It was "feature-complete week," and many developers were slightly more on edge than usual. Even Charlie, who was normally quite a calm, Zen-like character, was feeling the tension. He was a senior product owner, managing the projects of various development teams and being the go-between for the tech world and the customer. He was English and had moved to Berlin after meeting his German wife during their studies back in the United Kingdom. They now had two children, and Charlie seemed to approach both parenting and his work in a happy-go-lucky, shit-happens sort of way, not getting too overwhelmed by anything, knowing everything can be tackled with a good chuckle and a bit of eye-rolling. He balanced his cynicism and jokiness with a deep knowledge of how the company worked. I noticed that he was one of the rare product owners who had a sociological sensibility, a bird's-eye view of what was going on around him. He spoke knowledgeably about code, bugs, breakdowns, and updates, but he also knew a lot about the mobility industry he was in and always had something interesting to say on various topics, like the social consequences of managing knowledge workers.

That day in the office, I noticed Charlie in various parts of the office—in the kitchen and hallways, pacing around as if he were late for a meeting, his eyes wide as if he were thinking about something very important. I walked up to him and asked him what was wrong. He said that he was trying to put out a fire.

Later that afternoon, after I asked him a few times about the "fire" that he was trying to put out, he offered to show me what his work was all about. He grabbed his cup and his laptop, and we walked over to the common coffee area near the staircase. He opened up his laptop to an internal site called "Gerrit," a free, Web-based team code collaboration tool that many software companies use for reviewing code. This site displayed a list of "merges," meaning updates or additions to the code base. This list included the type of update, who updated it, and the status of the update (if it passed or failed). As one developer explained, the Gerrit code review system is a way in which other developers are forced to look at the code, review it, and say, "'Oh it's good enough, we want it in' or 'No, they have to improve it,' and then they write their remarks about what has to be improved."

Good-Enough Code Review

As I have now explained the various human and technical ways that things can go wrong in software development, I would like to note that there are attempts to fix and contain these mistakes before code gets shipped to the customer or user, yet problems still slip through the cracks, resulting in good-enough code. One important mechanism for trying to prevent stuff from going wrong is the code review system, which, as we learned from the previous chapter, acts as a peer review process when developing software. While in the last chapter I addressed how code review can be a mechanism for collective style acquisition and encourages closeness among developers, I'd also like to highlight that code review can be a way of writing good enoughness into the software system, leading to stuff going wrong.

If we go back to the Electric Vehicle (EV) team comprised of around five developers, we can understand that collectively, they often have to solve a routing problem typical of electric vehicles: how to optimize a driving route for a car that has to secure charging stations every few hours. Before their project is finalized and implemented into a vehicle's software system, their work is split into small subtasks. At the start of the project (the project's "sprint period"), the group of developers would sit together in a room with their manager or product owner, and together they would define the subtasks that needed to be done to complete the project. These subtasks are called "tickets." The next day, each developer would take a ticket and start working on it. A ticket, in the case of the EV team, could be, for example, to match the library for EV charging stations to a route library. Jelena would then take this ticket, work on it, and then upload it or "push it" to the Gerrit code review system for review. Her colleagues would then give her a score between +2 and –2, a rating system we encountered in my introduction.

Ori once explained that the main purpose of the code review was to monitor collectively whether each line of code that a developer uploads into their team's main repository actually fits and will work with the code that the other team members have created. Developers often peek over their desktop screens and yell out to a colleague, "Can you review my code please?" or "Hey, why did you give me a −1!" Ori's lines of code have to speak to another developer's lines of code, and these collections of lines have to communicate with one another when running within the entire system.

The code review systems are an inherent part of a corporate software environment, a crucial part of a production pipeline. This code review system is necessary because a software product has to be "shipped" to its users within a certain time frame in order for the software company to remain competitive on the market, and that product has to work without major bugs or breakdowns. Here is where the nuance lies: what is good enough to be shipped? How does a collective group of software developers negotiate what is good enough, especially on such a large scale?

Large-scale corporate software environments, made up of teams of dozens of developers, need code review systems to make collaboration and communication with a large amount of software updates easier. This is where a system like Gerrit comes in. Michael, a developer who used to work at MiddleTech and who has since moved to a small start-up company, explained that the code review system at MiddleTech is a good example of how a big company deals with the review process. After moving jobs, Michael and his new team of two or three people don't have a review process, but rather the team members communicate with one another before starting their job, agreeing what to work on that day, and cooperating throughout the development process. Merging a change into the whole system becomes more of a formality in his case rather than a necessity.

In noncorporate contexts, software developers working in a small team without a strict deadline might use an informal code review system, giving each other feedback much like a band of musicians would give each other tips and tricks on how to make a song better. But a code review system in a corporate large-scale software project environment is a formalized, software-based assembly-line.

James, a team leader, explained to me: "Gerrit is a key part of our culture. If a developer has a piece of code, he uploads it to Gerrit. You collaborate together to make one commit [the act of uploading a piece of code] happen. This is not a competition for making code. It is trying to work together. Trying to transfer information and knowledge." Sebastian, another iOS developer (building the application for iPhones), uses the metaphor of a tree to explain how code review works: "It's like a tree and every coder adds another branch to that tree. In order to merge their changes (branches), there [have] to be certain tests done. Only after these tests can the branches be really incorporated as part of this tree."

Using Sebastian's metaphor, when a programmer adds a "branch" to Gerrit, it is visible to other developers, and the code waits for at least two developers, plus an automated bot, to approve the code. At MiddleTech's front-end team, developers were encouraged to look at an incoming review every one to two hours, although one developer informed me that this rule "often didn't happen anyways, but a review of your work did take place every twenty-four hours." A review in the Gerrit system has five variables:

−2: Do not submit
−1: I would prefer that you didn't submit this
 0: No score
+1: Looks good to me, but someone else must approve
+2: Looks good to me, approved

As I mentioned in the introduction, Michael, a web developer, half-jokingly once confessed that on Fridays, when he feels like leaving work and running off for a beer, he would quickly go through the code review system and just add +2, +2, +2 to all the tickets waiting to be reviewed. How much of this is actually true is a mystery, but it shows how variables such as fatigue, the weather, the time of day, and the relationship between the developers themselves actually factor into their ratings.

While Michael was joking, a bit of his humor was of course true in describing what was happening in the field. Many developers I spoke to do not uphold strict excellence standards but just assume that the code will be good enough to work somehow. The more rushed developers are, the more sleepy they are, and the more focused they are on other things (like their family issues, their presentation for their boss that day, or what they will have for lunch), the easier it is for them to let certain code slide through the code review system, making way for merely good-enough software. The code review system is thus a collective way that good enoughness becomes ingrained into the software system as no software moves forward without peer approval. While undoubtedly some developers are strict reviewers and aim for certain forms of perfection, others can just click +2 for code that might not work. Even if some developers review in a "this-code-is-good-enough-for-now" way, it will impact the entire software system.

Firefighting

Yet after the code is uploaded to Gerrit, there are still people like Charlie whose job is to monitor these updates and changes, especially during the last week of production, which in this case was Week 44. This was feature-complete day, which meant that all features or changes should be finished and merged into the code base. Merging doesn't happen seamlessly. Charlie often anticipates that something will go wrong, and during days like these he always keeps his computer open in order to monitor the progress of each merge. During merging, Charlie explained, the code is automatically tested, or reviewed by fellow programmers, and because code tests can go wrong, or code review can overlook some mistakes, various problems can arise.

I asked Charlie, "So is it kind of like putting two pieces of a puzzle together, but one person chopped off one arm of the puzzle piece, so it doesn't fit into the other piece as it was intended to?"

Charlie explained, "You have to imagine something like a Google Doc that two people are working on. And one person makes the changes while the other person made changes already to what the other person was working on simultaneously. When they merge these two documents together, they can have a conflict."

Charlie also explained to me that "feature-complete day" is usually when people start "chucking stuff in," or roughly merging their code in, "and everything crashes." "Firefighting" is inevitable for Charlie. The term "firefighting" describes the attempt to make sure that not too many things crash at once in order to avoid "things getting really bad," which can include (as I mentioned earlier) calling on developers to build so-called "hacky-solutions" in order to fight a fire. It is obvious to Charlie that things will go wrong, but a product owner like him can monitor the situation, and such monitoring or firefighting helps mitigate any giant mishaps.

As we can learn from Charlie, firefighting is an inevitable part of software development. For Charlie, there will always be some sort of fire he is trying to put out. These moments of firefighting are neither shocking nor disappointing. Charlie explains this all to me quite matter-of-factly. I thought about the stereotypical image of the firefighter, who always seems quite calm in the face of the firestorm that is coming their way. Fires always happen, and firefighting isn't seen as annoying but as a natural part of living with fire. The same can be said of software—the reality that things will break is a natural part of living with software.

Good-enough software is, as Collins et al. (1994) highlighted, a principle that understands that every piece of new software can be assumed to contain errors, even after thousands or millions of executions. In the mid-1990s, the concept of good-enough software was "getting a lot of attention" in order to counteract the "we'll deliver high-quality, bug-free software on time" battle cry (Yourdon 1995, 78). Firefighting, chucking stuff in, and building quick hacks all help to illustrate that programmers and their managers, like Charlie, are not focusing their attention only on creating awesome software but are trying to keep stuff from going completely wrong or trying not to let the whole house burn to the ground, so to speak. Being just good enough to survive in the face of a huge fire is an achievement. In this culture of keeping stuff together, a development team understands that they cannot deliver perfect software and becomes satisfied with code that is good enough (as the programmer describing the Gerrit code review explained).

Conclusions

By this point, I hope you are getting a good picture of the various social and technical dynamics inherent in software development and the ways these dynamics can cause software to go wrong. This overview was in no way exhaustive, but its purpose was to give you a picture of the chaos, conflict, and misunderstanding inherent in software development.

This chapter zoomed in on the knowledge work of Aseem and his colleagues in order to show how conflict and controversy are unavoidable in the software development process and are an important part of understanding its culture. This inescapability stems from a variety of things: For one, working with software requires heterogeneous forms of knowledge that permeate the development process. Software developers often change jobs within a software company or between other software companies. Or while writing in the same programming language, another team might have a completely different task, requiring the programmer to possess a very different skill set. While these various forms of knowing might seem quite similar to those in any large complex company, the difference with software is the rapid speed of change within the industry, which is rooted in the update culture I mentioned earlier. A lot of software quickly becomes obsolete. A lot of programming languages have become redundant. Code becomes legacy code and has to be updated, often by programmers who know little about how this legacy code was programmed in the first place. This rapid speed of change during software development challenges the stability of the knowledge of the people involved. Aseem and other programmers I encountered spent a few hours a week studying, learning, and reading up on new programming trends. Programmers who take this kind of initiative further diversify the heterogeneity of knowledge within one team, dividing it into those who study, or whose knowledge evolves with the speed of change within their industry, and others who are left behind.

This chapter discussed how product owners, managers, and programmers give one another, as well as their customers, very vague and subjective estimations about how long a software project will take. This is also part of the myth of knowing as it involves pretending to understand the method of building a software project before it is actually built. These subjective estimations lead to misunderstandings and rushed "hacky solutions" (or a "stack of hacks"), which result in buggy code and general frustration for all parties involved.

This isn't to say that the myth of knowing is only about pretending and faking it. The myth of knowing also enforces a sense of trust between two parties. What I mean here is that a customer believes that their developer knows how to build their software product and trusts them to figure it out. In the case of Aseem's colleagues who voted on something they didn't fully understand, they trusted that Oleksiy, their team leader, would indeed know which solution would be best. This can also be seen as good-enough knowledge, where Oleksiy's team has a good-enough understanding of a system to follow along with what's happening but entrusts Oleksiy with knowing the details and carrying out the job.

But where does this myth of knowing come from? Why not just give up and give in to the utter chaos and unpredictability of programming a software system? I would argue that this myth of knowing is the result of tensions between those who demand full precision, transparency, and knowledge of the software system (like, at times, Aseem or the customers he was working for) and others who give in to the reality that development is messy, unpredictable, and unknowable (like, for instance, Jelena). These tensions of knowing and not knowing permeate the relationships between the customer, product owner, and the developer; between the older developer and younger developer; between the theoretical developer and practical developer; and between the manager and their developers, as well as the layers and layers of code that come between them.

This myth of knowing is the result of an engineering culture that follows a certain scientific method and craves intellectual security in the form of clarity, precision, "objectivity," and "truth." Engineers follow the principles of critical rationalism, which demand that they "take falsifications seriously; increase content; avoid ad hoc hypotheses; 'be honest'—whatever that means; and so on." Engineers are also taught the principles of logical empiricism: "be precise; base your theories on measurements; avoid vague and untestable ideas; and so on" (Feyerabend 1993, 218).

Yet, as Paul Feyerabend expressed, these scientific principles and methods give an inadequate account of science because science is much more "sloppy" and "irrational" than its methodological image (1993, 218). He states that there is "only one principle that can be defended under all circumstances and in all stages of human development. It is the principle: anything goes" (Feyerabend 1993, 39), which is really the only principle that does not inhibit progress. "Anything goes" allows for chaos, messiness, and mistakes.

So, as a software development culture is characterized by its heterogeneous forms of knowledge, moments of explanation and translation, and a permeating myth of knowing, stuff can clearly go wrong. Misunderstandings fall through the gaps between knowing and not knowing. Programmers and their team members mistranslate or do not fully explain something to other team members. A software system is not fully knowable, and code written one day mingles poorly with other pieces of code written tomorrow or years before. These are all symptoms of this culture of good-enough software—of the instability and imprecision that is software engineering.

In this chapter, I framed the software company as an "organized anarchy," where the purpose of the company or what it's working on is not entirely clear, where the company's "own processes are not understood by its members," and the boundaries of the organization are uncertain and changing (Cohen, March, and Olsen 1972, 2). In such conditions, it becomes quite inevitable that imperfection and good enoughness, rather than excellence and precision, become the status quo. In the next chapter, I'll turn to how corporate management and various methodologies try to tame this anarchy.

4

Managing Good Enoughness

It was warm on this particular August afternoon, and after a few meetings that day, I felt like walking home. I caught Simon's eye across the room and tilted my head toward the exit door. Like most days, he quickly and without hesitation nodded, immediately recognizing that I wanted to walk home. I grabbed my bike, and we started walking toward Prenzlauer Berg. The weather was sticky, the exact temperature of my skin, and Berlin's parks were buzzing with naked kids in water fountains and grannies eating ice cream.

When you work in a large institution like a corporation, you're often placed in situations in which you interact with people you would never have thought of meeting. Simon and I were an unlikely pair—a straight-talking, ambitious manager in charge of one hundred people, walking down the street with a slightly chaotic ethnographer. But there was something I instantly liked about Simon from the first moment I met him. It was the kind of feeling you have when you meet somebody you know you will be friends with for a long time. He was curious and inquisitive, which made me feel that he was interested in the things that I was saying and the world around him. He always had a response, almost before I could finish my sentence. Maybe it was also because he was Israeli, and I have always found Israelis familiar people too (a sense that somewhere down the line our great-great-grandmothers might have bumped into each other in a Polish shtetl somewhere).

Simon and his family lived on the third floor of a beautiful nineteenth-century apartment building on a small street in Prenzlauer Berg, the type of street that makes you want to walk up and down it a few times to imagine you are living on it and enjoying every minute. In 2015, Simon and his wife decided to leave the conservative confines of Israel for good and move to Berlin. Both he and his wife were rather timid people, quite the opposite of the adventure-seeking, globe-trotting types you might think would immigrate at the age of forty. Yet they exuded a "we did it" energy that perhaps stemmed from the fact that they successfully reinvented their lives in Berlin. Simon was quite happy with the city he was living in, filled with the excitement found among ex-pats who didn't take anything for granted. Every new café, every trip to the grocery store, every walk to work was something special because these experiences represented a break from the life he had left behind in Israel.

The friendship between us unfolded quickly and naturally. I found it a blessing to come across somebody in my field who wanted to discuss my insights and actually had something to say, something to interpret. "Okay, so what do you think about X?" he would ask me. As we walked, I asked him about his day. He grumbled a bit, frustrated at his managers who were "taking the company in directions" he thought were completely wrong. I asked him if this had anything to do with their company downsizing. "There is just so much waste in this company, Paula," he replied. The word "waste," when discussing a person or a group of people, will always make me shudder. He looked down at his feet and shook his head. "Months and months of people working on projects that don't work or not working on anything at all." I asked him what he would do to fix the problem, what he thought was a "good vision" of management. I also asked him what he hoped was happening in the company on a structural level but wasn't. He didn't really know. He just thought that people weren't being creative, weren't showing initiative. I probed him: "Maybe they do care, but management is just expecting too much from them." This notion prompted Simon to launch into a discussion about what great companies do to really motivate their workers.

I reminded Simon of the article he sent me a few days before about Amazon's "Leadership Principles." Many tech companies have slogans, principles, and rules, which permeate their office spaces and company Web sites. On its own Web site, Amazon states that the company "uses [its] Leadership Principles every day." Of the list of sixteen, some include "customer obsession," "leaders are right a lot," and "hire and develop the best."[1]

"Some of those principles creeped me out," I told Simon. He looked a bit surprised. "What do you mean? I genuinely think these are great principles."

---

1. "Leadership Principles," https://www.amazon.jobs/en-gb/principles.

I felt a bit awkward as if I had offended him. I chuckled nervously and said, "I can't recall the exact principle, but there was something in there about putting the customer first. I think if you start putting the customer first, there is no limit. Because you are providing a service for somebody who has limitless demands. And when somebody has limitless demands, they don't take into account that the person providing the service is limited. They have limited time and energy. You know what I mean?" He shook his head. "I just think there is a limit to everything," I continued, "and places like Amazon, with people crying at their desks, are not worth the ten, twenty, one hundred customers who will be very satisfied with a service. You have to care about the providers."

Simon responded, "Look [he always seemed to start with that word, "look"], there is a balance to everything. You don't want people crying at their desks. Or maybe not always crying."

I laughed, "Like the I-miss-my-mom crying is okay."

"True, exactly. But you know what I mean. You don't want people to feel crushed. But you also have to understand the customer, remember that you are doing something for them."

"I guess I agree with you to some extent. I just don't know how to ensure this balance will happen. When organizations get too big, things get lost along the way, people's emotions get forgotten."

Simon replied by sharing an anecdote about Amazon. They invited him for an interview. A recruiter contacted him and seemed mildly interested in Simon's profile. So Simon called them back. He was then bounced around from one recruitment officer to another, to another. All internal staff. "Their disregard for people was appalling. They just didn't care. They would have this American sort of vagueness to them when they said, 'Let me know what else I can do for you.' But you haven't done anything! And then I e-mailed them, and they said, 'Oh wait, wow, tomorrow a representative from the US is flying in; let's schedule you into an interview tomorrow.'"

"And did you go to the interview?"

"Yes, I did. But I just had to drop everything."

"So you agree with me? See! This company is so customer-first that they forget to think about their employees. Or future employees."

Simon just shook his head and chuckled. "You're right," he said, and we continued walking.

During my second year of fieldwork, I walked home with Simon almost every afternoon after work. But there were moments in my interaction with Simon that made me feel somewhat uneasy. This unease stemmed from the symbolic and actual power that Simon held as a manager of the one hundred developers I was researching. Simon could fire people. He could hire people. He could rearrange his employees' workspaces and decide who they worked with. Both Simon and I were cautious about expressing our friendship at work, as it would make my own role as their team ethnographer that much harder. I made it a rule not to talk about his employees; although, despite this rule, I still felt watched every time I snuck out the back door and wandered down the street with him. I worried sometimes that some of my interlocutors wouldn't talk to me if they found out how close Simon and I had become.

I knew Simon and I sometimes believed in different things, and the stories I would tell about his company were not necessarily the ones he was interested in hearing. He was also embedded within a management culture, while I was focused on critiquing the system he was part of and was building. Our discussion about Amazon is a perfect example: It was ingrained in me, as a sociologist, to look at the forms of exploitation within a company, while Simon was interested in how Amazon mobilizes efficiency. These were the times we agreed to disagree.

Managers Used to Be Developers Too

In the previous chapters, you saw the world through the eyes of the software developer. But in order to paint a more complete picture of corporate software development culture, I can't avoid describing managers, management culture, as well as certain key production narratives that permeate the software development workplace. Management, the people who directly report to management, and those who help managers implement software management methods are important to programmers. The people in these roles influence the flows of the programmers' work and attempt to reframe their work culture as well as the narratives of production. They care about performance and customer satisfaction. They also implement software development methodologies that help push this peak performance and customer satisfaction. To illustrate this latter function of management, I will explain a particular methodology used at the MiddleTech office that presents programmers with a set of schemes, stories, rituals, and routines that help enforce this narrative of peak performance.

At MiddleTech, Simon was a senior research and development manager of navigation, which meant that he managed all the software projects of around one hundred software developers who were working on navigation technology. These one hundred developers were then divided into ten different subteams who spent their days optimizing, fixing, and building the software that would help navigate users to their destination. Each of these subteams had one leader, the team lead, who would help them complete their tasks on time. And all these leaders would be under Simon's watch. His role was to plan the general direction of the work of all the teams and to make sure that these teams were "performing well," which meant that they were working on time and coming up with creative ideas and "innovating" while also creating software that would withstand the test of time.

Simon's career in software began with his job as an engineer for a company that was an integral part of Israel's tech boom of the late 1990s/early 2000s. Their main business was built around a centralized hardware system that supported voice and fax messaging, which was then sold to telecommunications companies and other large enterprises that sold the voice and fax services to their customers. Before the smartphone, one's voice in-box was a precious tool. Today, this type of technology is obviously obsolete.

Much like many tech managers, Simon started his career in software as a programmer. Having doubts about his ability to code, he progressed to being a team manager. Many developers try to avoid becoming managers because they know that the management path will take them away from the programming work they like so much. Some also want to avoid the stress of being a leader, or they lack leadership or organization skills. Simon didn't have these qualms, however, and he found that his ambition and competitive streak made him better suited to a managerial role. Promoted to director of research and development, he continued to work for this Israeli tech company until 2011, around the time of the company's collapse.

Simon's professional history is also typical within the computing industry. Middle managers are often sourced from a programming team. With enough skill to understand what a programmer was working on and enough drive and company loyalty to push efficiency, customer-facing innovation, and competition, programmers-turned-managers became figures who promised camaraderie and understanding among computer programmers, as well as the drive for excellence and ambition for upper management. The truth is a little messier, of course. As we know by now, software changes rapidly. The voice messaging software that Simon was building at the Israeli tech company is a perfect example. Practically nothing he was building in the 1990s and 2000s is still used today. The programming languages he was using are now obsolete or considered niche skills. Many programmers who have become managers have told me that their skills quickly turned rusty. This lack of knowledge (or partial knowledge) of how to program continues to challenge the management's authority, giving the "real" programmer an upper hand. So how does a manager gain control of a project and minimize the moments in which the programmer has this upper hand?

Organizing for What and for Whom?

Most days during my second year of fieldwork had a steady rhythm: I would spend my day in meetings, take lunches and breaks with software developers and their colleagues, and then end my workday with a forty-five-minute walk home with Simon. I noticed the contrast between the developers and the manager in my workday. Often Simon would have a completely different perspective on why something was built or why a project shut down. I recall a conversation we had about a few developers who felt frustrated when their work was ruined. It happened in another team the summer before I set foot on Simon's floor. A group of developers were working on one feature for an entire year. They loved what they had built, and they put a lot of creative energy into the project. One day, seemingly out of nowhere, their manager told them to abandon the project and start building something else. I asked Simon, "Isn't this tragic?" Simon didn't see it as tragic at all. He told me that developers see this type of occurrence as something sad only when they think that they're building for themselves. But if they remind themselves that we are all here for the customer, then they should recognize that these types of changes happen all the time.

From Simon's perspective, software development is about building a product for somebody. As he explained on our walk home, MiddleTech resides within a service industry in which its software serves customers, and according to Amazon, developers should be "obsessed" with their customers. What does this mean exactly? On the one hand, being obsessed with the customer means building software for somebody else, based on either the customer's or user's expectations. This product-oriented perspective, which Simon and many of his colleagues have, places demands on managers and their teams, and these demands help organize deadlines, requirements, standards, and the type of components that need to be completed for the customer.

On the other hand, if we take the perspective of the software developer, as I mainly did in the preceding chapters, software development is primarily done to build something cool. It's a creative, highly intimate, highly social sport that values beauty and elegance, with the developer at the center of all creation. This tension—between the developers (who want to create, code, hack, and break and fix stuff) and the managers and legal team (who have customers, deadlines, standards, and legal regulations to adhere to)—is a constant point of contention: how to care and compromise when building software, or how to function in a system of efficiency and excellence when sometimes good enoughness is all that is possible. Is the computer—the care and intimacy it demands and its shaky, annoying architecture, which constantly breaks down—the object at the center of a team's organization and organized practices? Or is profit at the center of a team's efforts to organize? Or is it perhaps both?

This chapter highlights the competing organizational tensions within a software development company and how good enoughness is both at the heart of software management methodologies as well as the outcome of these methodologies. I will focus on the role of the manager, as well as on one of the many methodologies of software project management. Revealing these competing organizational tensions also helps uncover the struggle to maintain control over the labor process. On the one hand, managers like Simon and his team of micromanagers use software development methodologies to break down and simplify the labor process in order to make production more transparent and tangible within their management team. On the other hand, software developers often attempt to retain control of the labor process and push back against these methodologies, explaining that no method of production can capture the complex, unforeseeable nature of software.

This chapter will focus specifically on how software development work is managed and organized, who does the organizing, and how organization is resisted. This will then help me explain how organizational methods struggle to capture the complex, unforeseeable nature of software. I will also highlight how developers engage with this unforeseeability to gain control of the labor process. Aside from telling you more about Simon, I will also introduce you to some of the people who work for him, including Chris, a "Scrum Master," who works directly with Simon to maintain productivity levels among the software developers. You will also meet a few developers who work for Simon, and we will return to some characters you already know, such as Aseem, the junior developer we met earlier; his software developer colleague Jelena, who was part of the EV team; and Ori, the data scientist/researcher.

The Team Reshuffle

Every second Thursday at around 10 a.m., Simon would host a Team Demo for his one hundred developers. This demo (short for "demonstration"), a widespread practice within the corporate software world, was an opportunity to share projects, accomplishments, and ideas with broader teams and/or departments. Each week a few teams would volunteer to show off their work, and for five to ten minutes would stand up in the large conference room at MiddleTech's seventh floor in front of about sixty of their colleagues and awkwardly point at a few slides. Christian, a more senior developer (the head of the algorithm team whom Aseem looked up to in an earlier chapter), would always buy breakfast for everybody. Rounding up a few friends from his team, Christian would lay out packages of cheeses, meats, jams, and breakfast rolls, and everyone would fill up their plates and sit around listening to the week's presentation. Buying food for the rest of the team might seem like an over-the-top biweekly gesture from any regular programmer, but Christian was widely respected as an astonishingly good developer (with some like Aseem saying he was the genius of the entire team), and his breakfast gesture fully established him as the unofficial king of Simon's navigation team.

Simon always opened these demos with a short pep talk. This particular week, he started the meeting with the topic of the team reshuffling, which would start the following week. The team reshuffle, which took place every six to eight months, is an "exercise" (as Simon called it) that gives developers the opportunity to switch teams as well as their seating arrangements. He began:

So, guys, we are a very large group, we need to break things down into small focused teams in order to be autonomous, agile, and well synchronized. It's about providing feedback. It's not about saying, "Yeah, just search in the Jira [online project management software], and you'll find what we do." Every decision we take is good for the time it was taken, but we need to reevaluate it periodically and look internally to ourselves and say, "Assuming everything is what it is, what can we do better? How can we be better aligned?" We need to deliver our [software product]. This is the main goal in our team. The other goal is to evolve our code base assets. We have a lot of assets. We need to improve our online services.Simon then clicked to a slide that outlined the structure of the Routing and Navigation team. The team substructure showed the various product owners (known as POs) who are responsible for each subsection. He also suggested that everybody look at a little Q&A sheet that he uploaded onto the team's internal site. There was a lot of commotion. This type of reshuffle was tricky to do as it challenged the stability of the team's social networks, ways of working together, and methods of self-management. After the meeting was over, I went back to my desk and copied the link into my browser and pulled up a page with the following explanation of how the team reshuffle would work in practice:

Q: What does the process look like in reality?

A: In the set week, the entire Navigation team will meet for 15 minutes every day, usually 13:45–14:00. There are posters for each team, each marking the number of available slots per team. There is a Post-it Note with the picture of each developer, and then each person places themselves in an open slot. The location can be changed each day.

Q: How do we know the process is over?

A: At the end of each daily session we have a vote—each developer should be either happy, or neutral, or come forward with an objection. The result of the vote is transparent to everyone. When we get to a point when there are no more objections, we wait an extra 24 hours, and if there are still no objections, we move on to the new setup. If you object, you don't have to provide a solution, but we will share your objection.

Q: What are the guidelines for selecting which team to join?

A: a) Do what is best for the company before what is best for you.
b) Each team should have the skill set to meet the delivery targets.

Q: What happens if I am away during the self-selection period?

A: You should ask for someone to act as your proxy.

Q: Is the process available for all developers or just for MiddleTech full-time employees?

A: Unfortunately, only people in the Berlin site are participating in the exercise.

Q: Will I change line managers when joining a new team?

A: Potentially, yes, the line managers are defined as part of the structure definition. If you join a new team that is managed by a different line manager than your current one, you will start working with her/him.

Q: I like working with my line manager. Why do I need to change?

A: We are trying to make sure that line managers are not just generic support functions but are involved in the day-to-day activity of their reports.

Q: Do I need to ask the team line manager for approval before joining it?

A: No.

Q: What happens if more developers want to join a specific team than available seats?

A: Some people will have to compromise and join their 2nd or 3rd preference.

Q: What should I do if I want to join a team, but all the spots are taken already?

A: You can either move one of the developers to another team or add yourself as a new developer. However, in the second option, this structure cannot be the final structure by definition.

Q: Do I have to move to a new team?

A: No, you don't have to move if your team continues to exist and the number of available slots in the team has not reduced.

Q: Do existing team members of a team have priority in joining it?

A: Yes and no. Everybody should have the same opportunity; however, existing teams with clear delivery objectives would benefit from continuity of at least some of its members. We would need to balance this if/when such a situation arises.

Q: Will I have to move my seat?

A: Likely, yes. After we finish the team self-selection process, we would like to arrange the seating so that all team members will sit together.

Q: What happens to current in-progress activities?

A: You need to bring existing activities to a state where they can be handed over to the new team members if you are not continuing with your current team.

Q: When would be the next re-shuffling exercise?

A: Usually, we have such an exercise every 6–8 months.

This list illustrates the entire process of the team reshuffle as well as how confusing it was for the developers. Many of these programmers were not accustomed to working in an office where their desks and teams changed twice a year. This list, which was created by Simon, also further cemented him as the person in power: He made his team move, and he, in the end, was the one with all the answers.

Under the Q&A, a few developers posted a number of new questions directed at Simon: "How do we know the skill sets necessary for each particular team? Let's say I've learned a bit about one team and would like to move there, but in the end, there is no place for me there and no place in my current team either. How do I learn where else I can fit if I am not a C++ developer required in most of the teams?"

Another developer asked, "Why do we need line managers to be involved in our day-to-day activities? What is their role there? And how does changing the line manager help when changing teams? When you change a line manager then the new manager doesn't know much about you, your skills, ambitions, performance and achievements, and it will take time for the line manager to learn about and start supporting you. Doesn't it make sense to make it more stable by line management not being dependent on the particular team you are part of?"

A third developer wrote, "Additionally, binding line management to the team membership is likely to cause a conflict of interest for the line manager (what is best for the team vs. what is best for the person within the company). It's a widespread natural thing, and I had such a negative experience in the past. Yet another developer wrote, "I'd also like to know, what is the role and what are the general responsibilities of line managers in the navigation team?"

These comments help illustrate how the team reshuffle stirred up some excitement and the underlying tension among the programmers and their managers.

The exercise had a mixed message: On the one hand, it gave developers the seeming autonomy of being in control, being able to choose the team that they wanted to be in. On the other hand, it delineated, top-down, that a rearrangement of their team was necessary. This was a sobering reminder that they were not, in fact, in control, and that Simon and the company were really in charge of the rhythms of their labor, something that programmers, as intellectual and creative laborers, had a hard time coming to terms with (as I will explain later). Simon was the one who decided they had to move. He was the one who decided that they needed to get up, stop what they were doing and building, and reshuffle their working order. The team reshuffle, was, as Simon mentioned in his demo pep talk, a way of "realigning" the teams and helping them "reevaluate" how they can work better on providing faster product "delivery."

Simon's reorganization caused a lot of social negotiation, and the guidelines he outlined in the Q&A established a way of working that he decided on, which might not necessarily work for the team. As the developers revealed in their responses to Simon's Q&A, they didn't fully understand the responsibilities of a line manager. One made it clear that "binding a line manager to a team"

```
1    2005: 2702 lines (0.15%)
2    2006: 671 lines (0.04%)
3    2007: 1296 lines (0.07%)
4    2008: 9692 lines (0.52%)
5    2009: 26075 lines (1.41%)
6    2010: 35579 lines (1.92%)
7    2011: 170494 lines (9.22%)
8    2012: 141467 lines (7.65%)
9    2013: 164942 lines (8.92%)
10   2014: 183079 lines (9.90%)
11   2015: 307694 lines (16.64%)
12   2016: 504015 lines (27.26%)
13   2017: 258404 lines (13.97%)
14   2018: 42962 lines (2.32%)
```

FIG. 4.1 The team reshuffle

created a "conflict of interest." What he meant here was something I mentioned earlier—that developers had different goals in mind than deadline-driven managers. Simon's team reorganization is an illustration of the competing powers at work as it is a top-down attempt to reshuffle the power structures at play within each team, to create new alliances among developers, and to abolish the alliances that were toxic or not working well.

History of Managing Expert Knowledge

This team reshuffle exemplifies a variety of wider themes in the modern corporate office, including shifting labor relations and the issue of how to control the knowledge worker in a postindustrial workplace. Indeed, the shift in programmer expertise, what programming looked like on a corporate level, and the management methodologies used in programming were part of a larger shift in ideas about expert power, organizational control, and occupational/class formation in late modernity, particularly in relation to the new class of knowledge workers.

In the middle of the twentieth century, organization studies scholars, labor scholars, and industrial sociologists all observed a shift in what the workplace looked like, how professions were shaped, and how power was constituted in the corporate setting, particularly because new professions (like programmers) were starting to emerge, and they possessed an expertise that was quite ephemeral and based on information and knowledge. The concern over the power of the expert was nothing new to the modern workplace. As some scholars have noted, experts have always been able to gain authority "if they can convince their society that they have access to esoteric matters only to be reached through their specialized skills and yet of general potential utility" (Schaffer 1994, 17). Yet, when it came to the modern organization, the key issue was the rise of knowledge workers (again, such as computer programmers), who possessed a certain professional expertise that their managers did not have. One of the core mechanisms of modern management is keeping control in the hands of managers (Braverman 1974), but how could this be achieved in light of the rise of the knowledge worker?

If we look back to Frederick Winslow Taylor's factory floor, the manager had a direct visual and conceptual connection to what was being built on the assembly-line. In postindustrial workplaces, however, as the workers' "practical skill grew out of an abstract system of knowledge," the workers' control of their occupation lay in the "control of the abstractions that generate the practical techniques." Here "control of knowledge and its application meant dominating outsiders who attack that control" (Abbott 2014, 25). These "abstractions" would be the theoretical knowledge behind the workers' practical, mechanical output, and the "outsiders" would be anybody without this abstract knowledge (like managers) hoping to take control.

Thus social and organizational researchers started to notice that in the postindustrial corporate workplace, expert power and control had begun to reemerge as a central theme, raising fundamental questions about the "longer-term impact of contemporary socio-economic restructuring on the forms of organizational and class control taking shape in 'late modernity'" (Reed 1996, 573).

Not surprisingly, management had a completely different set of challenges as the workplace began to shift from "capital-intensive industries, such as steel and automobiles, to information-intensive industries, such as financial services and logistics, and then towards innovation-driven industries, such as computer software and pharmaceutical companies" (Alvesson 2004, 5). When studying various knowledge professions, scholars started to notice that managers had begun to lose touch with what workers were working on and what was being created in the first place. As Alvesson explained, "the individual knowledge worker (or team) was often in the situation of having the best general insights into the problem area as well as being the person (or team) with most familiarity with the specifics of the actual problem. Superiors may have more general experience and overview but have less understanding of what can and should be done in specific situations" (2004, 23).

Managers made various attempts to reclaim power over the workers. One idea involved building a "humane" workplace, which in the 1980s and onward became a prevalent theme among management gurus who would train managers to "work with their 'hearts and minds' not structures and systems," focusing on the "human relations aspects of organizations" (Clark and Salaman 1996, 86; Woodworth and Nelson 1979, 29). This included at times invisible or more indirect employee-control structures, particularly with the help of various management methodologies and computer-assisted information-control systems (much like the team reshuffle). As Zuboff's (1988) research shows, more advanced information-control systems can enhance "the 'control at a distance' capacity available to modern organizations, but that very distancing capacity can have a debilitating impact on the capability of management to negotiate everyday order on the shopfloor and in the office" (Reed 1996, 578). In other words, the more management relies on management software, the more potential there is for them to be detached from what is being produced and how.

Thus, the expert-based information- and communication-control systems increasingly evident in the financial, commercial, technological, and organizational activities of modern corporations began to "signify a move towards an integration of 'planning and control on a systematic and regularized basis . . . A key point about new technologies is their increasing pervasiveness and intrusiveness, their capacity to penetrate even deeper into physical, social and personal areas. And, by virtue of these characteristics, what the new technologies offer is more flexible forms of surveillance" (Webster and Robins 1993, 248–49). Here, both managers and colleagues are able to monitor their workers and coworkers in new ways. As a result, expert groups often found themselves subjected to the more unobtrusive and pervasive control systems that they helped to design and introduce. This "enhanced organizational transparency and visibility makes it very difficult for anybody to hide from the 'supervisory gaze'" (Reed 1996, 582).

History of Managing Developers

Now, understanding how these particular power dynamics and forms of professional control shifted in programming would perhaps require a bit more explanation about the shifts in the professionalization of computing work throughout the past decades.

Programming evolved out of electrical engineering in the mid-1940s, and it used to require familiarity with the machine's electrical logic as well as its physical structure and operation. Early computing was highly integrated and highly skilled, requiring the programmer to understand machine-language programming, which meant having knowledge of logic and mathematics as well as familiarity with the machine being programmed (Kraft 1979). As Nathan Ensmenger explained, computer programming started to be recognized as a uniquely creative activity, a genuine "brain business," which was "often an agonizingly difficult intellectual effort—and therefore almost impossible to manage using conventional methods" (2010, 144). Ensmenger means that, as a manager, it was quite hard to monitor what developers were doing just by looking over their shoulders.

Moreover, as programming languages developed and software became more complex, a difference emerged between the "brain business" of one programmer and another, with some programmers needing to know much less about the computer in order to run it.

Following the 1950s, high-level programming languages implemented "translators," which triggered multiple machine operations with a single instruction. These higher-level languages allowed anybody who mastered the language to run the machine, making it unnecessary for all programmers to be quasi-engineers. Along with the development of these higher-level languages came the development of smaller, more packaged programs, which both expanded the employment of low-skilled specialists and finally freed the managers from depending on individual, highly skilled software workers. They also made possible, for the first time, a genuine task-based fragmentation of labor in programming (Kraft 1979, 148). As software production increasingly became big business throughout the 1960s until today, the division of labor and fragmentation of skills became a rational way to optimize output. At this point, software companies began to regard their workers as mere units of production and were concerned solely with the maximization of the profit extracted from them (Cooley 1980, 532).

This type of shift in fragmentation of programming work is nicely illustrated in Andrew Ross's *No-Collar* (2004). He recalls a story of a web developer named Paulsen, who worked in the early 1990s as a no-collar freelancer "renaissance man" within his field, hopping from one company to the next. Suddenly, in the late 1990s, when "projects became so complicated that a team needed to be specialized," he was forced to choose a specialty. In Paulsen's words, "Suddenly there was a factory, and you had Taylorization. . . . Now it only takes a tiny portion of my brain" (Ross 2004, 55).

This task-based fragmentation of labor gave management the false promise of scientific control over the "often-unpredictable processes of research and development" that software engineering involved (Ensmenger 2010, 59). Indeed, despite this task-based fragmentation in programming, a manager still did not have control over the full labor process, as there was still a large disconnect between how software was built and the complexity of a computer. Philip Kraft, a pioneer in the early sociology of computing, pointed out that while these new trends in computing, like structured programming, gave the software manager an "answer to the assembly line" (Kraft 1979, 145), they could not predict the massively rapid changes that the computer would undergo and the influence that the internet, including cloud storage, would have on the programming practice.

It seemed like the programmer and the software manager have been, since the beginning of their profession, in a subtle yet constant push-and-pull struggle over the control of their work organization.

Despite managers' many attempts to gain control of the labor process through various forms of task fragmentations and simplifications in programming styles, software developers were well aware that they had more control of the knowledge of their projects as computing gained more and more algorithmic and structural complexity. As programmers contend with the unprecedented unpredictability and complexity of computing, they must make decisions that are highly contingent on the task at hand. Controlling how to complete a task and how long a task will take depends on a variety of technical factors, such as the amount of legacy code that a given problem relies on, the robustness of the data being used (if it's cleaned up or not), as well as human factors (for example, if the one person who knows how to fix a bug is on vacation). As difficult as this task may be, managers like Simon still attempt to gain control over the decisions that are made in the course of work through strategies like a team reshuffle or a number of other management "methodologies." As I will also show, Simon's seating reshuffle was typical of the modern agile workplace, where movement and change become a catalyst for innovation and flexibility.

Scrumming Together

Up until the 1990s, conventional methods of developing software called for detailed upfront plans, precise prediction, and rigid control strategies. These methods seemed to stop working. Software developers themselves started to gain more status (and earn more money) and called into question these more rigid methods. In response to these changes, managers began opting for more subtle ways "to bound, direct, nudge, or confine, but not to control" (Highsmith 2013, 40).

Countless books and articles were then written—both by engineers (Ereiz and Mušić 2019; Mahanti 2006; Turk, France, and Rumpe 2002) and software project managers (Cervone 2011; Schwaber and Beedle 2008)—about how to best introduce more subtle software management methods. These texts outlined a number of methodologies that help manage complex (and reactive!) knowledge work, the most prominent within MiddleTech as well as throughout the global software industry being the Scrum methodology.

Scrum was introduced into the world of product development methodologies in 1986 by two Japanese professors of marketing who were looking for a way to make product development faster and more flexible, and reactive to the changing demands of the market. While Scrum was not originally intended for software development, the internet changed how software was built, deployed, and updated (as I mentioned in my discussion of "update culture" in a previous chapter). Basically, the internet allowed both software users and customers to demand updates to the software product any time they wanted (while also giving developers a way of delivering imperfect software, which could be tweaked, improved, or fixed weeks or months later through software updates, resulting in good-enough software. This development made software very reactive to the demands of the user and the market. A need for agility in software production teams emerged, meaning a way of being responsive to the changes that the update culture of the internet allowed.

This brought on a so-called "agile turn" (Gürses and Van Hoboken 2017) in software development, a response to the increased complexity of software and the shift in the distribution infrastructure of software. A new production order, characterized by short development cycles, continuous testing, and greater simplicity of design (Douglass 2015), also attempted to speed up the developers' work and deliver to their customers and their users quickly. Agile software companies encouraged teams to come up with solutions and customer requirements through self-organization and communication, and they advocated adaptive planning, evolutionary development, early delivery, and continual improvement to promote rapid and flexible response to change (Douglass 2015).

This push-and-pull dance over the control of the computing work process was also displayed in these production methodologies. As management gurus were coming up with ways of structuring their workers, Agile, which is very much linked to the Scrum methodology, originated in 2001 in the "Manifesto for Agile Software Development," which was, ironically enough, written by a team of seventeen software engineers after meeting at a conference. These self-professed "organizational anarchists," devised "12 principles" in their manifesto, which valued "individuals and interactions over processes and tools," "working software over comprehensive documentation," "customer collaboration over contract negotiation," and "responding to change over following a plan" (agilemanifesto.org). They explicitly stated that their approach was a response to their frustration with management: "Marketing, or management, or external customers, internal customers, and, yes, even developers—don't want to make hard trade-off decisions, so they impose irrational demands through the imposition of corporate power structures" (agilemanifesto.org). This fight between the "irrational" managers and the more realistic or rational programmers was a trope that seemed to repeat itself at MiddleTech twenty years after the manifesto was born.

It's worth noting that any methodology or technical tool that is implemented in a team comes with controversy and backlash. In Thomas Malaby's ethnographic look at programmers at Linden Labs and the development of Second Life, he described how the team moved from using a tool called Achievements and Objectives (or As & Os) for distributing information about the many projects going on within the company to using something called Jira (which is also used at MiddleTech). Supposedly "the transition to Jira from As & Os never sat well with some employees at Linden Lab, who felt the new technological conditions of their work ran counter to an established and flexible practice already in place" (Malaby 2009, 64). This struggle over freedom of choice and flexibility has a lot to do with the efforts to regain control over the labor process.

Scrum was thus just one methodology used to implement this so-called "agility." As I will show, Scrum is made up of microprocesses, defined roles, and rituals that help management regain control over the decisions that are made in the course of work, giving workers the illusion that they are in control.

To illustrate this struggle, I want to pinpoint the way in which Scrum was shaping the organization of software work at MiddleTech and give a concrete description of how MiddleTech's workers experienced this method. I will briefly pinpoint the basic principles of one methodology to illustrate how it can organize the labor process of developers while at the same time provide more units of control for the manager and reveal how methodologies struggle to capture the complex, unpredictable nature of software and how developers play upon this unpredictability. I will also show how Scrum becomes a way for developers to cooperate in order to establish certain criteria around what is good enough and what isn't.

Scrum "focuses on project management in situations where it's difficult to plan ahead" (Schwaber and Beedle 2008, 12), and development teams constantly work on versions of their software in small two-week "sprints," with developers given feedback following each sprint. This feedback comes either from their management, their customer, or analytical data (called Key Performance Metrics, which I will introduce later) gathered by MiddleTech's analyst team. This team reviews how the software is used and locates bugginess or breakdown.

Software is developed by a self-organizing team, and a manager like Simon is supposed to be quite hands-off. In fact, Simon relies on line managers who work for him, namely product owners (such as Liz, whom we met in the previous chapter, on the Electric Vehicle team) or Scrum Masters. A Scrum Master's role is to make sure teams are adhering to the Scrum production methodology. They are also sometimes called an "agile coach" or even, as Simon once pointed out, a "productivity coach." Their job is to attend all the developers' meetings and encourage them to meet their deadlines. Scrum Masters also often report back to managers like Simon, with the goal of making the developers' work explicit and transparent. When observing them in action, they sometimes reminded me of personal trainers, priests, coaches, or cheerleaders.

I also noticed that Scrum draws heavily on a vocabulary of "reflection," "sharing," and "transparency," pushing the developers to make their work explicit. This push for transparency stems from the fact that managers want to keep track of the speed of their developers' output. To this end, Scrum Masters not only cheer the developers on with their work but also help instill a culture of reflection through various daily or weekly meetings or rituals. As programmers engage in these moments of reflection, the Scrum Master collects information on the progress of the teams and the type of work they are doing and then provides this feedback to managers like Simon.

There are roughly 1,000 developers at MiddleTech, with around 150 developers working in the front-end team and 850 in the back-end team;

these developers are then further divided into smaller five-person teams that work on specific tasks, software products, or projects. Each of these small teams does not always need to know what another team is doing in order to complete their own task, so the deadlines for their projects are not always dependent on one another. Software development managers, therefore, structure the developers' production schedule using the Scrum methodology, with software developers working in sprints in which they have to deliver or update a piece of software to their customers. Within these sprints, the Scrum Master coordinates meetings to help temporally organize the developers' work. These meetings include a Sprint Planning session, which takes place once at the beginning of the sprint and lasts around two to four hours, during which developers plan what needs to be built in the next two weeks.

Midway through the sprint, the Scrum Master also organizes a weekly "grooming session," lasting from thirty minutes to one hour, to help refine the developers' work, acting as a check-in to see what still needs to be completed. Finally, at the end of the sprint, the Scrum Master holds a "retrospective meeting" to help developers reflect on the sprint and help improve it during the next iteration. Additionally, developers are expected (with or without the Scrum Master present) to hold a stand-up meeting every day for five to fifteen minutes, at which their team members stand in a circle and share what they are doing with the rest of the team. In order to help the developers visualize and make transparent both their work and their progress, a large whiteboard is hung up next to the team's desks. Each developer takes a ticket, usually written down on a Post-it Note, to work on and each day sticks it further along on the board until the task is completed. This ticket represents a small job a developer has to focus on, and the type of ticket depends on what the team is working on. This progress chart or Scrum task board is organized into vertical categories such as "To Do," "In Progress," "Blocked," and "Done."

For example, one team at MiddleTech was working on voice guidance for drivers, and one of the tickets on any given day would read, "Add voice command to speed limits." The developer would take a ticket, which meant they would commit to working on it and subjectively decide on the amount of time it would take to finish the ticket. One ticket can take a day, or it can take weeks. It is also worth noting that while sprints are small jobs that teams work on, a finished product takes an industry standard of forty-four weeks at MiddleTech. So Week 44 is known as feature-complete day, meaning that all features or changes created by individual teams should be finished and merged into the code base at that time.

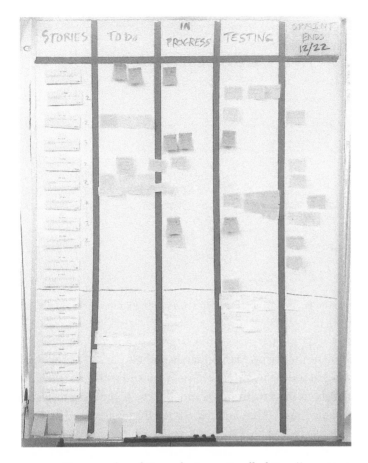

FIG. 4.2 The scrum board. Image by Logan Ingalls, https://commons
.wikimedia.org/wiki/File:Scrum_task_board.jpg. CC BY 2.0 license.

The Stand-Up

One key ritual in the implementation of Scrum is the daily stand-up. The daily
stand-up always made me feel like I was back in school or church. I would
arrive in the office, sit at my desk, and without even looking at my watch,
I would know it was 10 a.m. when a group of developers would get up and
walk over to a whiteboard. It was one of the first moments in a developer's
day. They would stand in a circle, like they were praying. The quiet tone in
which they all mumbled made their work even more prayer-like. Each of the
developers in the team was supposed to take a few seconds to discuss what
they did the previous day. Depending on the team, the developers would
either be silent and a bit annoyed, or they would laugh a lot, mainly at each

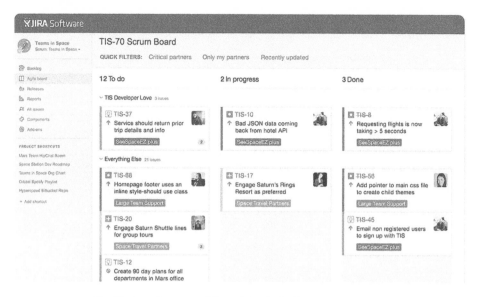

FIG. 4.3 The Jira board, accessed from Atlassian's Pinterest page, May 1, 2023.

other. Some of them stuffed their hands in their pockets. They would say, "I am trying to order the instances," or "I am still trying to reach the team in Chicago about the data from last month," or "I am trying to synchronize with the traffic team." "I am figuring out the FC5 issues," or "Bad news, ten thousand cases crashed," or "We had a meeting with the team from Tel Aviv." At times, I grasped what they were talking about. And at other times, I didn't understand at all. Their tasks were not always technical. They sometimes had communication issues with another team. Or they were waiting for some sort of process to happen. They often blamed their inactivity on something they called "blocks," which were both technical, human, and material.

Chris was the only Scrum Master in Simon's whole team of one hundred developers. He was in his mid-thirties and entered the tech scene after studying knowledge management and cultural studies and was certified as a Scrum Master in an official training course. He had a lot of energy and a kind aura about him. I liked him a lot, and he always welcomed me into his meetings with open arms, sharing details with me about the frustrations he was experiencing. Although he was engaged, excited, and highly organized, he was not always treated seriously, nor were the methods of working he was trying to implement. For example, one afternoon, Chris joined the Electric Vehicle team during their daily stand-up. We all gathered around a large screen, which was showing a Jira Scrum board (Jira is a software that illustrates a Scrum workflow setup).

In this stand-up, each member of the team took turns briefly explaining what they were working on. In this particular meeting, they were clearly not using the Scrum board.

After a few minutes, Chris became agitated and noticed that nobody was using the tickets, nor were they pointing at the board and moving the tickets from the "to do" to the "in progress" column. He started searching for the ticket on the screen that corresponded with Aseem's task.

"Can we see the 'dev drop' here?" He pointed at the screen with the Jira software, and at that moment I also noticed that nobody had really taken note of the screen at all in the past few minutes. Chris seemed more frustrated than ever. "Try to really reflect on the current work we are doing, otherwise we cannot see what is happening," he pleaded. The team then started talking again about some sort of terrain problems in northern Canada (the map in that area did not show the elevation). Chris got a bit annoyed again. "What will happen here? Can we move this?" he said as he pointed at a ticket. "Take your implements seriously, otherwise this does not make sense," he added, pointing again at the Jira board.

Aseem then started talking about a "bad scaling parameter" that he needed to fix. Chris looked at the board and said, "Okay, well, can we find this in here? Let's do a search. What should I search for?" Aseem replied, "Scaling," and Chris searched around in the Jira system. They didn't find anything.

The group moved over to the screen displaying the Jira board. They tried to work with it, but it was still not really part of their interaction. For the rest of the meeting, Chris struggled to get the team to use the correct procedures, while the team, lacking much enthusiasm for these procedures, shrugged, nodded, and promised to use the right procedures the following day.

The Unmanageable Art of Programming

This stand-up was relevant as it illustrated two themes that were repeated over and over again throughout my fieldwork at MiddleTech. Firstly, the programmers always seemed to resist meetings in general. While this might be the case for any worker in any organization, observing meeting resistance among programmers helped uncover a few tensions that played out within the software workplace.

While the stand-up was the shortest of the Scrum rituals, it revealed the sleepiness, the boredom, the unenthusiastic shrugs and yawns of the people attending. I have been to lunches, happy-hour beers, and Christmas parties where developers and their teammates were full of social camaraderie. What is different about these meetings? The problem was that these meetings were not conducted on the developers' terms. Developers at MiddleTech shared a lot about what they were working on with their teammates via their chat systems, in the coffee room, or through what I called "screen-tilting—tilting from behind their screen to catch the eye of the developer sitting across from them.

The Scrum ritual meetings were institutionalized, formalized, and pre-scribed top-down by managers like Simon. The "meeting"—any meeting—thus became a bit of a meme around the office: a joke, a waste of time, something that distracts from the "real" work, a mechanism to control the developers, etc. When Simon and Chris were absent for various reasons, meetings would be sleepier or not happen at all. One developer told me sarcastically, "We work on meeting-driven development—so for every four days of writing code, we sit the rest of the time confused in meetings."

I understood that the developers' lack of interest in meetings became a form of resistance to outsider power. Neither Simon nor Chris had a deep understanding of how to program a piece of software, being outsiders to the craft of programming. Because Simon and Chris lacked these skills, develop-ers had a hard time accepting their methods of order and organization—not because structure and organization are bad but because developers work with an object (software) that will inevitably go wrong, break down, or get more complicated as the project goes on. If an outsider like Simon or his proxy, Chris, attempted to organize the unforeseeable, complex matter that is soft-ware, they would inevitably come up against programmer resistance—not in the form of large explicit protests but small micropractices. In the case of the stand-up, this resistance took the form of changing the subject or steer-ing attention away from the organizational tool (in this case, the Jira board). During another meeting, after Simon left the room, a developer said, "I would say this is useless [he looked at the board that Simon suggested they look at]. The calculations are off. They aren't reflective." This comment clearly dem-onstrated this resistance to outsider power and the reaffirmation of one's own skill and superior technical competence.

This brings me to the second issue of this stand-up, which illustrated a more significant tension among programmers at large: the Scrum Master. Scrum Masters always had a tough time gaining respect and acceptance from the programmers, even if they were smiling, calm, and likable guys like Chris. All Scrum Masters I encountered were faced with an uphill battle.

Their job was to motivate a group of developers to finish a project, while at the same time having very little (or no) competency for building or maintaining the project itself. They were also the ones enforcing certain meetings like stand-ups, grooming sessions, and retrospectives, which were all met with outsider resistance as I mentioned above. Additionally, Scrum Masters were the direct proxies for the programming senior managers. They carried shiny boxes with colorful Post-it Notes to their meetings, trying to create a fun (multicolors!) and inclusive atmosphere (Post-it Notes allowed everyone to put their thoughts down and share them with others), but whatever was said in the stand-ups, grooming sessions, and retrospectives could at any point be relayed back to the manager. Retrospectives, in particular, were dressed up as venting sessions, drawing on pseudotherapeutic methods of introspection to look back at the mistakes that were made in the past programming sprint. In one retrospective I attended, Chris asked the team to write down their feedback under categories pasted up on the board on neon sticky notes. The categories were "I loved," "I learned," "I lacked," and "I longed for," all meant as ways of thinking through the team's work in the past sprint. These methods of introspection, typical of the Scrum methodology, place the Scrum Master in a difficult position: Chris is forced to ask for total honesty from his participants, while at the same time he might relay the programmers' feedback to management, who might use this feedback against them. Moreover, it seemed hard for developers to be very honest with their colleagues out of fear of creating conflict. On a more technical level, it also seemed hard for developers to write about their technical problems, or the technical things they "loved" and "learned" because the person asking them these questions (in this case, Chris) knew little about software development. Instead, if they responded at all, their answers were often on a very basic level of technical abstraction.

We can see how the Scrum Master is placed in a challenging role. They are either the object of ridicule or annoyance—or worse, they are ignored. I am not the first researcher to have noticed this (Ereiz and Mušić 2019). A developer once told me, "I don't even know what they do," which I interpreted as "I don't even make the effort to care about what they do in the first place."

Scrum Is Dumb

The problems with Scrum and Scrum Masters draw attention to how organizational methods struggle to control the complex, unforeseeable nature of software. The Scrum methodology breaks software production

into little tickets, the tiny colored boxes in the Jira image in figure 4.3. While
these tickets are meant to break down work into manageable chunks, in
reality, software developers struggle to contain the various problems that
arise in one ticket. As a front-end developer explained to me the year before
this meeting,

> There is a certain element of unpredictability to software. A car, for exam-
> ple, is predictable; you know how it's generally built. And it's stable . . .
> It's built in a quite unique way, on an assembly-line and then reproduced.
> But over time it doesn't become something else. With physical objects
> you don't move things around all the time. [He gestured to the wooden
> table we are sitting next to.] You can't make the table longer. With soft-
> ware things are often changing. Hence the name: soft-ware. It's malleable.
> Once you start with an idea for a product, you don't actually know if it's
> good or not. So that's why it changes.

This constant change and not knowing whether an idea is "good or not" is
what makes "reflecting on the current work" displayed on a Scrum board
(as Chris urged developers to do) a difficult practice.

Another Berlin-based programmer and blogger wrote the following in
one of his entries: "Scrum does not tell you how to organize interdependent
processes that mutate while they are in flux. It doesn't tell you how to match
domains to common abstractions. It doesn't tell you how to distinguish
important differences from superficial ones based on context."[2]

No matter how friendly and approachable the methodology is, its problem lies in its very makeup—that it is trying to predict, delineate, and quantify the interaction between humans and machines, something that is not
possible to put into tickets or short sentences during a stand-up meeting.
Moreover, as this blogger highlighted, when the method is put into practice, it ends up coming to superficial conclusions, something I also partially
blame on the great skill division between the Scrum Master and the software
workers.

Over my few years at MiddleTech, there were many other attempts to
tackle this unpredictable human-machine production process and make
methods more reactive and agile. During my first year of fieldwork at MiddleTech, the boss of the entire team even eliminated Scrum and implemented
his own methodology, which relied on programmer self-organization.

2. "OK I Give Up," https://okigiveup.net/blog/not-big-fan-of-scrum/.

This was the manager of the front-end team who was the first person to really give me a chance and be open to bringing an ethnographer into the company. Greg managed around ten developers, and he decided that Scrum was not working for the teams. He was well aware of the annoying and constraining nature of a top-down methodology (the way developers stopped appreciating the methodology in itself and saw only stifling management rules), so he and his colleague designed a new methodology called Tarzan. The Tarzan system was about self-organizing: Developers were meant to be the managers themselves, and each small team of five or six people was supposed to set out their own tasks, called Missions, which roughly defined their own deadlines. While Tarzan was intended to promote the autonomy of the teams, it went wrong when put into practice. First of all, it gave the developers the illusion that management was not needed, when in fact it was. When I spoke to Jake, another American Scrum Master working for one of Greg's teams, he was frustrated at the lack of structure that Tarzan brought into the teams and how certain management roles were deemed obsolete:

"I thought it was quite disorganized at my last job, but then I came here. With this way of doing things, nobody really knows what they are supposed to do. For example, how to write stories."

"What are stories? Are they like 'Jane needs to get to work and needs a faster route?' "

"Yes, actually they are sort of like that. They are just a long sentence explaining the problem of the user. Sometimes they are quite general. And sometimes they are very specific user stories. And then they even have usernames. Like a cyclist would be called 'James' or something. So there is this story, and then underneath the story there is this list of factors that need to be completed in order to fulfill the story."

"So if you don't like to write the story, then whose job is it to do this usually?"

"Well, in a normal company," Jake smiled a bit, "it's the product owner's job to write the story. But because of this Tarzan thing, then it's actually not the product owner's role to do this. So we have meetings sometimes at the beginning of our sprint, and people will be sitting around and twiddling their thumbs. And you ask them, 'Who wants to write the stories?' And nobody is raising their hands." Jake gestured pretending to be his colleagues and stares up at the sky and whistles, twiddling his thumbs. He leans toward me and says quietly:

"And so you know, this Tarzan thing castrated or neutered the product owners. They have no role really. Officially they have to just facilitate or intervene if there is a problem. But they don't have much responsibility. For example, in the statute of Tarzan it states, 'Product owners will not write stories.' And when I asked our bosses about this, they clarified that 'They don't have to write stories, but of course they can if the need arises.' But the product owners are like, 'Well, it says here in black ink that I don't, so I don't.'"

"Oh, so is that why Connie [a product owner] is sometimes so frustrated?"

"Yes exactly, because she doesn't really know what exactly she should be doing. Or where her boundaries are."

"I wonder if you can just talk to Greg about this. Like, this is a methodology-in-transition. I am sure there are things being tweaked throughout the process. It just seems like this methodology is still not complete. Like, what if you just had a meeting before each sprint that would get people to volunteer for jobs, or something like that?"

Jake chuckled. "You know that carnival game you play with the little cat head thing? And you hit one and the other pops up. It's sort of like that. Then it goes to shit. I started losing hope."

Tarzan showed that despite having another hands-off, self-organizing methodology, people still don't know what they are doing and needed organization. In the end, these alternative methodologies still required some quantified accountability from the programmers and product owners, as well as predictability regarding when a piece of software would be completed. This lack of structure created a lot of frustration for the programmers, who continued to complain that their work was highly unpredictable.

After my months at MiddleTech, I also started to consider the possibility that this tension is not in the method itself but in the conflicting goals of the manager and the developer. If you have a team of developers thinking through a method of organizing and working together in order to build robust, high-quality software with the least amount of personal conflict, and a manager who takes this methodology in order to maximize productivity, you have a train wreck waiting to happen. These are two conflicting goals: quality (over speed) and quantity. While I always got the feeling from Simon and Greg that they did care about their developers' happiness and cared that their developers felt fulfilled and respected as creators, what they cared most about was the amount of robust software they were able to squeeze out of their team in the shortest amount of time. At the end of the day, Greg and Simon, as middle managers, had to be accountable to their bosses, and their methods needed to provide the company with more value.

Any methodology sets the stage for a power game: management enforces an organizational framework and software developers push back or ignore it because it doesn't fit their technical constraints and the unpredictable contingencies they are working under. Developers also struggle with the fact that Scrum attempts to structure their labor process, taking control over the process away from those who understand the technical system best and placing it in the hands of people like Chris or Simon, who do not or need not understand the machine and its unpredictability.

Remember when I explained that developers were forced, in their producer-client relationship, to estimate the amount of time it will take them to complete a software project? In order to create this estimate, they need a methodology for how to build something before they start, which, as Jelena pointed out in the last chapter, they cannot. The method of building something often arises while building it and not beforehand. Thus, the struggle to regain or retain control over their production process is inherent to programmers' work ethic, as is the acceptance of the technical unpredictability of software. For many developers, it is impossible to manage the unmanageable art of programming.

Jan, another developer, once told me in relation to their work methodology, "There are so many things in the structure of how we do things that don't make sense, and we can't change them, even if we tried. I mean, I often think that some of the decisions that the company makes are done by product owners sitting in a chamber somewhere rolling dice and saying, 'Yeah, that's a great idea. Let's go for it.' There is a golden standard that everyone adheres to. Sometimes for no reason."

This "golden standard" is often a methodology like Scrum—something that software developers do not always find useful or see as being implemented "for no reason." As Brooks has explained, the unity of a team and the methods for organizing a project often contrast with "the conceptual integrity of the product itself" (1995, xii).

Software-Driven Uncertainty

The question in this chapter is thus not how to make the interaction between management and software developers more harmonious, but rather how this inevitable tension shapes corporate software development culture.

Let me explain this a bit further. In an ethnographic study that looked at how a software production method was implemented, Nahoko Kameo showed that despite management's affirmation of its commitment to a specific software production methodology, "software engineers produced and reproduced a 'culture of uncertainty'" toward Scrum (2017, 8). For Kameo, this culture was driven by the legacy of failed productivity schemes: "Workers remembered how other schemes had come and gone and understood the new scheme as another one of 'those' schemes that could be canceled at any point by managers' change of heart" (2). This was a product of "organizational memory," or the shared recognition of collective experience that is "reenacted every time workers interpret their current situation" (3).

Kameo showed well how this "culture of uncertainty" arises, but after observing the programmers at MiddleTech, I think we can further categorize the specific dimensions of uncertainty in practice. Building on Kameo's concept, I would also add that this culture of uncertainty has three faces:

The first could be understood as software-driven uncertainty. This stems from a collective memory of how the developers' software behaved in the past. As many of the programmers said, software development is a "Whac-A-Mole" game made up of "interdependent processes that mutate while they are in flux,"[3] and thus, developers collectively doubted that Scrum would be able to tame or address these complexities.

The second could be called skill-driven uncertainty. This stemmed from the developers' lack of trust in their manager's expertise. The developers collectively doubted that managers like Simon and their Scrum Masters would be able to deploy the method in a way that addressed the right technical issues.

The third I term "goal-oriented uncertainty." Here, developers become uncertain of methodologies like Scrum because they doubt the manager's motivations behind implementing the method. A common discourse among developers is that their managers are driven to increase the performance and efficiency of their workers. Programmers perceive their own development culture as constructed around a collective practice of engineering good software. These are two contrasting goals. When Simon or Chris implements Scrum, the developers become uncertain about Scrum as a premise. Developers start thinking, are we trying to build good software or build software quickly?

The latter two points are not specific to software development. Around a century ago, in *The Engineers and the Price System*, Thorstein Veblen (1921) highlighted how managers are detached from the work of their engineers:

> Business men are increasingly out of touch with that manner of thinking and those elements of knowledge that go to make up the logic and the relevant facts of the mechanical technology . . . the continued advance of

---

3. "OK I Give Up," https://okigiveup.net/blog/not-big-fan-of-scrum/.

the mechanical technology has called for an ever-increasing volume and diversity of special knowledge, and so has left the businesslike captains of finance continually farther in arrears, so that they have been less and less capable of comprehending what is required in the ordinary way of industrial equipment and personnel. (Veblen 1921, 16)

Elsewhere, he highlights the diverging goals of the manager and the engineer. While the manager is focused on value and profit, the engineer is interested in mechanical performance: "Addiction to a strict and unremitting valuation of all things in terms of price and profit leaves them, by settled habit, unfit to appreciate those technological facts and values that can be formulated only in terms of tangible mechanical performance" (Veblen 1921, 11).

He then goes on to explain that "the captains of finance, driven by an increasingly close application to the affairs of business, have been going farther out of touch with the ordinary realities of productive industry; and, it is to be admitted, they have also continued increasingly to distrust the technological specialists, whom they do not understand, but whom they can also not get along without" (Veblen 1921, 17).

As we can see from Veblen's observations, the tension between engineers and the managers attempting to organize them and the machines they are building has been an unresolved struggle lasting over a century. These uncertainties also serve a purpose. They help define the boundaries of the group of programmers (us versus the management), and they help instill a discourse of care for their software. (We care about having a robust infrastructure! These Scrum methods don't let us get into the detail of building something lasting and robust!) This boundary work and the care-for-software discourse is what gives power to the programmers, both at MiddleTech and beyond.

Good-Enough Methods: Some Conclusions

While these various uncertainties about a method of organizing software work help define the identity of software developers and what they care about (software!), they still have bosses and still have to live under Scrum or other methodological doctrines.

As Scrum presents the workers with sets of durable schemes, stories, rituals, and routines (Kameo 2017) that guide them through their workday, we witnessed how developers engage only partially in these practices. On the ground, developers construct another culture in which engineering (the computer) comes first, and "chaos is the reality" of software programming (Rising and Janoff 2000, 26).

Programmers hold on to the ability to be chaotic, sloppy, and uncertain. One explanation for this is that commercial software engineering sits somewhere between factory labor and scientific practice. While sometimes software developers' job description makes their job more repetitive (as in the case of a tester or a programmer in an outsourced team), or more scientific (as in the case of a researcher or data scientist), I would argue that most programmers at MiddleTech, at one point or another, no matter their job description, engage in forms of experimentation and computer "science." This "science" is much "sloppier" and more "irrational" than its methodological image (Feyerabend 1993, 218)—than what Scrum and other methods attempt to capture. And what appears as "sloppiness," "chaos," or "opportunism," when compared with methodologies, has a "most important function in the development of those very theories which we today regard as essential parts of our knowledge" (218).

Thus, in order to uphold this creative sloppiness and chaos, programmers engage in what I call "good-enough methodologies." As we saw with Scrum, most of the time developers go through the motions of engaging in that particular methodology or in mix-and-match methodologies (many told me that what they were doing was a general form of Agile and not Scrum per se) and only partially engage in certain rituals, all while rolling their eyes, not listening, or not using the various Scrum tools (as in the case of the stand-up). Good-enough methodologies allow developers to perform a methodology ritual to appease their managers and customers, while also preserving a sense of chaos and serendipity that is a key component of the corporate software development culture.

In the previous chapter I discussed the multiple ways in which stuff can go wrong during software development, mainly due to the diverse forms of knowledge inherent in building such a complex technical system. In this chapter, I build on this discussion and examine how managers implement methods into the software development process to help organize software workers and the machines they are working on (and to prevent stuff from going wrong). My goal was to highlight the tensions between developers, their managers, and their machines, as well as the ways in which power is exerted, performed, and achieved when building software.

In order to show these dynamics at play, I described how software project management methodology like Scrum can structure a software team's work process, delineating tasks into tickets for developers to work on and creating rituals for them to engage in. Scrum also sets forth a certain top-down narrative: No matter how developer-centric the method claims to be, it is still trying to provide "clients with deliverables faster" and to "maximize return on investment" (Schwaber and Beedle 2008). A method like Scrum becomes a management tool whose goal is to provide "breakthrough productivity" (Rising and Janoff 2000, 27) for software management. As I show in this chapter, this narrative of excellence and top performance permeates the corporate software environment, and methods like Scrum are a manifestation of this narrative. Scrum presents the workers with sets of durable schemes, stories, rituals, and routines that guide them, enforcing constant transparency with the goal of reaching peak performance.

These methodologies thus serve a number of purposes, which are at odds with the intended purpose of Scrum and other methods: They define the identity of software developers (as those whose work as well as the machines they work with cannot be "tamed" by a method) and help define the objects of their care (software comes first, not customers, users, or peak performance). In practice, methods like Scrum give developers rituals and daily routines that they thus only partially adhere to (in a good-enough way) in order to appease their management while at the same time reproducing a culture of unpredictability and care for their software.

One theme that I obviously kept ignoring in this chapter with terms like "agility," "sprints," and "deadlines" was the temporal order of software development. The next chapter will look at how efficiency is inherently part of corporate software development, and how this efficiency and various temporal orders impact the culture of unpredictability and creativity, the quality of software, and the culture of good enoughness in software development at large.

5

Slowdown

You might be wondering what I was doing sitting in a parking lot on a cold, early November morning in northern England with Pedro, one of the developers from MiddleTech. At that moment, so was I. I had almost finished my ethnographic stint at MiddleTech and had decided to move from the confines of the Berlin office into a more collaborative and spontaneous setting.

Pedro, one of the routing team's lead data scientists, looked cold, huddled on his little office chair in that parking lot. He was shivering a bit, and with every shiver, I felt a little more embarrassed that I brought him with me. That embarrassment was on top of my worry that nobody was coming to meet us, and that my whole idea to convince a software engineer I barely knew to fly with me to a conference in England and engage in a "thought experiment" was making me look weirder in the eyes of said engineer.

I didn't know Pedro well at all. He was a Portuguese developer in his midthirties who worked, like Ori, in a more research-related role, concerning himself with finding the right way to optimize the right algorithm to solve the various routing problems his team was trying to tackle. At the time of my fieldwork, he was working on optimizing an algorithm that would help clean up messy GPS data.

We were at the large "Mobile Utopias" conference hosted by my former PhD supervisor, who was head of the Centre for Mobilities Research (Cemore) at Lancaster University. Prof. Monika Buscher suggested that I engage somehow in a "Mobile Utopia Experiment," a subsection of her conference that was supposed to be "a creative enactment of a mobile utopia," which could be expressed through a game or performance. Excited to try my hand at game-and-performance-driven research, I decided to build a game that would help participants understand how a car sees the road, how it processes what is happening around it, and who is helping a driver drive.

But before I move on to the relevance of our parking lot experience and how I got Pedro to stop shivering, perhaps it would be useful to explain what this chapter is meant to do. By this point, you have learned that corporate software companies like MiddleTech function under a narrative of excellence and improvement that dominates various corporate industries. Excellence is measured by peak productivity and top performance, with managers implementing software management methodologies; workers being tracked, recorded, and ranked;[1] and software output being measured in Key Performance Indicators (KPIs) based on the least number of bugs or other criteria.

Market competition within the software industry helps dictate a certain temporal order of how quickly software should be produced, which includes the customer's product release time lines (like a new car being launched onto the market), as well as software industry-wide competition with other mapping software companies. All this competition enforces a company culture that values constant innovation and sprint-based production.

This commercial competition in the software company, and in the software industry at large, creates a culture of acceleration among software workers. Thus, another narrative dominant in the corporate computing culture, alongside excellence, improvement, and performance, is the narrative of speed. The idea that both workers and software should work quickly and efficiently is a key normative order within the industry.

In the last chapter, we learned that various software production methodologies like Scrum help enforce this narrative of speed and efficiency by organizing a developer's work practices. In this chapter, I will look more closely at this culture of acceleration and demonstrate that it does not (contrary to many hopes and dreams of the actors involved) constantly improve the efficiency of software workers or software innovation. Instead, we can witness good enoughness at work with constant stutters, blockages, breakdowns, and moments of slowness. I also felt I couldn't talk about speed without addressing the elephant in the room: I was researching people who

1. "The Rise of the Worker Productivity Score," https://www.nytimes.com/interactive/2022/08/14/business/worker-productivity-tracking.html.

made routing and navigations systems, the very technologies that sit in our cars and in our phones and accelerate us forward, optimizing our mobility.

I want to highlight in this chapter that slowdown has a lot to with good enoughness. While slowing down and focusing on a task at hand can lead to great discoveries and excellence, slowdowns do not happen because programmers choose to take their time to think through a topic. Instead, this chapter is about an imposed good enoughness. Slowdown—and often engaging in good enoughness—is imposed on programmers and their teams through various social and technical constraints. And once these constraints happen, programmers need to compromise on what they are creating and releasing to the public. It is precisely these slowdowns that lead developers into creating good-enough code. In this chapter, I wish to show how slowdown is the precursor to good enoughness. It's about halting the inertia of acceleration and stating, "I'm sorry, we have to stop; this has to just be good enough for now." The practice of halting, waiting, stopping, or canceling in order to do something else, figure something out, fix, or optimize is a key feature of code work. These slowdowns are not about stopping and thinking things through—they are about being interrupted or being forced to slow down for other reasons beyond their control.

In the following chapter, through the metaphor and practiced reality of the GPS navigation system, I will illustrate what causes slowdowns and good enoughness to happen in software development, and then what these slowdowns might look like in navigation software when software is then implemented into the world.

Back to Pedro

Pedro's work was devoted to optimization—getting your car from point A to point B in the most optimal amount of time possible. "Optimal," in the case of MiddleTech routing and navigation software, could have a variety of parameters but most often meant the quickest. Pedro's job was to figure out what could become a slowdown or hindrance along a route during navigation, fix it, and send the navigation system back into the world, helping a car get from point A to point B faster.

My research at MiddleTech taught me that a car ride is affected by a multitude of computer-mediated maneuvers and routing procedures, as well as by the behavior of software engineers optimizing a route. To me, the navigation software at MiddleTech became a metaphor for what was happening in the larger corporate software world. While we might plan and optimize for speed and efficiency, the reality is messy, and slowdowns and breakdowns happen all the time for a number of both social and technical reasons.

For our experiment at the Lancaster conference, I wanted to build a physical racecourse-like game that would help give users a better picture of the various sociotechnical issues that can cause slowdowns.

One afternoon in late August, I was having lunch with Pedro, and he mentioned that he was planning on taking a work sabbatical for one year starting in October. (At MiddleTech, developers are allowed to take an unpaid sabbatical every few years.) One of the first things he would do on his break would be to fly to Manchester with a group of his best friends and watch a football game. Again, I am not really sure why he was telling me all of this, but I remember that at that moment, my mind quickly put the date of his Manchester bro-hangout together with the date of my Lancaster mobilities conference and realized that the two were happening in relatively the same geographic region within one day of each other: on November 1 and 2, 2017.

One of the basic features in a car navigation system is an estimated time of arrival (ETA) system that can provide you, the driver, with a prediction of how long it will take to get from your starting point to your desired finish point. Once you have an ETA, the car routes you to your destination on a given path that coincides with your ETA. While driving, your car's software system communicates to satellite GPS waypoints that help position your car in a given spot on a road. These GPS points signal to the navigation software that you are, indeed, on the right route. To understand how this process works in practice, perhaps it would help if you imagined that your car is blind, and the GPS is like a cane that taps on a piece of road every few seconds to help position you in space. These taps are fed back into the car's software as a piece of data, and the software knows where the car is because the data from the satellite then correlates with cartographic map data in the car's software. These GPS points are often off by five meters, which can be substantial when driving through a city, as roads, buildings, lanes, and bridges are, at times, built on top of each other or very close to one another, which can mess up the road data. This is where Pedro and his algorithm come in. Long story short, Pedro was working on an algorithm that would help predict, more accurately, if a road is a road or a building is a building.

Pedro was quiet, but he had an approachable, friendly face that always seemed a little downhearted like he was going through something difficult in his life (which, I later found out, he was). During one of my first days at fieldwork, he agreed to go to lunch with me. I learned that he was living in Berlin with his girlfriend. Most of his free time was spent taking care of his mother, who had come to live with them from his hometown in Portugal. He would never call himself a programmer, preferring instead the more accurate titles of research engineer or data scientist. He studied physics and electrical engineering back in Portugal and loved living in Berlin.

Weeks before leaving Berlin, we spent a few afternoons planning what this experiment would be about. I wanted our game to do two things. Firstly, I wanted participants to understand that a seemingly simple and forgettable feature like an ETA in their navigation app is extremely complex and involves a multitude of factors and calculations. The game would give the participants a picture of this complexity as well as a few examples of the different factors and calculations that go into estimating a route. And secondly, I wanted to show the complex human-machine interdependency of the ETA system. All it takes is one bug or wrong calculation, and the ETA will be fully messed up, and the driver's drive will (at times) become more chaotic.

In order to achieve these goals in our little conference game, we decided that we would set up a trail on the Lancaster campus. Players would all start walking (or "driving") at the same point on the trail. Each "driver" would then have to stop at a waypoint station, where they would draw an instruction from a box.

This instruction would either (1) allow them to drive ahead, suggesting that their navigation software is working smoothly; (2) provide them with a bug or issue, which impedes their driving speed; or (3) provide them with an enhancement to their navigation, giving them a bonus or advantage over the other players, allowing them to run ahead. Each driver would, in the end, be timed to see how long it took them to get from start to finish, with the winner having the shortest arrival time. The game would be preceded by a short introduction from Pedro on how an ETA is calculated and the factors affecting an ETA calculation.

Stuttering

During our planning phase, Pedro and I spent a few lunch hours and e-mail exchanges thinking about the various factors that go into calculating and messing up an estimated time of arrival on a given route. The process of building the game also emerged as an unorthodox methodology for field expression. It forced Pedro to explain the problems in very simple-to-understand terms that not only I but the average person would understand.

He taught me that in order to gain a relatively accurate ETA, the developers building this feature need to plan out what algorithm to use and, as

1 You are driving a car which has an older MapNavi map version. This map uses an older technology of processing new changes to the road called "batch processing." This means that any changes to the road must go through long validation process (checking if the map data is up-to-date and correct) with your map validation team back at the MapNavi office. Thus, your map routed you to a road that closed 2 weeks ago. Penalty: wait back for 10 seconds as your car gets re-routed.

2 Oh no! Your software has a bug, and your software developer is on vacation and hasn't had a chance to fix it yet! Your map asks you to turn left at a junction when a left turn is not allowed (there is a one-way route coming in the opposite direction). You take the turn and have to veer off and make a U-turn. Penalty: wait back for 30 seconds.

3 Oh no! Your traffic rules have changed. But it's August, and half of MapNavi's map validation team (the team responsible for checking if the map data is up-to-date and correct) is on vacation and hasn't processed the change yet. The change: a left turn on is not allowed on the street you are driving on. On this junction, you can either turn right or continue straight. Penalty: wait back for 30 seconds.

4 You are driving an Electric Vehicle (EV)! Your car is low on battery. But oh no! Your EV routing team is using an algorithm that re-routed you the nearest charging station, but didn't account for dynamic traffic data (meaning changing traffic conditions updated live). You hit severe rush-hour traffic congestion. Penalty: wait back for 60 seconds.

5 Oh no! Your ETA team is not accounting for dynamic traffic data (so new data that emerges as the state of traffic changes). You keep hitting traffic jams. Penalty: wait back for 30 seconds.

6 Your ETA team is not accounting for traffic signals on the route. You keep landing on red lights. Penalty: wait back for 30 seconds.

7 You drive through a border, and the country you are now driving in has less accurate map data. Why? The research team who assures route quality in this country has not prioritized this region and is working on a more 'popular' region. You get routed to a road that doesn't exist. Penalty: wait back for 20 seconds

8 Although the route suggested to you was indeed the fastest possible at the time of departure, it is also a route with a high risk of accidents. Since you have not updated your app, you are still using the old MapNavi algorithm, which does not account for statistical risk on your ETA and are now stuck in a traffic jam. Penalty: wait back for 30 seconds

FIG. 5.1 The ETA game cards

I mentioned earlier, need to optimize this algorithm. In the process of optimization, they need to calculate "the sum of the car's speed, the length of the roads being traveled on, the traffic data, the turn cost (the number of right turns and left turns in the route, with a left turn taking longer than a right turn), etc." As a car doesn't travel in a bubble, software developers also take into account the fact that various human-related problems can mess up this data, such as the driver not obeying the routing guidance, or the driver being engaged in a certain action that makes them slower than the average driver.

Pedro and I then came up with a list of twenty-six playing cards, which each player would draw from a box among twelve waypoints. The scenarios that we wrote down on each playing card were derived from real examples that both Pedro and I had witnessed, real issues that arise in mobility software development and software in use. Pedro's expertise was invaluable as he gave me insight into what can go wrong when designing such a system. The following are just five examples of the twenty-six ETA issues that were written on each separate card (note that we gave the navigation system the fictional name of MapNavi):

1. You are driving a car that has an older MapNavi map version. This map uses an older technology of processing new changes to the road called "batch processing." This means that any changes to the road must go through a long validation process (checking if the map data is up-to-date and correct) with your map validation team back at the MapNavi office. Thus, your map routed you to a road that closed two weeks ago. Penalty: Wait back for ten seconds as your car gets rerouted.

2. Oh no! Your software has a bug, and your software developer is on vacation and hasn't had a chance to fix it yet! Your map asks you to turn left at a junction when a left turn is not allowed (there is a one-way route coming in the opposite direction). You take the turn and have to veer off and make a U-turn. Penalty: Wait back for thirty seconds.

3. You are driving an Electric Vehicle (EV)! Your car is low on battery. But oh no! Your EV routing team is using an algorithm that rerouted you to the nearest charging station but didn't account for dynamic traffic data (meaning changing traffic conditions that are updated live). You hit severe rush-hour traffic congestion. Penalty: Wait back for sixty seconds.

FIG. 5.2 The ETA game outdoor setup

4. Oh no! Your ETA team is not accounting for dynamic traffic data (that is, new data that emerge as the state of traffic changes). You keep hitting traffic jams. Penalty: Wait back for thirty seconds.
5. Your ETA team is not accounting for traffic signals on the route. You keep landing on red lights. Penalty: Wait back for thirty seconds.

Once in Lancaster, I printed out these instructions on little cards. The conference organizers suggested that I set up outside (despite the weather). I found a seven hundred–meter path between a few trees and a row of student dorms and set up our little waypoint boxes, filling them with cards. Pedro showed up right on time, clearly hungover from his Manchester post–football party and slightly confused about the whole parking lot setup and the conference setting.

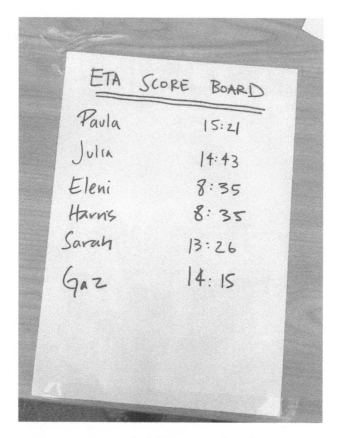

FIG. 5.3 The ETA game scoreboard

We then sat down on two office chairs outside and waited for conference goers to wander their way over to our "experiment." Nobody came for the first hour. I got anxious. Then a few stragglers wandered over. Then some friends of mine with their two teenagers stopped by. Our measly turnout and the early November Lancashire weather, with its windy half-drizzle, didn't make things easier for us.

But by the end of the game, I felt our tiny gathering of participants seemed to enjoy and learn something from the game, particularly after I nudged Pedro to give a lecture to our crowd about how software is essentially prone to bugs, prone to slowdowns. While our ETA game might not get pulled out at anybody's next family game night, the purpose of doing it at the Lancaster "Mobile Utopias" conference was to make visible the invisible sociotechnical constraints behind software systems. In this chapter, it functions as a way to show that slowdown results in good-enough systems that only sometimes make things more efficient.

The Need for Speed

Software-driven mobility is created by a group of people designing a system that mobilizes others. The tool we hold in our hands or the box that sits within our cars mobilizes us in specific ways. At times, it tells us to turn down one road and not another. At other times, it breaks down and messes up things. The experiment I just described was not only a story about how to awkwardly attempt collaborative ethnography with members of your field. If we look more closely at the playing cards, we will notice that these scenarios are full of stutters and slowdowns. But if we think about how MiddleTech software developers work and what they build, slowing down and stuttering contradict their larger narrative of speed and efficiency. As we learned from the earlier chapters, the dominant narrative in the software industry at large, and one that influences MiddleTech, is the drive for efficiency, velocity, or agility. Software development management tools or methodologies help drive this narrative.

Routing and navigation technologies are also an extension of this need for speed and speed and efficiency: They are designed to speed up our route to work or to school rather than slow us down. They are also in direct competition with similar products from other software companies; thus, the promise of creating a better navigation product with more efficient, quicker routes drives their software design.

With these stutters and slowdowns, Pedro's and my experiment became a larger metaphor for how digital mobilities are made. Instead of promising efficiency and speediness, routing and navigation software often stutters, gets blocked for one reason or another, and slows down or comes to a halt. Much like the larger MiddleTech ideology around performance and excellence, where our practiced reality includes good enoughness and breakdown, the reality of the GPS system is about the ideology of speed and its counterforce of slowdown.

Understanding the speed of software through my field at MiddleTech will also help illustrate the way in which software is an inherent part of the story of how our digitally driven mobilities are made and function—how the world moves and how we experience movement, flow, and acceleration in our daily lives. For most of us living with mobile technologies, we are experiencing an interdependency of physical space, mobility, and code, in which "flows, mobilities, and transactions; the folded geographies of inclusion and exclusion; [and] the construction, consumption and experience of place . . . all, very literally, are now performed—at least in part—through the continuous agency of vast realms of computer software" (Graham 2005, 4).

This networked urban mobility is experienced through software, which is now invisibly delegating our coordination to smart and intelligent environments, suggesting a fundamental change in the everyday practice of mobility (Freudendal-Pedersen and Kesselring 2017). The popular sentiment around smart cities or our networked digital cultures makes it seem that the temporal characteristics of material infrastructure that limited us in the past can be reconfigured, that transport can be made quicker and more seamless, and that capital can flow faster as the immateriality of bits absolves us from the messy burden of our material world. Against this ideology of speed, the reality is quite different.

The software industry is and has always been obsessed with speed, mainly in the context of software's processing speed, but also in the context of the speed of innovation, resulting in an obsession with production speed. In the previous chapter, I touched upon the latter topic in my discussion of the slew of production methodologies like Agile and Scrum, which aim to speed up and optimize production. But speed and productivity, one could argue, were always tied to the architecture of the computer and to how software works in general. A computer's success is based on its processing speed: A computer with a slower processing speed will lose to one with a faster processing speed. The road from the first general-purpose electronic digital computer's calculating circuits (of the ENIAC, the Electronic Numerical Integrator and Computer) in the 1940s to today's Japanese Fugaku Supercomputer with its 442,010 teraflops per second was a development road paved with an obsession with processing speed. Punch cards, magnetic tape or drums, disks, and drives were also all part of the inventive ways that engineers thought of speeding up the supply of instructions to the computer.

Then in 1964, Gordon Moore of Fairchild and soon-to-be cofounder of Intel noted something interesting. He observed that "from the time of the invention of integrated circuits in 1958, the number of circuits that one could place on a single integrated circuit was doubling every year." By sketching out this rate on a piece of semilog graph paper, he "predicted that by the mid-1970s one could buy a chip containing logic circuits equivalent to those used in a 1950s-era mainframe" (Ceruzzi 2003, 217). This rather specific estimation of market-driven forces and technological possibility was popularized as

Moore's Law. As the microchip became smaller through the design efforts of its engineers (who were driven by market competition), computers featured an accelerating computer power. This resulted in our computers, phones, and other devices running thousands of times faster than they did before. While critics of Moore saw that various fundamental physical constraints (such as the diameter of a hydrogen atom) would "interrupt the straight line that Moore observed" (Ceruzzi 2003, 585), Moore's Law nevertheless became central in highlighting the logic of acceleration dominating the computer industry from the twentieth century up until the present.

Another logic of speed within the software industry comes from the update culture. As I mentioned in previous chapters, commercial software is a product that can, especially through networked technologies, be constantly updated: "New media live and die by the update: the end of the update, the end of the object" (Chun 2017, 24).

Consequently, if software is meant to be updated, and there are two or more groups of people updating their software at the same time for profit, one could say that an inevitable race begins to see who can develop software the fastest. As operations management researchers explained, "dilatory software development can devastate the bottom line and shake the boardroom" (Blackburn et al. 1996, 1). From the perspective of a commercial software manager, updating fast is key.

Yet, paradoxically, building computer software and hardware quickly in order to produce fast products has sometimes slowed us down. For example, in the 1960s, the software industry faced a chronic "software crisis" (Ensmenger and Aspray 2002), stemming from the acceleration of software production and its too-hasty evolution for the infrastructure that contained it. Computing innovation was moving too quickly, causing a huge shortage of workers (Ensmenger 2010).

There were also other moments in history when speedy software design got us into trouble. Who can forget the Y2K hysteria in 1999, which arose from the fear that the speed of innovation in software development (specifically the adoption of IPv6, the new internet addressing standard) would cause total collapse of our critical infrastructures? Or the British Royal Mail software scandal, when the Horizon IT software system had an accountancy "bug," which resulted in over seven hundred postal workers being falsely accused and prosecuted between 2000 and 2014? These are merely a few in a multitude of incidents in which the speed of software development and the belief in flawless speedy software have messed with the software product, and in turn, messed with society.

This brief overview serves as a way of understanding that a narrative that values speed and speediness looms over the software industry. Instead of fulfilling this dream of acceleration, corporate software environments and their products experience various temporal orders that slow us all down. This chapter will provide a few examples from the field to explain the types of temporal orders inherent in programming. I will illustrate how slowdown works in software development, explaining what exactly slows down programmers with the examples of legacy code, the halting and scraping of projects, and blocks that bring projects to a halt. I will also explain a bit more about what slows down a navigation system, an issue that is often linked to the way in which programmers attempt to deal with these slowdowns.

Spaghetti Code and Time Travel

Let's rewind a year back to my first summer of fieldwork. I was on the third floor of the MiddleTech office building, which featured the same aqua-blue walls and gray carpets found on all the other floors. The open-office concept grouped small clusters of six developers in desks pushed together in a rectangular shape. This was the front-end team, who, as you recall, were building navigation software for either an Android phone, an iOS phone, or a Web site (and were thus grouped into teams according to the platform they were working on).

Amira and Otavio were on the iOS team, and they quickly became the developers who were closest to me. Amira was one of only a handful of women programmers working in the front-end team at MiddleTech. She was shy and soft-spoken but always had a heartfelt curiosity about what I was researching. She had been in Germany for only four months before I met her, and one afternoon over lunch, she explained how she managed to leave Alexandria and her freelance software development work in Egypt. She was alone in a foreign country and missed her mother and sisters the most. But what she loved about living in Berlin was the fact that she could take long walks on her own: "Like, just walk around the streets on my own. I had never experienced that. As a woman living in Egypt, you take taxis everywhere, and if you walk, you do so briefly, always chaperoned by a man." She explained that in Berlin she could get out and go to the park and spend her weekends exploring the city. She also taught me that a woman engineer in the Middle East, unlike in Europe or North America, is not an anomaly. Women made up the majority of software engineers in Egypt because software development is so "clean"—meaning free of any contact with men. She thought about her mother and father, who feared that if she became an architect or an industrial designer, she would have to interact with men—with construction workers, technicians, or foremen. These jobs weren't considered safe. And Amira added, "my parents are very protective and worried about me. But not in software engineering. It's just so clean. The whole environment is considered so clean."

Life in Berlin still had its challenges for Amira, however small. For one, she was still trying to find a voice among her developer colleagues, who were mostly men. To her, finding her voice meant having the courage to speak up and tell her colleagues that what they were building could be done differently. Even though she was new to the company, she had experience and wanted to share it, but she felt things moved too quickly for her, and everyone was too loud. She liked speaking slowly, quietly, and didn't have it in her to speak up. She feared that she would just sound awkward.

Otavio became a bit of a mentor for her, although she admitted that she often knew a lot more than the developers around her, including him. Otavio came from Porto Alegre in Brazil and moved to Berlin from San Francisco after working at Hewlett Packard (HP), building the company's photo app. After the app was shut down, Otavio lost his job and visa in San Francisco but said that "it was time to get out of SF anyways" due to its difficult socio-economic and housing situation. When working at HP, he was dealing with "huge technical infrastructure." He explained, "my role was building a small little component that was tucked away in the monstrosity of this one-million-dollar project. Nobody ever saw what I was doing because it was this one invisible project. But now they can see it. They can see what I'm building. And better, I can see what I'm building. I can use what I'm building, which is even better."

As a front-end developer, he preferred working on an aspect of software that relates to the user because, "after all, computers, in the end, don't care," implying that the user, in fact, does care. He loved being able to build something that "mothers can use." This desire to build something for mothers to use and understand was not only a desire to build something of use to users but also seemed like a desire for recognition and for the ability to become visible in a profession that is largely invisible to users. Programming is mostly a thankless, faceless, fameless job. But front-end developers would often take out their phones and point out a tiny little feature on the app they were building and say, "I built that. I did that. This is my piece of software." In these moments of showing and pointing, they gained notoriety as artifact-rousers, as agents, as magicians who made something out of nothing. I noticed that many developers liked watching my reaction to their work. It would actualize their artifact-in-the-world and legitimize their work as being of use.

I started going for lunch regularly with Amira and Otavio, about once a week. Some of their colleagues would occasionally join. Sometimes I would go out with just Amira. She and Otavio were working on a feature called the home button, which they were grappling with for a while. It was a specific feature in the mobile phone app that would bring the user home, a task that involved merging all sorts of data points, including the user's address as well as their given location. It didn't seem too difficult, but their work was very slow. They started nearly half a year before I joined them but still had not completed the project.

The slowness of their work stemmed from a variety of factors. Firstly, it had to do with various forms of legacy code. We already know a lot about legacy code, which I discussed in chapter 3. In this chapter, I am revisiting it to see how it affects the temporal orders of software work—how it forces developers to go back and forth in time, working their way through different moments and different coding styles in the present and past. Legacy code "is composed of multiple lifetimes of different parts of the system—hardware, software, code, organizational processes, programming languages, institutions, careers—all of which are entangled and are aging or obsolescing at different rates" (Leavitt Cohn 2016, 1513). These different lifetimes and rates of aging is what also influences slowdown.

This infrastructural decay is at times highly frustrating for developers as it makes them feel that they cannot move forward as the code they are faced with limits what they can build on top of it (for example, by ignoring the legacy code or not cleaning it up or refactoring it, the developers run the risk of their software collapsing altogether). At other times, legacy code, much like a road that has already been paved once, makes software development much more predictable for the developer, providing more stable foundations and resulting in fewer crashes and breakdowns. Any software developer will tell you that legacy code determines how they work. It also shapes or limits the speed of their engineering process—what they can and cannot do with their new code.

To illustrate this in my field, developers like Otavio and Amira told me that they have to slow down their own work in order to travel back in time and work on old code. This "time travel" is about understanding the mentality of a previous developer, their design choices, and the various entanglements resulting from their design choices. Developers told me that they feel as though they are mind-reading, trying to understand the logical order that previous programmers were working through.

Throughout many of their workdays, Amira and Otavio had to focus on combining old code with new and managing software change in ways that interoperate with legacy systems. This is work that Marissa Leavitt Cohn calls "keeping software present" (2019, 427). In this work, Amira and Otavio interact with the past, with the ghosts of programmers who came before them and the creativity and sloppiness they left behind. As we know, at MiddleTech, a finished product takes roughly forty-four weeks, and Week 44 is known as "feature-complete day," meaning that all features or changes created by individual teams should be finished and merged into the code base. Yet, while developers like Amira and Otavio do work within this time frame, their time sometimes goes backward in the sense that they have to rewind and work with old code, code that not only holds them in place but forces them to look back and work on something that was built years before. In these instances, when working with spaghetti code, they aren't innovating and moving forward but rather slowly digging and attempting to figure out what is going wrong or not making sense.

This "work of keeping software present (maintaining its currency, know-ability, relevance)" highlights the constant tension between the new, speedy innovation-driven software and the old software, which constantly has to be brought up to speed so to speak. It is not just software workers' sociality, their multiple moments of competition and negotiation over how to optimize a feature, and their dependence and synchronization with live, real-world traffic systems that slow them down but also their interaction with "software's lived durations" (Leavitt Cohn 2019, 426).

These moments of moving backward that Amira and Otavio experience when working with spaghetti code are present in all legacy work. More explicitly speaking, the amount of legacy code in a system has a direct impact on how software is built. Older companies like MiddleTech are bound to have a large stack of code (called a legacy stack) piled up under them, often using older programming languages, older programming methods, and foreign design choices. As one of my informants explained, these older, "dinosaur" companies have a hard time innovating and moving with the demands of the technology market, mainly because they focus their efforts backward in time on maintenance and refactoring or adapting older code to fit a new system.

Halting and Scrapping

I kept in touch with Amira and Otavio, and the following summer during my fieldwork we went out for lunch. We sat in a sushi restaurant around the corner from the office, and I felt that pang of nostalgia that many ethnographers feel when reconnecting with their informants after leaving the field. A year had gone by since my fieldwork ended and a lot had changed. I was surprised to hear that the entire mobile and web app of MiddleTech had been scrapped, along with the teams I had been working with during my first summer of fieldwork in 2016. Only twenty developers kept their positions in order to keep the app running in maintenance mode, which meant that the app would remain as is and not receive any new features.

Amira and Otavio started telling me that they were, in fact, happy the entire project had been scrapped. Years of work, including their home button project, went into the ether. They had spent hours thinking about their code, fixing things, tweaking things, cleaning up spaghetti code. So much time was wasted, I told them. But they didn't see it that way. They told me that software changes all the time, and the demands of the market also change. Developers can't get too attached to their product because it will soon be gone. Otavio experienced this with the HP app he was building in San Francisco, which no longer existed. It was just part of the profession. Software, for Amira and Otavio, was temporary and disposable. Building a piece of software took a long time, sometimes years, but the product of this work could be thrown away, leaving nothing behind. In a large company like MiddleTech, a project can be scrapped for various reasons. Firstly, a customer might disapprove of it. Secondly, it can happen because the users dislike it: Various forms of market research and so-called "A/B testing" (where one section of users gets one version of the app, and another group gets another version) reveal that the feature is not being adopted by the user for various reasons. Thirdly, project scrapping comes from internal factors: for example, if the company wants to rebrand itself and go in another design direction, where certain features are no longer necessary.

Other forms of scrapping that happen in corporate software environments include team scrapping, where an entire team stops working on something and has to pivot to work on something else. Team scrapping also happens for various reasons. Firstly, a company like MiddleTech can acquire a software team and their product: let's say, a small start-up of ten people based in Tel Aviv, who built a successful product that helps optimize a routing system. MiddleTech acquires this app and either uses their team's innovation internally to strengthen their own product or scraps the product entirely in order to squash the competition. These ten workers in Tel Aviv are either assigned to another project, or they can be made redundant due to the lack of synergy with the rest of the MiddleTech office. (Note that letting go of these workers is easier if they are not yet employed by MiddleTech, or were originally based in another country like Israel, which is often the case.) Team scrapping also happens if a company like MiddleTech wants to rebrand itself in a much larger way and no longer needs a particular product. This happened to Amira and Otavio. In the time between my fieldwork with them and our lunch the following year, not only was their home button scrapped, but MiddleTech decided to stop producing a user-facing mapping app for mobile devices. Hundreds of developers were moved around as their projects were scrapped. After this happened, Amira and Otavio, like most of the developers in the front-end team, were redistributed throughout the company into other teams. Some built internet-of-things technologies, and others built indoor maps. But as you can imagine, scrapping a project or a team means that a multitude of people have to start over, which involves retraining and doing additional research and planning—things that take time.

The process of scrapping projects and teams was in complete contrast to the efficiency and speed-obsessed managers and their methods of production described in the last chapter. On the one hand, companies like MiddleTech attempt to create rapid and reactive forms of software delivery and promote a certain commercially driven narrative that software has to be produced quickly, and that speed is of utmost importance to beat the competition. So, on the one hand, a defining characteristic of the software industry is its treatment of time as a scarce good, whereby methods are implemented to foster a categorical economization of time; yet, on the other hand, a programmer's time is often completely wasted, as in the case of Amira and Otavio's project. Programmers are told time is valuable, while years of software work is thrown away in the blink of an eye or with the loss of a customer.

Blocked and Waiting

Until this point, we learned that developers are slowed down by going back in time when working with legacy code, and that their work slows down when projects are halted and scrapped. Another common issue is being blocked, a term used by both programmers and managers when work cannot get done for some reason. A block might happen because the legal team is stalling a project for legal reasons, more information from a customer is needed to complete something, a key programmer is sick, or a problem is too tricky. When fixing bugs, developers can be blocked from getting to the core of the problem because a fix is too complicated, the piece of software where the bug is located is too entangled with another piece of code, or the person who created the bug in the first place is away. Fixing one end would mean taking apart another end. Some developers explain that blocks arise because of "a design defect inherited from others," meaning another team, years ago, designed something in a way that causes a bug to occur in the current code (as I said, code is entangled with other legacy code). Blocks also arise when developers do not want to do the work that their product owners ask them to do because it's too tedious, too tricky, or too hard. In another instance, Ori was attempting to complete a research project that used the personal mobility data of MiddleTech's users, but he was blocked from moving forward with the project while waiting for legal approval from the company's privacy team. Other blocks include waiting for code review from other programmers or approval from a team leader to ship a finished product.

I would often notice programmers loitering around in the kitchen or browsing the internet. When I asked them what they were doing, they would say they were blocked for one of these reasons. This process of waiting around is again at odds with the narrative that software has to be produced quickly and efficiently. While some blocks happen in microprotest, to procrastinate or find an excuse not to work, I observed that most blocks are the inevitable result of working in a complex team that is building a complex system.

Waiting is deeply entangled with digital media. As users, we often refresh our screens, buffer, or wait for updates. Infrastructural latency is also sometimes built into our devices where there is a "commodification of waiting." Neta Alexander gives the example of "Apple's annual launch of the latest version of its iPhone, or Facebook's decision to slow down a 'security check' feature to convince users that it is thorough and therefore trustworthy," cases in which "false latency is therefore a feature, rather than a bug, of the digital infrastructure" (Alexander 2020, 28). Being blocked and kept waiting are not only part of the story of how users engage with software but also how producers of our software become entrenched in a culture of waiting around.

One of the developers in the back-end routing team once explained that "there is a concept of undone work," where a programming sprint is over, and a product needs to be shipped, but work is not done because it's blocked by various people or factors (for example, a team is waiting for approval or

FIG. 5.4 Blocked tips in the lunchroom

information from the product owner, the privacy team, etc.). This undone work then goes back into the so-called backlog of code work, waiting to be unblocked during the next sprint and software update.

This process of waiting around, being blocked, and leaving undone work means that once a deadline approaches, programmers have to compromise and either finish the project without the component they were waiting for, completely amend the project, or omit something from their final project, leading, again, to good-enough software. Thus, blocked and undone work is part of the culture of good enoughness.

Different Programmer Times

When speaking of the speeds of software development, it's also important to mention that corporate programmers' time is valued differently by their employer in relation to their job description or status, and the speed at which they work is different too. There are also moments when time speeds up for some and slows down for others. Time can be treated as a value or a commodity at one moment, while in the next, entire projects can be scrapped, thus wasting time.

For example, a software developer like Pedro would rarely look at his watch to make sure his project was finished on time. Pedro's colleague explained that he didn't need a ticket system in his team: "We develop features more long term. It takes us a longer period of time to find a solution." Pedro explained that the development process for him includes "design debates," which take time, with a lot of back-and-forth discussions between developers. Pedro reads, researches, and tests; sometimes the test doesn't work, so he goes back to thinking and reading. He said, "The data scientist's job is so vague. We don't really have a clear problem. It would be like 'Make an ETA that's better than Google.' But what does 'better' mean? What are they doing that we can or cannot do? This takes a lot of research to get precise."

Pedro, as a researcher, had the privilege of going at his own speed because of his research role. The privilege to slow down doesn't happen only in relation to the software project one is building. Sometimes, different paces of work emerge because there is a different level of attention that employees can give to their work. Let me illustrate this with another example. I attended one of the breakfast demos of the routing and navigation team. It was Thursday morning in early August and the atmosphere in the large conference meeting room was quite relaxed and friendly. Everyone was spreading camembert and prosciutto onto their fresh breakfast rolls and sitting around in a circle chatting. As I mentioned in one of the last chapters, these meetings were an important ritual of team-building. The minutes before the demo were as important as the demo itself, with developers awkwardly standing around having breakfast and forming pseudofriendships that would, in the end, fill the room with a team-like spirit. It is already telling that these particular workers had the opportunity to slow down and hang out for an hour eating breakfast together, while others, like those in Charlie's team in Bangalore, did not.

After it was over, I walked upstairs and saw Youssef, Pedro's colleague and a research-based developer who was just unpacking his bag. He had clearly just arrived at work, skipping the breakfast demo altogether. I asked him why he wasn't there. Youssef replied, "Oh, I don't go to those kinds of things."

The last time we met, Youssef told me about his wife and child and how they were away for three weeks without him after flying back home. This was the fifth time they returned to Syria since the war started. He was originally supposed to go with them but was advised to stay in Berlin, out of fear that the regime would recruit him into the army. I could see that his attention, his care or affective labor was placed less on his work at MiddleTech and more on his family's needs. Here, Youssef was able to come to work at his own speed and not attend the company demo because of the status of his software development position.

Not only are there different temporal cultures among developers within MiddleTech, but different global work cultures have different approaches to software project deadlines stemming from work competition, company culture, or the necessity (or lack thereof) to prove oneself out of fear of losing one's position. Charlie more recently explained that he had two developers from Bangalore working on his team. He was surprised that they had a completely different approach to efficiency and speedy project delivery. He said, "They were like 'We can do this overnight!' And I was like 'Or you can take four days?' Their work culture is just used to fast delivery and intense competition."

How time is experienced by software developers depends on their global economic status (as in the case of the outsourcing team), and various divisions of labor, which are generally either more creative or more mechanical, repetitive, and focused on maintenance work. Not all developers' time is equal both in terms of the type of work they do and the amount they are paid.

As Amrute highlighted, Indian programmers in particular feel they are hired especially for the purpose of bringing work in on schedule, leaving their "German counterparts surprised as to why they work so hard" (Amrute 2016, 103). While not written explicitly into their contract, some of Amrute's respondents engaged in long work hours as they felt it was expected of Indian programmers precisely because they had been brought in to produce reliable code on time.

Conclusions

All these moments of slowing down—going backward to work on legacy code, scrapping or halting projects, being blocked and standing in place, or even caring for one's family or enjoying the privilege of a long lunch or breakfast gathering—also affect the routing and navigation user or driver. If we travel back to the parking lot scene with Pedro, our game in the Lancaster parking lot showed that what happens to developers directly affects how software will run, resulting in moments of software refreshing, waiting, updating, and processing. These moments, which I unpacked in detail over the last pages, have the potential to shift the temporal order of a mobility system that promises speed and efficiency.

If we circle back to the game cards that Pedro and I created, we'll notice that on the first card, Pedro came up with an example that read,

You are driving a car that has an older MapNavi map version. This map uses an older technology of processing new changes to the road called "batch processing." This means that any changes to the road must go through a long validation process (checking if the map data is up-to-date and correct) with your map validation team back at the MapNavi office. Thus, your map routed you to a road that closed two weeks ago. Penalty: Wait back for ten seconds as your car gets rerouted.

Pedro explained that some cars still use older software, while others use newer software. An older MiddleTech map version processes changes to road data through batch processing. Batch processing takes more time, so any changes to the road must go through a long testing or authentication process to find out if the map data being used is up-to-date and correct. There are currently more modern or faster ways of validating new map data, but batch processing is still widely used. While roads are being updated, and new road data is quickly flowing into the MiddleTech system, an older legacy component slows down the system. This slowness, in turn, can slow down traffic, for example, if a car takes the wrong turn onto a closed road (as the playing card suggests), thus affecting the driver.

The following is another example of how programmers' work can directly affect the user. Another playing card reads,

Oh no! Your traffic rules have changed. But it's August, and half of MapNavi's map validation team (the team responsible for checking if the map data is up-to-date and correct) is on vacation and hasn't processed the change yet. The change: A left turn is not allowed on the street you are driving on. At this junction, you can either turn right or continue straight. Penalty: Wait back for thirty seconds.

While being on vacation might seem completely arbitrary, software, much like writing, can be deeply personal. When somebody like Pedro works on a project and then leaves the office for a week to go on a football-vacation-in-Manchester-turned-parking-lot-hangout-with-weird-ethnographer, his fellow programmers might have to wait around until he returns to process the change. And it's not just vacation. As I tried to illustrate in this chapter, slowdowns also happen due to personal factors. When Youssef is too concerned with his personal life to care about thoroughly reviewing his colleagues' code, mistakes can also happen.

Moreover, our apps, like our routing and navigation software, rely on live data fed to the software team via regular updates. In the case of MiddleTech, this data might be information about new traffic rules sent from the traffic ministry of Bavaria. In this instance, there are at least three (or even more) temporal orders at play: the temporality of a city's urban development, the temporal orders of travel through a given region (like Bavaria), as well as the temporal orders of the software developer's work and personal/leisure time. These all intermingle and mutually influence one another.

Each of the twenty-four playing cards Pedro and I came up with was just the tip of the iceberg in a slew of events that can mess up a software's ETA system. This brings me to one of my main points in this chapter: The story of infrastructural latency, infrastructural decay, and infrastructural slowdown is complete only if we also talk about where this slowness originates and take into account the various temporal orders at play, both in the use of software as well as in software production. The temporal orders of software development greatly affect the temporalities of mobility software, as well as the temporality of a user's mobility. This slowness is deeply entangled in good-enough software development, which then results in good-enough navigation software that gets us from point A to point B—we hope.

Too often as users, we start to detach ourselves from what really happens behind our screens, imagining that bugs or glitches just happen or are inherently part of the infrastructure: The cloud is updating our software, or a bug came out of nowhere and created a glitch. Yet the reality is that the temporal orders of software production directly impact glitches and breakdowns. My fieldwork and my discussion with Pedro illustrated that the routing and navigation back-end developers who work on an ETA system also experience a lot of slowness and waiting in their work, which then directly affects the slowdown, waiting, and breakdown of the software itself and its ETA system. To study mobilities, we must focus on *both* the fast and slow lanes of social life (Sheller and Urry 2006). An ETA is, thus, a sociotechnical object that involves a temporal assemblage of a variety of factors, including the developers' slowdowns and accelerations, and a software artifact that encapsulates good enoughness, both in how it was made and how it functions for its users.

One can now piece together how the entire ETA game experience mirrored the same moments of waiting, confusion, and breakdown that are experienced when driving and building software. What mobility systems and software systems have in common is that they both battle various cultures of speed that are inherent within their systems.

Pedro's and my ETA game cards highlighted the actual issues and practices that happen when building software. So when we ask ourselves what slows down an ETA, we will also get answers to a broader question of what slows down a software project. Not only does stuff not go according to plan (as I highlighted in chapter 2), but the process of software development involves multiple temporal forces—sometimes accelerating, but at other times slowing down, stuttering, moving in reverse, or completely coming to a halt in breakdown, shifting the pace of any idealized or desired technological progress. These temporalities often happen simultaneously and on different scales.

This chapter used routing and navigation software as a metaphor for what also happens during software production. Neither the culture of speed and efficiency in software production nor the logic of speed and efficiency in navigation software creates a constant improvement in the efficiency of movement or software innovation. Much like how drivers are faced with traffic jams, breakdowns, delays, waiting, and time wastage, software development is also inherently slow, blocked, moves backward into legacy code, and stutters. Software development is an inherently slow process, functioning within a contrasting culture of seamless agility and digital acceleration.

There are thus a number of mixed messages and tensions when it comes to how software is produced and the temporal orders in which it is produced. On the one hand, programmers understand that development needs to happen quickly, but they are also forced to slow down because of the material resistance of software and/or the social factors surrounding it.

This chapter shows how slowdown is the precursor to good enoughness: Faced with moments of halting, waiting, stopping, or canceling, programmers have to compromise on their initial ideas and release good-enough code.

Over two years later, long after our ETA game parking lot adventure, I wrote to Pedro to check up on him. He recalled the weirdness of our ETA game, replying, "That campus was somewhat empty for some reason, and that I wasn't entirely sure whether I was helping or not—this was mainly where the cluelessness stemmed from . . . I couldn't figure out the intersection between my expertise, that activity, and, say, digital sociology, and at some point just gave up trying to figure that out and just rolled with it. I thought maybe this was akin to you sitting beside me while I debugged some complex algorithm, which related to my experience, not knowing exactly why I was doing that and how."

Conclusion

Two years after my fieldwork ended at MiddleTech, I boarded the train from my new home in Switzerland, got off in Berlin, and took a taxi directly to the Prater, an expansive beer garden in the Prenzlauerberg district. Now seemingly devoid of much overt political action, the Prater was once the meeting ground for the German left: in the late 1860s, it was the location of the festivities celebrating the foundation of the General German Workers' Association, Germany's first labor party.

That evening, the ghosts of former revolutionaries and activists were replaced by teenagers, tourists, and locals rubbing shoulders in a postpandemic frenzy during happy hour. You could tell it was one of the warmest evenings of the year. I stopped at the entrance to look around for my party. I scanned the crowd and found Ori sitting next to Pierre and Charlie, with a group of MiddleTech software developers huddled around, drinking and clinking glasses. Some of them I knew, and some of them were people I had never seen before.

We were all there for Ori, Pierre, and Charlie's joint MiddleTech farewell party. Each of them had acquired jobs in different places and was moving on from the company to work elsewhere. Ori decided to try out life back home in Tel Aviv and got a job with one of the Big Tech companies there, which he had interviewed arduously for. Pierre, Ori's former boss in the R&D group and one of the most talented researchers at MiddleTech, got a prestigious research job at another Big Tech office in Zurich. Charlie, on the other hand, decided to stay in mobility technologies but got a job working for a rising new German ride-sharing start-up. None of them was staying at a quiet Medium Tech company.

With the same nervousness I felt during my first day of fieldwork, I waved at the table, which was packed with around fifteen software developers, designers, and product owners, and Charlie came up to greet me with a warm hug. During the COVID-19 pandemic, Charlie, Ori, and I started a biweekly online reading group with a few other colleagues, reading various books about computing cultures. We had all become quite close, but it was one of the first times that I had seen him face-to-face in years.

I took a seat at the long wooden beer garden table next to Anton, a Slovenian researcher and data scientist whom I met during his time working in Ori and Pierre's team, but who had since moved on to work for a financial technology (Fintech) start-up. Anton started telling me about his new job, and I found it striking how naturally we both fell back into our researcher-interlocutor roles. He knew I'd be interested in hearing about the type of problems he was facing when automating financial transaction software with a machine learning system he didn't fully understand. I sat listening to him, wishing I had brought my notepad. I felt a nostalgic yearning to do more fieldwork.

I got up for some more beers and sat back down next to Ori and Pierre. On the other side of me sat a new group of about four software developers and designers I didn't know. They were older, maybe in their mid- to late forties, and had been working at the company for a long time. Some of them had been there for over fifteen years. Ori and Pierre introduced me to them as "somebody who researched us for a few years and is writing a book about us." Looking skeptical, they started asking me questions: "Why did you research MiddleTech? What's so exciting about software developers? Did you finish your book yet? What was your main takeaway?"

I admit I was not prepared for the most obvious question a software developer at MiddleTech would ask when first meeting me. But I started to explain to them, slowly and delicately, how my book circled around the idea of *good enough*:

"Throughout my years studying you guys, I always felt that there was another logic at work in software engineering. When you don't know much about software, you just think it's a magical seamless object that is made in quick sprints by hackers in hoodies trying to appease their Steve Ballmer or Elon Musk–type bosses. But your work showed me . . . that, well . . . there are software companies out there that just make software that's just good enough to function. Not perfect, not special, just . . . good enough."

As soon as I said "good enough," the guys started gasping. I heard semiof-fended cries saying, "What!?" Some guys started laughing.

"I don't want to offend you guys! I just mean that there is something realistic about working in a good-enough way and making software that's good enough. Think of all the times you hacked something together to meet a deadline or pushed code out without a feature or component because you were blocked or didn't understand something or couldn't manage to untangle some spaghetti code. Software is also meant to be good enough. Because you can just go and update it later. No other object can be as regu-larly updated as the software object!" Some of them nodded. "Also, there is another side of good enough—it's the good-enough work culture. Working in a good-enough company gives you time to go home to your family and not be stressed. It becomes just a job."

I looked at one developer who was in his late forties and who had been at the company for over ten years. Earlier, he had been complaining about how mediocre MiddleTech had become, and I asked him, "For example, why did you decide to stay for so long if MiddleTech is so mediocre? Why are you still there?" He answered, "You're right. It's because it's quite relaxed. And familiar. I don't really have to think about my job. And that's a good thing."

"Exactly," I responded. "Like, who has the energy to actually go work at Microsoft or Google or some flashy new start-up?" I said, gesturing to the other side of the table at the three guys leaving the company. The rest chuckled a bit nervously.

While good enoughness is about being realistic with how a software developer works and what type of software they can produce, I won't deny that there was a part of the concept that sounded offensive that evening. While I might have been reading too much into the faces looking back at me around the table, I sensed some of the developers felt a pang of jealousy when looking over at Ori or Charlie's good-bye glory.

The Silicon Valley work culture celebrates those who move on. Whether at in-house barbecues on the MiddleTech roof or after-work beer garden parties like the one I was sitting at, these are rituals celebrating success and at times shaming those who stay behind. While this notion may seem counterintuitive (why would a company celebrate those who leave?), the farewell ritual communicates that individual workers are loved and cared for (and will be missed), and if you work hard, you will be rewarded (whether in the company or elsewhere with another job). It is also a ritual that high-lights the mismatch of discourses circulating around the office: The ritual appears to celebrate excellence and success (the value system of the Silicon Valley), but it also speaks to the people who stand for preservation, maintenance, and staying in place.

In describing this good-enough culture, it was my intention to highlight an alternative and at times resistant narrative to the go-getter workplace, which is so focused on achievement, excellence, efficiency, and improvement. Especially under the light of these slogans of corporate success, there is a tendency to look at good-enough culture and to understand it as subpar or "mediocre." Yet it is important that we take the terms "good" and "enough" seriously. Good enough is still good. It's not a failure or a falling behind (and being left in the shadows of the Big Tech giants or start-ups). During that biergarten good-bye party, I wanted to express to the guys sitting around the table that the "good" in good enough is about sufficiency and a feeling of adequacy. It is about their fluctuating negotiation between care for their work and their software and, at times, a necessary compromise to move on to care about something else. And the "enough" in good enough is, well, enough. It is about both individually and collectively negotiating a limitation to more innovation, more maintenance, or generally to more work. It represents the easing of a tension that drives us, a cessation of our endless illusion of endurance. Rather than moving fast and innovating, it is about relinquishing and maintaining.

In this concluding chapter, I will present the conditions of good enoughness, drawing on what we learned from MiddleTech. I have split this chapter into four sections: The first section will illustrate the diverse and complex fields where good enoughness plays out. To explain this, I introduce what I call "constellations" within which an actor negotiates what good enoughness is at any given moment. I then move on to complicate these constellations, showing that good enoughness is achieved in a negotiation between various constellations and cannot be achieved in isolation. The third section will highlight why and how good enoughness is under threat, namely by the forces of capitalism that work against its logic. The fourth section will return to our party in the biergarten to explore how good enoughness is stabilized while being under constant threat of extinction. While we will encounter new theoretical themes and analyses here, I deliberately saved these until the end in order to let each chapter's empirical descriptions stand on their own and work their way into various directions of the reader's thoughts. Coming back to the theme of good enough here will hopefully help readers "discern what is at stake politically and normatively for my informants" (Vogel 2021, 62).

Constellations of Good Enoughness

In this book, I demonstrated that good enoughness is a negotiated practice that is informed by unfolding constellations of actors (both human and nonhuman) interacting with one another at any given moment. As I draw this story to a close, I'd like to end by giving an overview of these constellations and highlighting that good enoughness arises in many fields and work practices beyond just software. The concept of the "constellation of good enoughness" might help us in this final endeavor and allow us to understand what "good enough for what" and "good enough for whom" can mean at any given moment. I define "constellation" as a set of relations between human actors (for example, the programmer) and other human actors (for example, other programmers), imagined actors (for example, a client whom one has never met), or nonhuman actors (for example, code). For instance, as we witnessed at MiddleTech, a programmer is faced with different constellations of relations that determine good enoughness on a daily basis—other programmers, their colleagues, their customers, their code, and beyond—and each of these constellations has different notions and thresholds of what good enough means. Taking the viewpoint of programmers at MiddleTech, I'd like to highlight eight constellations that we came across in earlier chapters, in which good enoughness was negotiated:[1]

The first constellation of good enoughness unfolds in relation to one's status as an employee, where the worker negotiates, in practice, if they are a good-enough programmer for the company. When hired, a corporate software developer signs a contract with the employer that delineates the labor power sold for a specific amount of time (for example, thirty-six hours). Work contracts set expectations about the kind of work and length of work that a programmer should carry out. Yet, in a culture of flexible work hours, contracts set certain expectations that are then interpreted by the programmer. Ori, when asked, said that there was nothing in his contract about the quality of his work, the length of his work breaks, or his intensity of work. Thus, we can assume that if nothing is explicitly stated in Ori's and his colleagues' work contracts, what happens during their workday must still be negotiated. Here, I mean how much labor power their workday entails, how fast their code has to be written, how much time is spent writing code or

---

1. I define these constellations from the perspective of the programmer, although good enoughness can also be approached from the perspective of other actors such as the product, the customer, or the company, which, for the sake of keeping my argument brief, I don't do here.

in meetings, what counts as a work break, what is an acceptable length for a work break, how much overtime is expected, and generally how much "filling-up of the pores of the working-day" (Marx 1990, 534) is required. In short, how much labor power is expended during a given workday differs from worker to worker and company to company and must be negotiated.

The second constellation arises between the programmer and the client, where the programmer negotiates whether what they are making is good enough for client X or meets their expectations.[2] While these contracts with the client are signed by the company rather than the programmer, they greatly affect the programmer's work. Much like the previous constellation, this one also involves a contract outlining what has to be worked on and under what deadline but still leaves a lot of room for negotiation. As I showed in earlier chapters, MiddleTech might get a contract to carry out a software project for a German car company. This contract also has certain deadlines and delineates what is to be produced (for example, software for an electric vehicle), which then influences the type of contractual pressure a manager places on their workers (for example, "this software product has too many bugs, which is not good enough for the customer," or "we are not working fast enough for the customer," or even "ignore the bugs, this software is good enough, we have to ship it now to the customer!" etc.). Additionally, certain contractual requirements can shift if deadlines and specifications are updated by the customer. The programmer has an imagined relation to the client, as well as those brokered through other employees, such as the program managers like Charlie. While they never meet their clients, programmers at MiddleTech often speak about them in relation to the software they are building, worry about them, or argue about what they need.

The third constellation emerges in the relation between the programmer and the product they work toward building or maintaining—where the programmer or manager involved negotiates whether or not the product they are building is good enough as a software artifact. At MiddleTech, the routing and navigation team would (implicitly and explicitly) ask the following questions: Is the software product safe enough? Robust enough? Bug-free enough? Is the software of good quality? We might recall Aseem being in this exact situation: He had an imagined solution to an EV routing system, but instead of pursuing this solution, his colleagues resorted to (in his view) "hacky solutions" and shipped the project to the customer in a half-baked state. Here, Aseem worried

2. As we might recall, at MiddleTech, this relation was mediated through the programmer's manager or the team's product managers.

about the quality of the product and had a different product standard of good enoughness compared to his colleagues. The product relation also includes imagining how the product will be used in the world by the user. In the case of MiddleTech, not ensuring a software product is good enough can have dramatic results: bad navigation software can lead at its worst to catastrophic incidents (Lin et al. 2017). In turn, good enoughness can mean that, most likely, no one will get hurt.

The fourth constellation relates to the programmer's professional ethos, where they negotiate if what they are building will be good enough to be respected professionally by their peers. The sense of professional ethos, or what Noble (2011) calls "professional habit," which informs technical and scientific work itself, affects not only the "lives of technical people but their imaginations as well, their notion of what is possible" (Noble 2011, 43). The so-called "engineerial mindset" is part of a professional ethos of building something solid, well crafted, safe, and sometimes even exciting, complex, interesting, new, or disruptive. This ethos is often acquired through their professional communities (their teammates, hackathons, conferences and congresses, and platforms like Slashdot or Hacker News) or formal training (university, workshops, coding camps, etc.). Within the Open Source community, this comes to the fore especially clearly. When developers add to an open source project, the open source community will evaluate programmers' work according to a certain standard of participating in the project. Here, programmers will ask themselves if what they are contributing is good enough to adhere to a set of shared goals (Kelty 2008).

The fifth constellation relates to the affordances of their tools, which inform a certain standard of use. As we encountered, the Scrum board, the Gerrit ticketing system, and the software within which developers write their code (IDE) have certain frames, protocols, requirements, and standards of "good" use. For example, within the programmer's development environment, programmers have to negotiate whether their code is good enough. If the code has mistakes, the IDE highlights them in red or often does not allow the programmer to keep writing. Here, it's harder for a programmer to get away with writing bad or wrong code, but they can get away with something that is good enough in a certain frame of the IDE.

The sixth constellation is a set of relations with the programmer's colleagues, where the programmer negotiates whether they are a good-enough coworker: whether they are helpful to others, whether they evade work at the expense of others, etc. This includes a relationship with current colleagues and future colleagues. As Leavitt (2019) explained, working with code involves working across time, meaning that whatever a developer writes today will also interact with other developers in the future through their legacy code. As I also mentioned, lines of code have documentation attached to them, including the developer's name. Thus, many programmers do not want to leave behind bad code for others to deal with as it becomes obvious, via the documentation, who wrote the faulty code.

Beyond their workplace, programmers are entangled in constellations that produce their own fields of negotiation of what is good (enough) or not. The seventh constellation unfolds between family and friends, involving strong affective ties and care work (Abel and Nelson 1990) in particular. The work assessments of what is good enough for now arise because a programmer has to leave a project in order to engage with other relations: programmers go on vacation, have to leave work earlier to pick up their kids from school, or feel like going out for a beer with friends on a Friday afternoon. When accountable to their work, to the product they are building, or to their professional ethics, programmers are faced with these other forces that help them negotiate the question, "Is this product or is my work good enough for now, so that I can leave to be a good-enough family member or friend?" As we might remember, Marek, a web developer, half-jokingly once confessed that on Fridays, when he feels like leaving work and running off for a beer, he quickly goes through the code review system and just adds +2, +2, +2 to all the tickets waiting to be reviewed. Here, Marek was compromising his professional ethics and, perhaps in the long run, on the quality of his software product to engage with his friends on a Friday afternoon and be a good friend or colleague.

The eighth is a constellation relating to an envisioned "good life," where developers negotiate the leisure time they engage in, in order to achieve a sense of meaning, pleasure, and participation in a social life outside of work (McKenzie 2016), as well as the social status and cultural capital that come with it. This includes various forms of leisure, such as going out with friends, engaging in clubs or sports, or participating in political or civil society organizations. Amrute, for example, highlighted how Indian programmers in Berlin push back against certain work demands and do not let work encroach on leisure time, which enforces their middle-class imaginary of a good life (Amrute 2016). This dynamic is fueled by class politics, which are situated in India just as much as in Berlin. Aseem's desire to engage in his photography club in order to meet new people and not be deemed a lonely geek programmer was also part of this constellation. This meant that work was sometimes dropped, and software projects were left in a good-enough state, in order for Aseem to leave work for a photography club meeting. The opposite is also possible: programmers might also deem their personal life good enough for now and pass on a party with friends, while working overtime at the office.

These eight constellations, which I presented from the perspective of the programmer only, are not an exhaustive list. If we take the perspective of the company or the manager at MiddleTech, further constellations might arise (such as the existence of other competitors, libel laws, company auditors, or privacy regulations, etc.). In short, this preliminary outline does not give an understanding of good enough in its full intricacy.

The Dynamics of Good Enoughness

We now have a partial idea of the enormous complexity that good enoughness entails in a corporate context such as MiddleTech. While simply asking "good enough for whom" or "good enough for what" is a start, it is not . . . well . . . good enough(!), as there are so many "whoms" and so many "whats" that interact with each other and have to be negotiated at the same time.

That said, each of the aforementioned constellations comes with internal tensions, and further tensions arise between various constellations. Our analysis here would be half-baked if we reduce this complex landscape to one constellation—let's say, we took the first constellation around class struggle and subsumed the manifold struggles in the other constellations to the logic of this one constellation. We'd risk overlooking the fact that programmers do not judge only what is good enough in relation to their employer but rather judges what is good enough through the conflicting constellations between their employment, their product, their professional ethos, their obligations to their families, etc.

One way of describing this conflicting dynamic is through the notion of care: at any given moment, a programmer has to care for one thing (for example, picking up a child from school) and compromise on care for another (for example, finishing a software feature). We can understand care as maintaining a focus on one constellation and compromise as pausing an abundance of care in a way that allows the other constellation to function. Actors must individually and collectively balance how much care is necessary and how much compromise is possible at any given moment within and between these constellations. It takes both care and compromise to decide that something is good enough: care for good software means sometimes compromising on a client deadline (that is, "our relationship with our client doesn't have to be great: it can be good enough"). The opposite can also happen: care for a client deadline can mean compromising on software (that is, "Well, this project can be just good enough for now because we have to meet our deadline and care for the needs of our client"). Good enough is not the same as striking or "quiet quitting" because compromising is really about pausing (not completely halting) care for one relation to care about another.[3]

The type of care one gives to any given constellation at any one time fluctuates and differs from programmer to programmer. In my own field, Youssef the data scientist defines his sense of what good-enough work output is when he shows up to work and skips the team breakfast demo. He knows his management accepts the vagueness of his role as a researcher and, quite often, the vagueness of his work output. While not done explicitly, Youssef judges what good enough is or is not. He will skip the team demo because his contract doesn't delineate his engagement in these types of events, and his research will be good enough to present to his colleagues and management at a later stage. In another situation, Charlie decided to stay at work late to "firefight" and fix a few bugs because he understands his software project well enough to know that it will cause bigger mishaps if he just leaves the bugs running. Different workers judge, at different moments and based on their job descriptions and contracts, their relationship to their product, what is happening in their private lives, and their professional ethics. They also judge how they distribute their care and compromise in relation to their own expectations, their contract obligations, and their product's limitations. Some people have more agency over how they distribute their care (for example, researchers like Youssef whose work is not quantified or monitored using the Scrum or other methodologies), and others have less agency (for example, Charlie's team, whose members had to finish a product for their customer by a certain deadline).

When becoming accountable to any of these constellations (for example, to the product they are building, to their professional ethics, etc.), dynamic forces other than care and compromise come to the fore as well: programmers also cooperate with others, compare themselves to others, and are already part of various relational networks that help them negotiate what good enough is for that given moment or task. In short, it's not enough to

3. "If Your Co-Workers Are 'Quiet Quitting,' Here's What That Means," *Wall Street Journal*, https://www.wsj.com/articles/if-your-gen-z-co-workers-are-quiet-quitting-heres-what-that-means-11660260608.

define good enough for what and for whom, but each of these constellations is further negotiated through various dynamic forces.

For example, no single actor has full agency over which constellation to engage in at a particular time. Good enoughness is a collective endeavor, one that includes not only programmers but their managers, customers, imagined users, as well as the material object of software and other tools that call out for care at any given time. When negotiating good enough, this collective all works together, stresses together, fixes code together, all in the name of gaining a cooperative sense of what is good enough to ship to completion. This collective negotiation is sometimes done explicitly through something like the Gerrit code review through which, as we learned, programmers collectively review one another's code and decide what is good enough and what isn't (by asking, "Will this piece of code create a bug? Will this line of code crash the system?"). In other instances, a consensus of good enough is implicitly stabilized through mutual trust (between managers and software developers, between customers and managers, etc.) that a piece of code will run properly, or that a software project will be good enough to function.

When figuring out whether something is good enough, programmers will compare themselves to others. This comparison sometimes resembles what Groth (2019b) would call a sort of competition to be mediocre. Again, this comparison can be made explicitly through certain metrics like KPIs, where, as we might recall from my introductory chapter, managers quantify and visualize the "bug velocity," showing how many bugs each team produced. More frequently, a comparative good enough emerges in an implicit way, where various collaborative forms—discussions with other programmers, pair programming, hackathons and fixathons, code review, code documentation (where programmers reveal who wrote what line of code on their IDE), or other team events—all create a sense of what one programmer is doing in comparison with other programmers. Questions such as, "Am I slower or faster than the rest?" or "Do I produce more bugs than the others?" or "Is my code as robust as my colleague's?" might lead a programmer (or a programmer's colleague or manager) to decide if their work is good enough or too good or too bad in comparison to the work of their colleagues.

Good enoughness is also affected by the amount of agency an actor has to act, as good enoughness is often imposed through certain constraints. With an "imposed" good enough, software workers experience external constraints that enforce a good-enough product, no matter their intentions, the intentions of their team, their contract, their professional ethics, and so on. Remember when Ori was attempting to complete a research project that used the personal mobility data of MiddleTech's users, but he was blocked from moving forward with the project while waiting for legal approval from the company's privacy team? Not only software but privacy regulations, legal regulations, deadlines, the downsizing of teams, the scrapping of projects, the material constraints of code, and other blocks and slowdowns can cause projects to remain good enough. Despite even the worker's best efforts, sometimes the material condition of the product being built or the infrastructure within which it is embedded causes the product to be just good enough. As we have learned, software contains an inherent resistance to the logics of excellence and efficiency (through, for example, its complexity, breakdown, unpredictability, and slowdown). Moments when software developers are faced with legacy code, spaghetti code, monolithic software architectures, hard-to-find bugs, messy databases, or code that's not been properly optimized are just a few examples of a long list of product-oriented reasons that a project will stay good enough (and not excellent).

Throughout any of these constellations, the practice of judging a good-enough piece of software or good-enough work output also requires imaginary relations, which can inspire empathy: it forces the programmer to imagine the customer, the user, the manager, fellow programmers, and so on. In these imaginary relational practices, the programmer, either alone or collectively with colleagues, has to negotiate and predict that something is good enough in the eyes of the client, manager, user, other colleague, etc. This then sets the stage for a specific social gesture that combines an understanding of the other (What will they think?), and when it comes to software, a confidence in one's own expertise (that is, "This piece of software won't hurt anyone!"), with a certain utilitarian attitude (that is, "More work on this piece of software would be a waste of my time/more work on this would not really make it that much better").

Good Enoughness under Threat

That afternoon in the Prater Biergarten, I felt a clear contrast between Ori, Charlie, and Pierre, who were celebrated for moving on from MiddleTech, and the people who were staying behind, accepting their position as veterans of MiddleTech. These two groups, to me, represented two contrasting logics at play at a company like MiddleTech: on the one hand, there were those who represented the dominant discourse of success; on the other hand, there were those who had to justify their reasons for staying behind and not succeeding, in light of this dominant discourse. Ori admitted to me that he wanted to leave because it was "not okay" to stay at a company for so long, and he felt like he was staying stagnant by sticking around at MiddleTech. Here, the logic of ambition was at play. Improvement through upward mobility, change, and personal growth were important, versus staying still in a good-enough job.

Good enoughness is always under threat of being subsumed by the logics of postindustrial capitalism, and in a way, when you state that something is good enough, you imply that it could be better (somehow). The way in which achieving good enoughness becomes a constant negotiation between care (for a piece of software, for a project, etc.) and compromise (for a customer's deadline, for leaving work early, for a team member's idea, etc.) helps highlight the underlying tensions of capitalism. On the one hand, MiddleTech was filled with the pressure to uphold a fast-paced, innovation-oriented work ethic in sync with a global capitalist logic. Awesomeness and not mediocrity has certainly become one of the overarching values in corporate culture that has stayed with modern companies for the past century.[4] Working in any company has become about striving for excellence: about adapting to the market, being reactive, constantly innovating, and incessantly wowing and amazing others, and, of course, succeeding at what you do and moving on. On the other hand, good enoughness is real. Many MiddleTech employees are interested in staying around and maintaining software while moving between various constellations of good enoughness all the time, caring about certain relations while compromising on others.

These two contrasting logics function together under one roof at MiddleTech. This is something Nancy Fraser describes as an inherent contradiction of care within the capitalist structure: "On the one hand, social reproduction is a condition of possibility for sustained capital accumulation; on the other, capitalism's orientation to unlimited accumulation tends to destabilize the very processes of social reproduction on which it relies. This social-reproductive contradiction of capitalism lies at the root of the so-called crisis of care" (Fraser 2016, 100). Throughout these past years, I encountered the software industry's obsession with eliminating the good-enough culture, both in my interactions with managers in my field and in industry books written in the past half-century, which grappled with the various moments of complexity or lethargy that led to a good-enough software culture.

---

4. Adrian Chiles, "When Did Everything Become 'Awesome' and 'Amazing'? I Blame the Americans," https://www.theguardian.com/commentisfree/2022/sep/01/when-did-everything-become-awesome-and-amazing-i-blame-the-americans.

While good enoughness cannot be reduced to the relations between employee and company, this first constellation plays a special role because it is the one that makes good enoughness most fragile, the one where it is attacked the most. With every new wave of unionization, we can witness a pushback from large corporate tech companies (Boewe and Schulten 2017), and antiunion rhetoric can begin to mix with antigood-enough sentiments too. In a more recent study on the unionization efforts in the global high-tech sector in Israel, some workers and managers feared unionization because "work councils would encourage mediocrity, since it would . . . undercut management's ability to dismiss under-performing workers in order to improve the firm" (Fisher and Fisher 2019, 318). These workers believed that work councils could "undermine the value of excellence," and they perceived councils as organizations that "protected failing workers, and objected to this based on a radical meritocratic ethos that argues that talented workers do not need a union at all" (318).

This effort to overcome good enoughness is rooted in an inherent desire to make capitalism work more seamlessly through boasting narratives of excellence, improving "creativity," squashing union activity, and exploiting personal quests of ambition. Therefore, capitalist logic will always undermine any good-enough solutions because niche situations like the one at MiddleTech are very hard to come by and, per system design, are meant to be broken apart. And once they are disrupted, this compromise that works for so many—for the ones who stay or who stayed for a long time—will not last.

MiddleTech teaches us that regardless of the efforts of these cheerleaders of capitalism to abolish good enoughness, it will continue to exist under certain conditions and in opposition to certain capitalist logics. The culture of good enough can't be sought out or abolished by any programmer or manager but is the result of a deep intermingling of software and sociality, which emerges in certain places over time. A company like MiddleTech doesn't strive to be good enough, nor can it try to abolish good-enough culture. No amount of rebranding or off-site weekend workshopping can help make or break good-enough software culture. As my book has shown, good-enough software is a culture that emerges over time and in the right conditions.

Good enoughness is thus a concept that is full of contradictions and will always undermine itself by evoking its own opposite, thus never staying stable on its own. In short, it is a concept that needs to be achieved, to be made and remade through various practices that fight capitalist logic.

Good Enough Is Here to Stay

If the dominant postindustrial capitalist logic desires an excellent and not a good-enough worker, the question remains: How do workers stabilize their good-enough condition?

While I found very little evidence at MiddleTech of explicit class politics in the narrower Marxist sense, one answer to this question could be witnessed in the achieved stability of good enoughness, where a certain form of middle-ground stability becomes a goal in itself (Groth 2020a).

What I mean here is that knowing when something is good enough to finish, or good enough not to fail, is a collective and learned skill that is delicately negotiated and achieved over time. As we've seen in earlier chapters, teams of programmers work together for months, if not years, to push out code that's good enough not to disappoint the customer, not to drive a car off the road when given a certain route, and not to embarrass their manager. So, more specifically, understanding the limits of what is "good" and what is "enough" is an achieved collective skill. While they might not consciously realize it, software developers are connected by this knowledge, involved in their collective achieved stability.

Software workers also stabilize good enoughness through a technical dependency on good enough. As I've explained in the past chapters, software cannot be perfect in practice due to certain forms of complexity and constraint in software production (in particular with its update culture), software's architecture, and how software functions. As Collins et al. (1994) and Yourdon (1995) highlighted, software projects can't be awesome or perfect because of the material resistance of software. All the sketches, plans, and theoretical blueprints might point to a perfect project, but once faced with the infrastructure of the material and social world, software will fail (Jackson 2014), and as a result, it will always be just good enough to function, with lots of mishaps and bugs popping up along the way. Programmers know this, and no desire to escape and follow the light into bigger and better-paid tech companies will help get around the fact that any software project, anywhere, will always be just good enough.

Good enoughness also prevails at MiddleTech through the notion of reasonableness. As I highlighted in my introductory chapter, Collins et al. argued that the software industry should "encourage reasonable expectations about software capabilities and limitations" (1994, 89), both among users and producers of software. This call to be "reasonable," as Collins and his colleagues explain, is about understanding "how good is good enough," a responsibility that lies in the hands of the software provider or the programmers and their team. It is also a way of defending one's position against a capitalist discourse (that is, "because how awesome can software be anyway?"). Knowing what is reasonably good enough is learned, meaning that software developers acquire expertise over the years of working with software and understand that the boundaries between what is reasonably good enough and what is not good enough can lead to critical, at times dangerous, software failure. It is important also to add that this collective learned negotiation of what is "reasonable" or not doesn't have to be so clean-cut, polite, and safe. Software developers also acquire a sensibility of what is good enough to get away with, which can also entail a more risk-taking gamble, where the outcome of one's actions is not so clearly known as the term "reasonable" might suggest.

Another related way that the good-enough condition perseveres is through the commons and collegiality of good enough. This is a form of sociality where a group of people—in our case, engineers—find a sense of social belonging and collegiality (Bachmann 2014) in a workplace commons (Korczynski and Wittel 2020) where their colleagues have a similar goal of maintaining a state of good enoughness. In this sense, the achievement is not moving on to bigger and better Big Tech worlds or creating one's own start-up, but sticking together to practice good enoughness. As Silvia Gherardi explained, "learning how to do and learning how to be are part of the same social process, and a community of practitioners can be read as the enactment of a locus not only of identity, belonging and engagement but also of socio-technological knowledge" (2009, 110). In other words, programmers collectively learn the process of programming something in a good-enough way, push back against deadlines, and do quick code reviews in order to go out for beers. This is all part of the tricks-of-the-trade of the workplace commons and enforces their sense of belonging and engagement in their sociotechnical worlds. Negotiating, discussing, arguing, laughing at late deadlines, sneering at faulty code, or posting memes about the impossibility of solving spaghetti code—things we observed in the past chapters—all make up the collegiality of good enough.

Software developers additionally stabilize their good-enough condition through the notion of contentment. In contrast to workers who competitively strive to advance in their fields, workers who orient themselves "towards the middle" do not seek the best but rather a medium position, "a 'good average' or a 'happy medium' with which one is content (or claims to be content)" (Groth 2019a, 31). This is a sentiment of good enough where people justify their position against their dominant workplace ideology by being happy with being in the middle, where a certain form of middleness ensures calmness, low risk, or restraint. I remember that during a lunch break, Pierre, Ori, and Charlie were laughing at their US office for pushing new hoodies on them. Their argument for not getting new hoodies and getting hyped by more company team spirit was that one hoodie was enough. They already had one hoodie, so why get more? This "enoughness" is about being sufficient. For those coming from the sustainability corner of science, good-enough culture—one that promotes slowdown, modesty, or mediocrity—might remind us of the recent discussion around the economic theory of degrowth. This approach, generally derived from economics and sustainability studies, understands that the world is in a period of economic stagnation and sees that there are limits to growth. Thus, degrowth is, among other things, about "maintaining prosperity without growth" (D'Alisa et al. 2014, 54), based on a democratically led shrinking of production and consumption and acceptance of the slowdown or exhaustion of technical innovation. Although degrowth is unlikely to be a widespread ethos anytime soon, old aging software companies can embrace their inertia and stability and accept that their enterprise is not based on producing endless wasteful apps and speedy innovations but instead on providing stable infrastructure.

This sentiment is also shared by those who study maintenance work, who showed us that focusing on the way in which our existing technologies, inventions, and infrastructures "get put back together" through the everyday work of maintenance, caretaking, and repair is a welcome alternative to the stress caused by a delusional culture of industriousness and competition (Denis et al. 2016; Mattern 2018; Vinsel and Russell 2020). If we fit good enough into the discourse around maintenance, we can see that within a good-enough culture, software developers are resisting shiny innovation and overproduction and focusing on the task at hand. Making a judgment that something like software is good enough to be released into the world also gives software workers a repair-oriented perspective: Imperfect, good-enough software will be released into the world and will come back with bugs, which is okay because software developers will be around to fix it.

Yet another way of preserving a good-enough culture is through a belief that being good enough can ensure a sense of freedom from excellence. What I mean here is that building software in a good-enough way also absolves the software developer of the pressure to strive for perfection and the pressure not to fail. Striving to be awesome can lead to stress for the software providers and disappointment for the users and customers. Leaving something good enough is a freeing gesture, absolving the developer from the strict focus on perfection and excellence. This type of approach is not uncommon in approaches to parenthood, where a "good enough mother" (Winnicott 1953 in Ratnapalan and Batty 2009, 239) is freer and more relaxed than a mother who constantly strives for her vision of perfection. This is an illustration of how good enough can create a better experience for all involved: The mother reduces her pressure to achieve the impossible, and the child is then listened to.

Additionally, and somewhat related to the former, is that programmers preserve a good-enough culture by making it part of their lifeworlds. Being good enough can also be associated with the state of mediocrity, which, as Groth (2019a) highlighted, is increasingly becoming a positive point of reference in different fields of practice. Keeping up with the midfield, earning a middle-range income, or being part of the middle class are powerful models for socioeconomic behavior and lifeworld interpretations (Groth 2019a). Perhaps it became a postpandemic trend, perhaps the younger generation cares more about the climate crisis than their day hustle, but since I began writing this book, various journalists and authors started talking about the good-enough job (Stolzoff 2023), where Gen Z workers were rejecting the idea of going above and beyond in their careers, happy to do just the bare minimum to get by, caring about their own well-being and that of their colleagues before profit or advancement. If we care about our own well-being as workers, we won't have a problem shipping a good-enough project at 5 p.m. rather than working late to improve upon it. Because why not? In a good-enough culture, the workday is over, the software is good enough to run, and we would rather spend time with our families or friends or caring about our own health and happiness.

Yet the most obvious way of keeping good enough alive at the workplace is to not openly speak out about good enoughness. Speaking out about a cultural practice that challenges a dominant discourse is bound to be criticized. MiddleTech employees know that good enoughness exists but consciously choose to ignore its existence. The silence around good enoughness remains, for now, a crucial part of good enoughness.

Good-bye MiddleTech

Three months after the MiddleTech good-bye party in Prater's Biergarten, I called Ori and Charlie to find out how they were doing in their new jobs. Ori was already three months into his Big Tech job in Tel Aviv, and I would get photos of him on the beach or short video messages of him strolling down the streets on warm evenings wearing his usual button-down vintage shirts. He explained, with a bit of excitement, that he hadn't done that much in the past few months. Describing his Big Tech workday thus far, he said that it was over-flowing with a variety of corporate events and social gatherings: onboarding meetings, frequent rooftop parties celebrating a company achievement or holiday, and colleagues coming back from vacation and sharing treats around the office. "There is just a lot of social activity all the time, so it's quite hard to get any work done," explained Ori. The days he worked from home were the most productive. He didn't know if this buzz around the office was due to the Israeli social culture or just the culture around the Big Tech office. Their company kitchens are run by one of Israel's top chefs, and he is regularly invited to different food tastings and other events. He boasted that there is even a "bring-your-friend-to-work" scheme, and the office is filled with friends and family members roaming around. While his company life is incredibly social, his software work is done completely alone. He was hired to develop a special machine learning tool for a specific branch of the Big Tech product, and the software he builds assists teams in Singapore and London (teams that he says he barely interacts with). Nobody really watches over his work, and if the software he builds goes wrong, nothing critical will happen—no driver will swerve off the road; no parent will be late to pick up her kid from school.

Charlie, on the other hand, started working in a much smaller hyped Ger-man ride-sharing start-up where the "stakes were higher." He described the culture in his office as being "intense" and "driven to achieve." He had already experienced his colleagues coming in at 7 a.m. to fix something. He was recently required to work on the weekends during a "crisis." "We all get stressed because we own the end-to-end. So it's like we own the stress. We don't sell our technology for somebody else to build it into their system and just ignore the pressure of our system potentially failing. There is a higher bar," he explained. His fellow product owners were also very ambitious. While at MiddleTech he stood out as somebody smart, at his new start-up he felt he blended in with the crowd of ambitious, young go-getters, and he constantly had to prove himself. "I sometimes miss the laziness of [MiddleTech] . . . Last week I was exhausted . . . but I am also much more challenged." While Charlie didn't regret moving to his start-up, he did so knowing he would have to work harder and be more engaged, giving up his propensity for good enoughness.

Ori and Charlie helped highlight that good enoughness is everywhere. Whether surrounded by good enoughness in Big Tech companies (as in Ori's case), or nostalgically longing for a culture of good enoughness (as in Charlie's case), the tension between good enoughness and the drive for excellence and achievement is one that exists in many software companies. Ori had encountered a work culture where the bar of good enoughness seemed to be set even lower in Israel, a place that has become known in the global tech industry as a hotspot for ambitious tech culture, whereas Charlie had encountered the bar of good enoughness that was significantly raised in a German start-up firm operating in the same industry. I would like to highlight that there wasn't a presence or absence of good enoughness in either the Israeli-based Big Tech or the German start-up company but rather different (and contrasting) constellations, different internal balances between constellations, and different balances between constellations.

While this book was about a specific company in a specific region of the world, building a specific type of software, my hunch is that good enoughness is everywhere. More optimistically, I believe that the capacity to preserve a good-enough culture in which slowness and care overcome our desires to build fast and break things is a sociotechnical achievement that allows for workers to have certain freedoms and for software to be cared for and maintained. This is a call for the acceptance of one of the many fallacies of capitalism in which acceleration and innovation inadvertently lead to slowdown and maintenance.

Paradoxically, while also being an achievement, good enoughness can often be a privilege. This is the case not only for workers who get away with doing a good-enough job, which is possible in a culture that provides safe working environments, and have been able to gain employment at a company like MiddleTech. Another point of privilege here is the mere possibility to achieve good enough in any relation or production process, breaking through a threshold of just being "bad" or constantly failing. Whether practically or just subjectively, the experience that one is "never good enough," or that the object one is working on should be good enough but is instead a failure, is not an uncommon feeling. This inability to be good enough or to judge what is good enough might have to do with one's class background, the forms of discrimination somebody is experiencing, or one's access to education. Underfunded care work, for example, is a notorious example of work that leaves its workers in a constant state of not being able to deliver good-enough care.[5] In software development, I can also speculate that an

---

5. For example, in her ethnographic research of nursing home workers in the United Kingdom, Eleanor Johnson described the "shortfall" of funding, leading to care workers merely "getting the job done," which in turn led to damaging impacts on residents and care workers (2022, 7).

outsourcing team in Krakow or Bangalore, working to meet deadlines and fearing for their job security, can feel that their work is never really good enough for their employer.

While our past was rooted in expansion and the demand for bigger, better, and greater, it is my hope that the skills and tactics of good enoughness will be necessary to build a livable future. Resistance to the narratives of capitalism can include care, compromise, balance, safety, contentment, or collegiality. Knowing how to be good enough can give us the skill to maintain our infrastructures and keep them running and stable. Accepting a good-enough work culture can be productive as it leaves time for the realignment of power relations, and the reconfiguration of what is important at a given moment. What I aimed to illustrate is the overarching need for managers, workers, and software users to accept the inherent bugginess and lethargy of working with technical systems. It was my hope for us to get out of the mindset that traps us into thinking that new technology will be able to save us from the problems of older technology. Doing so can help us embrace endurance over newness, maintenance and repair over quick innovation, and prepare us for a highly adversarial world that is yet to come. A good-enough future would be a substantial feat, and getting there would have to entail the art of being good enough.

Good Enough beyond MiddleTech

Although my research was centered around one specific corporate software development office, during the process of writing this book, I was bombarded by examples of how good enoughness—as both a way of making software and a work practice—existed beyond the walls of MiddleTech.

During the first few months as I started writing this book, Ori sent me a discussion thread he found on Hacker News, one of the sites many developers I encountered enjoyed reading with their morning coffee. For some software engineers and other techies, the Web site is the front page of the internet: a simple compendium of news sites, opinions, and hacker-related factoids posted by users, all organized into one list. The list is organized by popularity and shifts by popularity on a daily basis. On April 7, 2021, Ori sent me a post that was getting significant traction that day. I am including it here in its entirety (with original spelling and grammar retained). It read:

Hey HN [Hackernews],

I'll probably get a lot of flak for this. Sorry.

I'm an average developer looking for ways to work as little as humanely possible.

The pandemic made me realize that I do not care about working anymore. The software I build is useless. Time flies real fast and I have to focus on my passions (which are not monetizable).

Unfortunately, I require shelter, calories and hobby materials. Thus the need for some kind of job.

Which leads me to ask my fellow tech workers, what kind of job (if any) do you think would fit the following requirements:

- No / very little involvement in the product itself (I do not care.)
- Fully remote (You can't do much when stuck in the office. Ideally being done in 2 hours in the morning then chilling would be perfect.)
- Low expectations / vague job description.
- Salary can be on the lower side.
- No career advancement possibilities required. Only tech, I do not want to manage people.
- Can be about helping other developers, setting up infrastructure/ deploy or pure data management since this is fun.

I think the only possible jobs would be some kind of backend-only dev or devops/sysadmin work. But I'm not sure these exist anymore, it seems like you always end up having to think about the product itself. Web dev jobs always required some involvement in the frontend.

Thanks for any advice (or hate, which I can't really blame you for).

—LMUEONGOQX (APRIL 7, 20211)

Both the post and the comments that responded to it (over a thousand—a lot for one post on the site) were a testament to what I have been hinting at all along in this book: that good enoughness exists not only in MiddleTech but is everywhere: in lmueongoqx's world, and in the lifeworlds of the thousands of developers in San Francisco, Tel Aviv, Bangalore, and beyond who responded to this post.

This post, and the responses that followed, were laced with a multitude of meanings. Hacker News is an online space that celebrates engineerial culture, promoting mostly the success of technological perfection, celebrating new forms of innovation, or sharing tips on how to complete a project or learn something. The purpose of the site is to promote hacker culture. In lmueongoqx's post, he expresses an appeal and even suggests that there is an art to being average. On the one hand, lmueongoqx seemed to be honestly asking for advice and honestly searching for a different way of working as an engineer. On the other hand, lmueongoqx's question and its answers (which I will get to below) were laced with cynicism, as if these programmers were responding to the shattering of a taboo that usually prevented them from speaking out about their slowness, slacking, and good-enough work culture.

1. *Hacker News*, Apr. 7, 2021, https://news.ycombinator.com/item?id=26721951.

Implicitly, this post denounced the mainstream engineering culture, which they normally believed in and were supposed to follow on Hacker News within their work practices and beyond.

Coincidentally, this post spoke to various moments in my field, where the escape from good enoughness (and into the arms of Big Tech or start-ups) was celebrated. If we look more closely into some of the meanings behind this post, we'll notice that the celebratory ritual is somehow flipped on its head: The programmers who stay at MiddleTech, who engage in good-enough jobs, and who are able to get away with making good-enough software, are celebrated as the winners or achievers. Yet with every sentence these Hacker News programmers write, you can see how this approach goes against the discourses of excellence that inform their field and reveals a back-stage reality of a work culture that normally remains hidden.

Good-Enough Job Tactics

As I read Hacker News, it was as if the results of my ethnographic research were mirrored in programmer message boards beyond the corridors of MiddleTech. The comments were uncanny. They resembled the practices, experiences, and conversations I had observed.

I noticed too that the advice for lmueongoqx was practical and quite tactical—almost summarizing the various experiences of the developers at MiddleTech. By "tactical" I mean having a practice-based orientation, the way in which de Certeau defined "everyday practices" and "ways of operating" as "tactical in character" (de Certeau 1984, xix). While I won't share the entire list, I grouped the comments into two different tactical themes that make direct connections to my other chapters, addressing what good-enough work in software development entails.

The first theme of advice for lmueongoqx circles around "tactics" for identifying the type of company to work for and the kind of job that allows a worker to "not care" at work. The second set of themes can be grouped around the "tactics" of engaging in a good-enough job, where programmers suggested ways for lmueongoqx to engage in good-enough practices while already at the workplace. I will include these comments below, again retaining their original spelling and grammar.

Regarding the former set of advice on accessing a good-enough job, some highlighted that start-ups are not recommended as "the owners watch costs like hawks and there's zero chance of slacking off." Rather, older, more established, "medium-sized" companies are best because they have a "local monopoly" and aren't really forced to "compete in their market" and "have had dominance for more than a decade" (Hacker News, April 8, 2021). The user recommending medium-size companies; XCoderX, added that the best companies are the ones whose "business model does not depend on innovation or moving fast . . . The development dept. is known for saying 'good things take time' because they can afford to." Another user, Hamcha, added, "If you're a developer in a big/mid company (or a consultant regardless of company size) your input to the product will be minimum to non-existent. And even if it wasn't, maybe the problem at the base is something you don't believe is worth solving or being solved properly." These comments resonated with how I characterized Medium Tech companies as those that structure their workdays around maintenance and repair rather than around innovation. The sentiment among these Hacker News programmers was that environments that focus on maintenance and repair give rise to a culture of "mellow and chilled co-workers" rather than "career-hungry overachievers"—a phenomenon that was present at MiddleTech.

A different user, burnoutguru, highlighted the importance of working in an older, "stagnant" company, explaining, "[I'm a] Senior DevOps Engineer at a mid-sized, stagnant Californian 'startup' . . . My last three jobs were at companies which were 10–15 years old, had burned through $75m–$150m in VC and had flat revenues of $12–$15m for years . . . The thing about companies this size is you have a good sized team managing a medium workload and very low expectations." As I noted in chapter 1, Medium Tech software companies can be characterized by their age and the older software assets they hold. While older companies in any industry are often replaced by new ones that build better or more innovative products, there are a select few that keep surviving for years as the company is able to build up a stable revenue from a software product that is embedded in the market (for example, the routing and navigation system in German vehicles). This lack of pressure to build a flashy, innovative product leads to a good-enough product.

Additionally, some of these comments noted the link between the age and size of the company and its propensity for promoting good-enough work cultures. In particular, many of lmueongoqx's advice-givers noted that a culture of underachievement could be found in companies that are "mid-sized and older."

While I characterize MiddleTech as the older, less sexy software companies building more invisible products, providing a "medium workload and very low expectations," many developers on Hacker News also wrote about the BigTech/FAANG (Facebook, Amazon, Apple, Netflix, Google) companies. These companies are also older, and some of their departments and teams are also slower and focus more on maintenance than on innovation. Some Hacker News users wrote that these companies have gotten so big that it has become easy to "fall through the cracks." Natch wrote, "Work at Google. They seem to have many thousands of people who do very little. Just look at their product quality." Others, like Quartus, suggest going for larger, more "dinosaur" companies, writing, "Try some of the old school tech companies: Cisco, Oracle, IBM, etc." These larger companies get "so big" because they hold a monopoly on a certain software product. As I mentioned throughout this book, MiddleTech builds a stable product with a "local monopoly," meaning that not many other companies have such a robust mapping engine and have mapped the world to the same extent as MiddleTech. This monopoly gives MiddleTech an edge on the market, meaning that they do not have to be "innovation-driven" but rather maintenance-driven, making sure they keep the dominance that they have had for more than a decade by maintaining and repairing an existing product. This logic is precisely what helps drive BigTech/FAANG companies too, also fostering a good-enough work ethic.

Good-Enough Work Tactics

In addition to this advice on finding a good-enough job, hundreds of programmers gave lmueongoqx precise tactics for engaging in good-enough work practices while at his good-enough job. I chose a select few themes (which often repeated themselves throughout the Hacker News posts) and grouped them into work tactics for creating a good-enough culture in a commercial software company. While seemingly cynical and offered with a sense of humor, these "tactics" help highlight that good enoughness is a real practice at the tech workplace, resonating with many programmers in their everyday corporate environments. Again, the cynical and jokey tone of these "tactics" doesn't mean that they aren't real but rather helps highlight the taboo of actually speaking out about good enoughness. If we link these tactics with what we've learned throughout these chapters, we'll find that they resonate with real backstage practices that are not usually openly discussed.

The first tactic involves helping others all the time: "Pick a role where spending time on other people's tasks is justified. During stand-ups when you have to explain what you did, you can say that you worked on your own thing, and that you helped the other person. This is not just a way to cheat: I care more about what I do, if I'm helping someone who cares more. I invented this coping strategy at points where I didn't care at all myself."[2] This resonates with many moments we encountered in the past chapters. Pedro, my Lancaster ETA data scientist, once explained the other side of the coin: that you get "punished" for caring because people are so often unloading their own work on those who do "care": "Developers are punished for being caring: for reading e-mails, for doing more experiments, for being involved. If you do not care, you are allowed to be in your corner and just plug away at whatever it is you are assigned to do. But if you care, you will keep getting more problems to solve. I'm the type of person who cares, but I just have to start saying 'no' and stop caring." Care here is like a ball that keeps bouncing back and forth between programmers, stopping with the programmer who is actually willing to do more work. Many programmers know this, and as Pedro explained, deflect their care onto somebody else to "hide in a corner."

The second tactic involves working "in research, where the final product is vague and intangible . . . Pick more research-y tasks: People don't know exactly what to expect, the work isn't as easily quantified. So when you spend longer or don't have as much to show for it, that may make sense." Here, we can recall engineers like Youssef, Ori, and Pedro, who often embraced a very different work speed than other more product-driven developers. As I also suggested, having a lot of revenue based on older assets meant that MiddleTech did not worry about wasting it on employees who did nothing at all. Simultaneously, many of the teams at MiddleTech didn't work on maintaining their software assets but were employed to research and test new map-related business ideas. These business ideas did not necessarily have to provide any financial returns because the cash-cow map software was securing the majority of the employees' salaries. As many researchers in particular weren't building anything tangible that needed to be finished by a certain time, it was easy to lose track of an employee.

Another tactic that can lead to management losing track of its workers (and the worker thus getting away with working on a good-enough level) is to first "work diligently for a while and then become invisible. You have to work for some time and then count on 'falling into the cracks'—landing in a place where there's less work than people capable of doing it."

2. All quotations from the Hacker News post come directly from *Hacker News* and were gathered in Apr. 2021.

This relates to a fourth tactic, which suggested working with clueless managers. "Select somewhere with a new CTO/tech lead: They're super busy learning how to juggle management and mentoring, so if you're stuck onboarding for more time than normal, they won't blame you. This may sound leechy, but just make sure you provide some kind of value to everyone else other than your full attention." In many places in this book, particularly in chapter 4, "Managing Good Enoughness," I explored the knowledge divide between the programmers and their managers, where management was often left clueless as to what was being built and how long the project would actually take. Working at a good-enough company should be understood as an interplay of understanding and misunderstanding, communication and miscommunication, and knowing and not knowing. This interplay of understanding relates to a fifth tactic that I highlighted above, which involves blinding management with vague language around "digitization" and technosolutionism: "Show off your AI and offer to 'digitize' their workflow across the board? Could make big bucks off of that."

Moments of going backward to work on legacy code, scrapping projects and halting, or being blocked and standing in place are also part of the practice of knowing and not knowing characterizing software work. A sixth tactic that I could identify within the Hacker News post suggested "getting blocked": "Pick a role where you're constantly blocked by other people. So, working in a big company, where every function (renting a [virtual machine], setting up a [database] schema) . . . is centralized in one team, possibly overloaded and not too competent . . . These folks can take months to complete simple tasks and you can always say you can't move forward until they deliver." In particular in chapter 5, "Slowdown," I explained that being blocked and kept waiting is not only part of the story of how users engage with software but also how producers of our software become entrenched in a culture of waiting around.

Complexity is also an underlying theme in good-enough software development, and another tactic that the Hacker News engineers identified was to get entangled in complex chaos: "Work in an integration-heavy project. If your codebase calls 8 different systems in your company, they will all fail, have incomplete documentation, unresponsive teams etc. and will result in a lot of waiting and lost time on your end (which is what you're after)." At MiddleTech (or any large software company) we noted that projects get so complex, so intricate, and involve so many layers of code and so many ideas that they stop being understandable. Creating software is always, in some way, about encountering ideas beyond one's capacity, and it demands care and time that do not fit into a speedy mode of production, leaving the developer building merely good-enough software.

As I also discussed in chapter 1, "Welcome to MiddleTech," good-enough corporations are often "anarchic organizations" (Cohen, March, and Olsen 1972) characterized, among other things, by organizational complexity that neither employees nor their managers can fully comprehend. Somewhat related to the anarchic organization is the Hacker News tactic that suggests choosing a large and dysfunctional company: "If the organization is big enough and dysfunctional enough, your absence will not be noticed for long periods of time. Just make sure whenever you are seen you have the appearance of being in a huge rush."

Anarchic organizations, and in particular knowledge organizations like software companies, also feature work that is defined in vague terms. Vagueness was also very ingrained within the work practices of our MiddleTech programmers, with vague, highly subjective methods of estimating the amount of time that a project will take to complete. Vagueness can also be achieved, as another tactic suggested, by gaining expertise in a very "esoteric or depreciated" programming language. With nobody knowing how to control a worker using an outdated language, "you may only be asked to help once a month (or even once a year) but when they need you they really need you, and are willing to pay handsomely." As we recall, particularly in the chapter on how stuff goes wrong, product owners, managers, and programmers give one another, as well as their customers, vague and subjective estimations about how long a software project will take, or what needs to be done to finish a project. These vague estimations are an integral part of how different parties interact in good-enough software cultures.

It is worth noting that the Hacker News comments included tactics that I did not witness at MiddleTech, highlighting other significant tactics that were perhaps more prevalent in other corporate fields. For example, as one Hacker News engineer suggested, making oneself available in an emergency is also key: "Show high effort once in a while: This counts against not making an effort, but people will remember you for fixing things when it matters, and they tolerate you working at your own pace most of the time." Others suggested finding a job based on repetition and then automating this repetition: "If you found a job that required a lot of repetitive manual tasks and you could write a little program or script and automate it (and not tell the company that you did so) you would suddenly find yourself with a lot of free time." Some of these additional tactics help highlight that good enoughness exists beyond MiddleTech and encompasses various practices dependent on the software being made and the way software production is organized. While this book is a focused study of a mid-sized company in Berlin, I have no doubt that programmers and their colleagues in all sorts of tech companies across the globe are practicing these tactics of good enoughness and coming up with more every day.

—*Paula Bialski*
May 1, 2023 (the German Labor Day)

REFERENCES

Abbott, Andrew. 2014. *The System of Professions: An Essay on the Division of Expert Labor*. Chicago: University of Chicago Press.

Abel, Emily K., and Margaret K. Nelson, eds. 1990. *Circles of Care: Work and Identity in Women's Lives*. Albany: State University of New York Press.

Alexander, Neta. 2020. "The Waiting Room: Rethinking Latency after COVID-19." In *Pandemic Media*, edited by Philipp Dominik Keidl, Laliv Melamed, Vinzenz Hediger, and Antonio Somaini, 25–31. Luneburg, Germany: Meson Press.

Allaire, Yvan, and Mihaela E. Firsirotu. 1984. "Theories of Organizational Culture." *Organization Studies* 5, no. 3: 193–226.

Alpert, Avram. 2022. *The Good-Enough Life*. Princeton, NJ: Princeton University Press.

Alvesson, Mats. 2004. *Knowledge Work and Knowledge-Intensive Firms*. Oxford: Oxford University Press.

Ames, Morgan G. 2019. *The Charisma Machine: The Life, Death, and Legacy of One Laptop per Child*. Cambridge, MA: MIT Press.

Amrute, Sareeta. 2016. *Encoding Race, Encoding Class: Indian IT Workers in Berlin*. Durham, NC: Duke University Press.

Anders, Gerhard. 2015. "The Normativity of Numbers in Practice: Technologies of Counting, Accounting and Auditing in Malawi's Civil Service Reform." *Social Anthropology / Anthropologie Sociale* 23, no. 1: 29–41.

Bachmann, Götz. 2014. *Kollegialität: Eine Ethnografie Der Belegschaftskultur Im Kaufhaus* [Collegiality: An ethnography of workplace culture in a department store]. Frankfurt am Main: Campus Verlag.

Barbrook, Richard, and Andy Cameron. 1996. "The Californian Ideology." *Science as Culture* 6, no. 1: 44–72.

Barley, Stephen R. 2005. "What We Know (and Mostly Don't Know) about Technical Work." In *The Oxford Handbook of Work and Organization*, edited by Stephen Ackroyd, Rosemary Batt, and Paul Thompson, 376–403. Oxford: Oxford University Press.

Barley, Stephen R., and Beth A. Bechky. 1994. "In the Backrooms of Science: The Work of Technicians in Science Labs." *Work and Occupations* 21, no. 1: 85–126.

Berlant, Lauren. 1998. "Intimacy: A Special Issue." *Critical Inquiry* 24, no. 2: 281–88.

Beverungen, Armin. 2019. "Executive Dashboard." In *Oxford Handbook of Technology, Media and Organization*, edited by Timon Beyes, Robin Holt, and Claus Pias, 225–37. Oxford: Oxford University Press.

Bietz, Matthew J., Toni Ferro, and Charlotte P. Lee. 2012. "Sustaining the Development of Cyberinfrastructure: An Organization Adapting to Change." In *Proceedings of the ACM 2012 Conference on Computer Supported Cooperative Work*, 901–10. New York: Association for Computing Machinery.

Bijker, Wiebe E., Thomas P. Hughes, and Trevor Pinch. 1989. *The Social Construction of Technological Systems: New Directions in the Sociology and History of Technology*. Cambridge, MA: MIT Press.

Blackburn, Joseph D., Gary D. Scudder, and Luk N. Van Wassenhove. 1996. "Improving Speed and Productivity of Software Development: A Global Survey of Software Developers." *IEEE Transactions on Software Engineering* 22, no. 12: 875–85.

Blunden, Bill. 2003. *Software Exorcism: A Handbook for Debugging and Optimizing Legacy Code*. New York: Apress.

Boenig-Liptsin, Margarita, and J. Benjamin Hurlbut. 2016. "Technologies of Transcendence at Singularity University." In *Perfecting Human Futures*, 239–67. Wiesbaden, Germany: Springer.

Boewe, Jörn, and Johannes Schulten. 2017. *The Long Struggle of the Amazon Employees*. Berlin: Rosa Luxemburg Stiftung.

Boltanski, Luc, and Eve Chiapello. 2018. *The New Spirit of Capitalism*. New Updated ed. London: Verso Books.

Bowker, Geoffrey C., and Susan Leigh Star. 2000. *Sorting Things Out: Classification and Its Consequences*. Cambridge, MA: MIT Press.

Braverman, Harry. 1974. *Labor and Monopoly Capital: The Degradation of Work in the Twentieth Century*. New York: Monthly Review Press.

Brooks, Frederick P., Jr. 1995. *The Mythical Man-Month: Essays on Software Engineering*. Anniversary ed. Boston: Addison Wesley Longman.

Burawoy, Michael. 1982. *Manufacturing Consent: Changes in the Labor Process under Monopoly Capitalism*. Chicago: University of Chicago Press.

Burke, Ronald J., Marina N. Astakhova, and Hongli Hang. 2015. "Work Passion through the Lens of Culture: Harmonious Work Passion, Obsessive Work Passion, and Work Outcomes in Russia and China." *Journal of Business and Psychology* 30, no. 3: 457–71.

Casper, Steven. 2007. *Creating Silicon Valley in Europe: Public Policy towards New Technology Industries*. Oxford: Oxford University Press on Demand.

Certeau, Michel de. 1984. *The Practice of Everyday Life*. Berkeley: University of California Press.

Ceruzzi, Paul E. 2003. *A History of Modern Computing*. Cambridge, MA: MIT Press.

Cervone, H. Frank. 2011. "Understanding Agile Project Management Methods Using Scrum." *OCLC Systems & Services: International Digital Library Perspectives* 27, no. 1: 18–22.

Chandra, Vikram. 2014. *Geek Sublime: The Beauty of Code, the Code of Beauty*. Minneapolis: Graywolf Press.

Chun, Wendy Hui Kyong. 2017. *Updating to Remain the Same: Habitual New Media*. Cambridge, MA: MIT Press.

Clark, Timothy, and Graeme Salaman. 1996. "The Management Guru as Organizational Witchdoctor." *Organization* 3, no. 1: 85–107.

Cohen, Michael D., James G. March, and Johan P. Olsen. 1972. "A Garbage Can Model of Organizational Choice." *Administrative Science Quarterly* 17, no. 1: 1–25.

Coleman, Enid Gabriella. 2012. *Coding Freedom: The Ethics and Aesthetics of Hacking*. Princeton, NJ: Princeton University Press.

———. 2014. *Hacker, Hoaxer, Whistleblower, Spy: The Many Faces of Anonymous*. London: Verso Books.

Collins, W. Robert, Keith W. Miller, Bethany J. Spielman, and Phillip Wherry. 1994. "How Good Is Good Enough? An Ethical Analysis of Software Construction and Use." *Communications of the ACM* 37, no. 1: 81–91.

Cooley, Mike. 1980. "Computerization Taylor's Latest Disguise." *Economic and Industrial Democracy* 1, no. 4: 523–39.

Courpasson, David, Françoise Dany, and Stewart Clegg. 2012. "Resisters at Work: Generating Productive Resistance in the Workplace." *Organization Science* 23, no. 3: 801–19.

Crain, Marion, Winifred Poster, and Miriam Cherry. 2016. *Invisible Labor: Hidden Work in the Contemporary World*. Berkeley: University of California Press.

Cram, David, and Paul Hedley. 2005. "Pronouns and Procedural Meaning: The Relevance of Spaghetti Code and Paranoid Delusion." *Oxford University Working Papers in Linguistics, Philology and Phonetics* 10: 179–210.

Csikszentmihalyi, Mihaly. 1997. *Finding Flow: The Psychology of Engagement with Everyday Life*. New York: Basic Books.

D'Alisa, Giacomo, Federico Demaria, and Giorgos Kallis. 2014. *Degrowth: A Vocabulary for a New Era*. London: Routledge.

Darr, Asaf, and Chris Warhurst. 2008. "Assumptions, Assertions and the Need for Evidence: Debugging Debates about Knowledge Workers." *Current Sociology* 56, no. 1: 25–45.

Darrah, Charles N. 2001. "Techno-missionaries Doing Good at the Center." *Anthropology of Work Review* 22, no. 1: 4–7.

Deal, Terrence E., and Allan A. Kennedy. 1983. "Corporate Cultures: The Rites and Rituals of Corporate Life." *Business Horizons* 26, no. 2: 82–85.

Denis, Jérôme, Alessandro Mongili, and David Pontille. 2016. "Maintenance & Repair in Science and Technology Studies." *TECNOSCIENZA: Italian Journal of Science & Technology Studies* 6, no. 2: 5–16.

Doane, Janice L., and Devon L. Hodges. 1992. *From Klein to Kristeva: Psychoanalytic Feminism and the Search for the "Good Enough" Mother*. Ann Arbor: University of Michigan Press.

Douglass, Bruce Powel. 2015. *Agile Systems Engineering*. Waltham, MA: Morgan Kaufmann.

Downey, Gary Lee. 1998. *The Machine in Me: An Anthropologist Sits among Computer Engineers*. London: Routledge.

du Gay, Paul. 1991. "Enterprise Culture and the Ideology of Excellence." *New Formations* 13, no. 1: 45–61.

Dunbar-Hester, Christina. 2019. *Hacking Diversity: The Politics of Inclusion in Open Technology Cultures*. Princeton, NJ: Princeton University Press.

Dybå, Tore, and Torgeir Dingsøyr. 2008. "Empirical Studies of Agile Software Development: A Systematic Review." *Information and Software Technology* 50, no. 9–10: 833–59.

Edgerton, David. 2008. *The Shock of the Old: Technology and Global History Since 1900*. London: Profile Books.

Engelbart, Douglas C. 1961. "Games That Teach the Fundamentals of Computer Operation." *IRE Transactions on Electronic Computers* EC-10, no. 1: 31–41.

Engels, Franziska, Alexander Wentland, and Sebastian M. Pfotenhauer. 2019. "Testing Future Societies? Developing a Framework for Test Beds and Living Labs as Instruments of Innovation Governance." *Research Policy* 48, no. 9, 103826: 1–11.

Ensmenger, Nathan. 2010. *The Computer Boys Take Over: Computers, Programmers, and the Politics of Technical Expertise*. Cambridge, MA: MIT Press.

———. 2015. "'Beards, Sandals, and Other Signs of Rugged Individualism': Masculine Culture within the Computing Professions." *Osiris* 30, no. 1: 38–65.

Ensmenger, Nathan, and William Aspray. 2002. "Software as Labor Process." In *History of Computing: Software Issues*, edited by Ulf Hashagen, Reinhard Keil-Slawik, and Arthur L. Norberg, 139–65. Heidelberg, Germany: Springer.

Ereiz, Zoran, and Denis Mušić. 2019. "Scrum Without a Scrum Master." Paper presented at the 2019 IEEE International Conference on Computer Science and Educational Informatization (CSEI), Kunming, China, August 16–18. 1

Farman, Jason. 2017. "Repair and Software: Updates, Obsolescence, and Mobile Culture's Operating Systems." *Continent* 6, no. 1: 20–24.

Feathers, Michael. 2004. *Working Effectively with Legacy Code*. Upper Saddle River, NJ: Prentice Hall Professional.

Feyerabend, Paul. 1993. *Against Method*. London: Verso.

Fisher, Ben, and Eran Fisher. 2019. "When Push Comes to Shove: Dynamics of Unionising in the Israeli High-Tech Sector." *Work Organisation, Labour & Globalisation* 13, no. 2: 37–56.

Fisher, Eran, and Ben Fisher. 2019. "Shifting Capitalist Critiques: The Discourse about Unionisation in the Hi-Tech Sector." *Triple C: Communication, Capitalism & Critique. Open Access Journal for a Global Sustainable Information Society* 17, no. 2: 308–26.

Foroohar, Rana. 2021. *Don't Be Evil: The Case Against Big Tech*. New York: Penguin Random House.

Forstie, Clare. 2017. "A New Framing for an Old Sociology of Intimacy." *Sociology Compass* 11, no. 4: e12467.

Forsythe, Diana. 2001. *Studying Those Who Study Us: An Anthropologist in the World of Artificial Intelligence*. Stanford, CA: Stanford University Press.

Fraser, Nancy. 2016. "Contradictions of Capital and Care." *New Left Review* 100, no. 100: 99–117.

Freudendal-Pedersen, Malene, and Sven Kesselring, eds. 2017. *Exploring Networked Urban Mobilities: Theories, Concepts, Ideas*. New York: Routledge.

Gherardi, Silvia. 2009. *Organizational Knowledge: The Texture of Workplace Learning*. Hoboken, NJ: John Wiley & Sons.

Goldstine, Herman Heine, and John von Neumann. 1947. *Planning and Coding of Problems for an Electronic Computing Instrument* 1–3, Part 2. Princeton, NJ: Institute for Advanced Study.

Goodwin, Charles. 1994. "Professional Vision." *American Anthropologist* 96, no. 3: 606–33.

Graeber, David. 2018. *Bullshit Jobs: A Theory*. London: Penguin Random House UK.

Graham, Stephen. 2005. "Software-Sorted Geographies." *Progress in Human Geography* 29, no. 5: 562–80.

Graham, Stephen, and Nigel Thrift. 2007. "Out of Order: Understanding Repair and Maintenance." *Theory, Culture & Society* 24, no. 3: 1–25.

Green, Ben. 2020. *The Smart Enough City: Putting Technology in Its Place to Reclaim Our Urban Future*. Cambridge, MA: MIT Press.

Gregg, Melissa. 2011. *Work's Intimacy*. Cambridge, MA: John Wiley & Sons.

Groth, Stefan. 2019a. "Of Good Averages and Happy Mediums: Orientations towards an Average in Urban Housing." In *The Vulnerable Middle Class? Strategies of Housing in Prospering Cities*, edited by Johannes Moser and Simone Egger, 29–48. Munich: utzverlag GmbH.

———. 2019b. "Wettbewerb Ums Mittelmaß? Kompetitive Orientierungen Im Breitensportlichen Rennradfahren" [Competition for mediocrity? Competitive orientations in recreational racing cycling]. In *Auf Den Spuren Der Konkurrenz. Kultur- Und Sozialwissenschaftliche Perspektiven*, edited by Karin Bürkert, Alexander Engel, Timo Heimerdinger, Markus Tauschek and Tobias Werron, 199–219. Münster: Waxmann Verlag GmbH.

———. 2020a. "Comparison as Reflective and Affective Practice: Orientations towards the Middle in Recreational Road Cycling." *Cultural Analysis* 18, no. 1: 63–75.

———. 2020b. "Mitte und Mittelmass: zwischen privilegierter Gleichheit und kompetitiver Differenz" [The middle and mediocrity: between privileged equality and competitive difference]. *Bulletin Schweizerische Akademie der Geistes-und Sozialwissenschaften (SAGW)* 1: 45–47.

Groth, Stefan, Karl Braun, Johannes Moser, and Christian Schönholz. 2019. *Zwischen Ermöglichung und Begrenzung: Zur subjektiven Plausibilisierung des Mittelmaßes als normative Orientierung* [Between enabling and limiting: On the subjective plausibility of mediocrity as a normative orientation]. Marburg, Germany: MakuFEE.

Gürses, Seda, and Joris Van Hoboken. 2017. "Privacy after the Agile Turn." In *Cambridge Handbook of Consumer Privacy*, edited by Jules Polonetsky, Omer Tene, and Evan Selinger, 579–601. Cambridge: Cambridge University Press.

Haigh, Thomas, and Mark Priestley. "Innovators Assemble: Ada Lovelace, Walter Isaacson, and the Superheroines of Computing." *Communications of the ACM* 58, no. 9 (2015): 20–27.

Halpern, Orit, and Robert Mitchell. 2023. *The Smartness Mandate*. Cambridge, MA: MIT Press.

Hasse, Raimund, and Eva Passarge. 2015. "Silicon Valley und sonst nichts Neues? Biotechnologie in der Schweiz als Beispiel für neue Organisationsformen und deren Legitimierun" [Silicon Valley and nothing new anywhere else? Biotechnology in Switzerland as an example of new organizational forms and their legitimation]. *Zeitschrift für Soziologie* 44, no. 1: 6–21.

Highsmith, James A. 2013. *Adaptive Software Development: A Collaborative Approach to Managing Complex Systems*. New York: Dorset House Publishing.

Hochschild, Arlie Russell. 1983. *The Managed Heart: Commercialization of Human Feeling*. Berkeley: University of California Press.

Ingold, Tim. 2002. *The Perception of the Environment: Essays on Livelihood, Dwelling and Skill*. London: Routledge.

Irani, Lilly. 2019. *Chasing Innovation: Making Entrepreneurial Citizens in Modern India*. Princeton, NJ: Princeton University Press.

Jackson, Steven J. 2014. "Rethinking Repair." *Media Technologies: Essays on Communication, Materiality, and Society*: 221–39.

Jamieson, Lynn. 1988. *Intimacy: Personal Relationships in Modern Societies*. Cambridge, MA: Polity Press.

Jasanoff, Sheila, and Sang-Hyun Kim. 2015. *Dreamscapes of Modernity: Sociotechnical Imaginaries and the Fabrication of Power*. Chicago: University of Chicago Press.

Johnson, Eleanor K. 2022. "The Costs of Care: An Ethnography of Care Work in Residential Homes for Older People." *Sociology of Health & Illness* 45, no 1: 54–69.

Kaldrack, Irina, and Martina Leeker. 2015. "Introduction." In *There Is No Software, There Are Just Services*, edited by Irina Kaldrack and Martina Leeker, 9–19. Luneburg, Germany: Meson Press.

Kameo, Nahoko. 2017. "A Culture of Uncertainty: Interaction and Organizational Memory in Software Engineering Teams under a Productivity Scheme." *Organization Studies* 38, no. 6: 733–52. https://doi.org/10.1177/0170840616685357. https://journals.sagepub.com/doi/abs/10.1177/0170840616685357.

Kelty, Christopher M. 2008. *Two Bits: The Cultural Significance of Free Software*. Durham, NC: Duke University Press.

———. 2019. *The Participant*. Chicago: University of Chicago Press.

Kelty, Christopher, and Seth Erickson. 2015. "The Durability of Software." In *There Is No Software, There Are Only Services*, edited by Irina Kaldrack and Martina Leeker, 39–56. Luneburg, Germany: Meson Press.

Kidder, Tracy. 1981. *The Soul of a New Machine*. New York: Penguin Books.

Kirchner, Jens, Pascal R. Kremp, and Michael Magotsch. 2010. *Key Aspects of German Employment and Labour Law*. Berlin: Springer.

Knorr-Cetina, Karin. 1997. "Sociality with Objects: Social Relations in Postsocial Knowledge Societies." *Theory, Culture & Society* 14, no. 4: 1–30.

Korczynski, Marek, and Andreas Wittel. 2020. "The Workplace Commons: Towards Understanding Commoning within Work Relations." *Sociology* 54, no. 4: 711–26.

Kraft, Philip. 1979. "The Routinizing of Computer Programming." *Sociology of Work and Occupations* 6, no. 2: 139–55.

Kunda, Gideon. 1992. *Engineering Culture: Control and Commitment in a High-Tech Corporation*. Philadelphia: Temple University Press.

———. 2009. *Engineering Culture: Control and Commitment in a High-Tech Corporation*. Pennsylvania: Temple University Press.

Lafargue, Paul. 1883. *The Right to Be Lazy*. Auckland, New Zealand: Floating Press. http://theanarchistlibrary.org/library/paul-lafargue-the-right-to-be-lazy.

Larson, Selena. 2017. "Why Do Hackers Always Wear Hoodies? Behind the Stereotype." *CNN Business*, May 26.

Latour, Bruno. 1990. "Technology Is Society Made Durable." Supplement, *The Sociological Review* 38, no. 1: 103–31.

———. 2005. *Reassembling the Social: An Introduction to Actor-Network-Theory*. Oxford: Oxford University Press.

———. 2013. *An Enquiry into the Modes of Existence: An Anthropology of the Moderns*. Cambridge, MA: Harvard University Press.

Law, John, and Annemarie Mol. 1995. "Notes on Materiality and Sociality." *The Sociological Review* 43, no. 2: 274–94.

Leavitt Cohn, Marisa. 2016. "Convivial Decay: Entangled Lifetimes in a Geriatric Infrastructure." In *Proceedings of the 19th ACM Conference on Computer-Supported Cooperative Work & Social Computing*, 1511–23. San Francisco: ACM Digital Library.

———. 2019. "Keeping Software Present: Software as a Timely Object for STS Studies of the Digital." In *DigitalSTS: A Field Guide for Science & Technology Studies*, edited by Janet Vertesi and David Ribes, 423–45. Princeton, NJ: Princeton University Press.

Leveson, Nancy G. 2016. *Engineering a Safer World: Systems Thinking Applied to Safety*. Cambridge, MA: MIT Press.

Levy, Karen. 2022. *Data Driven: Truckers, Technology, and the New Workplace Surveillance*. Princeton, NJ: Princeton University Press.

Levy, Karen E. C. 2016. "Digital Surveillance in the Hypermasculine Workplace." *Feminist Media Studies* 16, no. 2: 361–65. https://doi.org/10.1080/14680777.2016.1138607.

Lin, Allen Yilun, Kate Kuehl, Johannes Schöning, and Brent Hecht. 2017. "Understanding 'Death by GPS': A Systematic Study of Catastrophic Incidents Associated with Personal Navigation Technologies." In *Proceedings of the 2017 CHI Conference on Human Factors in Computing Systems*, 1154–66. Denver, CO: ACM Digital Library. https://doi.org/10.1145/3025453.3025737.

Lupton, Deborah. 2014. *Digital Sociology*. London: Routledge.

Lynd, Robert Staughton, and Helen Merrell Lynd. 1929. *Middletown: A Study in Contemporary American Culture*. New York: Harcourt, Brace.

Mackenzie, Adrian. 2006. *Cutting Code: Software and Sociality*. Vol. 30, Digital Formations. Frankfurt am Main: Peter Lang.

———. 2017. *Machine Learners: Archaeology of a Data Practice*. Cambridge, MA: MIT Press.

MacKenzie, Donald, and Judy Wajcman, eds. 1985. *The Social Shaping of Technology: How the Refrigerator Got Its Hum*. Milton Keynes, England: Open University Press.

Mahanti, Aniket. 2006. "Challenges in Enterprise Adoption of Agile Methods—A Survey." *Journal of Computing and Information Technology* 14, no. 3: 197–206.

Malaby, Thomas M. 2009. *Making Virtual Worlds: Linden Lab and Second Life*. Ithaca, NY: Cornell University Press.

Marx, Karl. 1867. *Das Kapital. Kritik der politischen Ökonomie* [Capital: A critique of political economy]. Buch 1, *Der Produktionsprocess des Kapitals* [Book 1, The production process of capital]. Hamburg: Otto Meissner.

———. 1990. *Capital*. London: Penguin Classics.

Mattern, Shannon. 2018. "Maintenance and Care." *Places Journal*, November. https://doi.org/10.22269/181120.

McGaughey, Ewan. 2016. "The Codetermination Bargains: The History of German Corporate and Labor Law." *Columbia Journal of European Law* 23: 135–76.

McKenzie, Jordan. 2016. "Happiness vs Contentment? A Case for a Sociology of the Good Life." *Journal for the Theory of Social Behaviour* 46, no. 3: 252–67.

Meadows, Donella H., Dennis L. Meadows, Jorgen Randers, and William W. Behrens. 1972. *The Limits to Growth: A Report for the Club of Rome's Project on the Predicament of Mankind.* New York: Universe Books.

Milo, Daniel S. 2019. *Good Enough: The Tolerance for Mediocrity in Nature and Society.* Cambridge, MA: Harvard University Press.

Mitropoulos, Angela. 2012. "The Time of the Contract: Insurance, Contingency, and the Arrangement of Risk." *South Atlantic Quarterly* 111, no. 4: 763–81.

Morozov, Evgeny. 2013. *To Save Everything, Click Here: The Folly of Technological Solutionism.* New York: Public Affairs.

Noble, David Franklin. 2011. *Forces of Production: A Social History of Industrial Automation.* London: Routledge.

O'Donnell, Casey. 2014. *Developer's Dilemma: The Secret World of Videogame Creators.* Cambridge, MA: MIT Press.

O'Mara, Margaret. 2019. *The Code: Silicon Valley and the Remaking of America.* New York: Penguin.

Parmiggiani, Elena, Thomas Østerlie, and Petter Grytten Almklov. 2022. "In the Backrooms of Data Science." *Journal of the Association for Information Systems* 23, no. 1: 139–64.

Paulsen, Roland. 2015. "Non-work at Work: Resistance or What?" *Organization* 22, no. 3: 351–67.

Pelizza, Annalisa, and Rob Hoppe. 2018. "Birth of a Failure: Consequences of Framing ICT Projects for the Centralization of Inter-departmental Relations." *Administration & Society*, no. 50 (1): 101–30.

Peters, Thomas J., and Robert H. Waterman. 1982. *In Search of Excellence: Lessons from America's Best-Run Companies.* New York: Harper & Row.

Pettigrew, Andrew M., and Evelyn M. Fenton. 2000. *The Innovating Organization.* London: Sage.

Pfotenhauer, Sebastian, and Sheila Jasanoff. 2017a. "Panacea or Diagnosis? Imaginaries of Innovation and the 'MIT Model' in Three Political Cultures." *Social Studies of Science* 47, no. 6: 783–810. https://doi.org/10.1177/0306312717706110. https://journals.sagepub.com/doi/abs/10.1177/0306312717706110.

———. 2017b. "Traveling Imaginaries: The 'Practice Turn' in Innovation Policy and the Global Circulation of Innovation Models." In *The Routledge Handbook of the Political Economy of Science*, 416–28. London: Routledge.

Pinch, Trevor. 2010. "The Invisible Technologies of Goffman's Sociology from the Merry-Go-Round to the Internet." *Technology and Culture* 51, no. 2: 409–24.

Porter, Theodore M. 1995. *Trust in Numbers: The Pursuit of Objectivity in Science and Public Life.* Princeton, NJ: Princeton University Press.

Posner, Miriam. 2022. "Agile and the Long Crisis of Software." *Logic Magazine* no. 16. https://logicmag.io/clouds/agile-and-the-long-crisis-of-software/.

Ratnapalan, Savithiri, and Helen Batty. 2009. "To Be Good Enough." *Canadian Family Physician* 55, no. 3: 239–40.

Reckwitz, Andreas. 2017. *The Invention of Creativity: Modern Society and the Culture of the New.* Cambridge, MA: Polity Press.

Reed, Michael I. 1996. "Expert Power and Control in Late Modernity: An Empirical Review and Theoretical Synthesis." *Organization Studies* 17, no. 4: 573–97.

Rising, Linda, and Norman S. Janoff. 2000. "The Scrum Software Development Process for Small Teams." *IEEE Software* 17, no. 4: 26–32.

Roberts, Lissa, Simon Schaffer, and Peter Dear, eds. 2007. *The Mindful Hand, History of Science and Scholarship in the Netherlands.* Amsterdam: Edita Knaw.

Rosa, Hartmut. 2013. *Social Acceleration: A New Theory of Modernity*. New York: Columbia University Press.

Ross, Andrew. 2004. *No-Collar: The Humane Workplace and Its Hidden Costs*. New York: Temple University Press.

Rousseau, Denise. 1995. *Psychological Contracts in Organizations: Understanding Written and Unwritten Agreements*. Thousand Oaks, CA: Sage Publications.

Russell, Andrew L., and Lee Vinsel. 2016. "Hail the Maintainers." *Aeon Online*. https://aeon.co /essays/innovation-is-overvalued-maintenance-often-matters-more.

———. 2020. *The Innovation Delusion: How Our Obsession with the New Has Disrupted the Work That Matters Most*. New York: Currency/Random House.

Russell, Bertrand. 1935. *In Praise of Idleness*. London: George Allen & Unwin Ltd.

Russell, Stewart. 1986. "The Social Construction of Artefacts: A Response to Pinch and Bijker." *Social Studies of Science* 16, no. 2: 331–46.

Salecl, Renata. 2011. *The Tyranny of Choice*. London: Profile Books.

Schaffer, Simon. 1994. "In the Know." *London Review of Books* 16, no. 21 (November 10): 17–18.

Schimroszik, Nadine. 2015. *Silicon Valley in Berlin: Erfolge und Stolpersteine für Start-ups* [The Silicon Valley in Berlin: Success and a steppingstone for start-ups]. Konstanz, Germany: UVK Verlag.

Schwaber, Ken, and Mike Beedle. 2008. *Agile Software Development with Scrum*. Upper Saddle River, NJ: Pearson Prentice Hall.

Sennett, Richard. 2008. *The Craftsman*. New Haven, CT: Yale University Press.

Serlin, Ronald C., and Daniel K. Lapsley. 1985. "Rationality in Psychological Research: The Good-Enough Principle." *The American Psychologist* 40, no. 1: 73–83.

Sheller, Mimi, and John Urry. 2006. "The New Mobilities Paradigm." *Environment and Planning A* 38, no. 2: 207–26.

Simon, Herbert A. 1956. "Rational Choice and the Structure of the Environment." *Psychological Review* 63, no. 2: 129–38.

Star, Susan Leigh. 1999. "The Ethnography of Infrastructure." *American Behavioral Scientist* 43, no. 3: 377–91.

Stolzoff, Simone. 2023. *The Good Enough Job*. New York: Portfolio/Penguin Random House.

Suchman, Lucy A. 1987. *Plans and Situated Actions: The Problem of Human-Machine Communication*. Cambridge, MA: Cambridge University Press.

———. 2007. *Human-Machine Reconfigurations: Plans and Situated Actions*. Cambridge, MA: Cambridge University Press.

Sutton, Robert I., and Hayagreeva Rao. 2014. *Scaling Up Excellence: Getting to More Without Settling for Less*. New York: Crown Business.

Taylor, Claire, and Tony Dobbins. 2021. "Social Media: A (New) Contested Terrain between Sousveillance and Surveillance in the Digital Workplace." *New Technology, Work and Employment* 36, no. 3: 263–84.

Thompson, Clive. 2019. *Coders: Who They Are, What They Think and How They Are Changing Our World*. London: Picador.

Turk, Dan, Robert France, and Bernhard Rumpe. 2002. "Limitations of Agile Software Processes." Third International Conference on eXtreme Programming and Agile Processes in Software Engineering, Alghero, Italy, May 26–30, 43–46.

Turkle, Sherry. 1984. *The Second Self: Computers and the Human Spirit*. New York: Simon & Schuster.

———. 2005. *The Second Self: Computers and the Human Spirit*. Cambridge, MA: MIT Press.

Turner, Fred. 2009. "Burning Man at Google: A Cultural Infrastructure for New Media Production." *New Media & Society* 11, no. 1–2: 73–94.

Ullman, Ellen. 1997. *Close to the Machine: Technophilia and Its Discontents*. San Francisco: City Lights Books.

Veblen, Thorstein. 1921. *The Engineers and the Price System*. New York: BW Huebsch.

Vinsel, Lee, and Andrew L. Russell. 2018. "After Innovation, Turn to Maintenance." *Technology and Culture* 59, no. 1: 1–25.

———. 2020. *The Innovation Delusion: How Our Obsession with the New Has Disrupted the Work That Matters Most*. New York: Penguin Random House.

Visaggio, Giuseppe. 2001. "Ageing of a Data-Intensive Legacy System: Symptoms and Remedies." *Journal of Software Maintenance and Evolution: Research and Practice* 13, no. 5: 281–308.

Vogel, Else. 2021. "Juxtaposition: Differences That Matter." In *Experimenting with Ethnography: A Companion to Analysis*, edited by Andrea Ballestero and Brit Ross Winthereik, 53–65. Durham, NC: Duke University Press.

Wajcman, Judy. 2014. *Pressed for Time*. Chicago: University of Chicago Press.

Wajcman, Judy, and Nigel Dodd, eds. 2017. *The Sociology of Speed: Digital, Organizational, and Social Temporalities*. Oxford: Oxford University Press.

Webster, Frank, and Kevin Robins. 1993. "'I'll Be Watching You': Comment on Sewell and Wilkinson." *Sociology* 27, no. 2: 243–52.

Weiss, Manfred, and Marlene Schmidt. 2008. *Labour Law and Industrial Relations in Germany*. Austin, TX: Wolters Kluwer.

Weizenbaum, Joseph. 1976. *Computer Power and Human Reason: From Judgment to Calculation*. San Francisco: W. H. Freeman.

Wiener, Anna. 2020. *Uncanny Valley: A Memoir*. New York: MCD Books.

Willmott, Hugh. 1993. "Strength Is Ignorance; Slavery Is Freedom: Managing Culture in Modern Organizations." *Journal of Management Studies* 30, no. 4: 515–52.

Winner, Langdon. 1993. "Upon Opening the Black Box and Finding It Empty: Social Constructivism and the Philosophy of Technology." *Science, Technology, & Human Values* 18, no. 3: 362–78.

Winnicott, Donald W. 1987. *Babies and Their Mothers*. Edited by Clare Winnicott, Ray Shepherd and Madeleine Davis. Reading, MA: Addison-Wesley Publishing Company.

Wittel, Andreas. 1997. *Belegschaftskultur Im Schatten Der Firmenideologie. Eine Ethnographische Studie* [Workplace culture in the shadow of company ideology]. Berlin: Edition Stigma.

Woodworth, Warner, and Reed Nelson. 1979. "Witch Doctors, Messianics, Sorcerers, and OD Consultants: Parallels and Paradigms." *Organizational Dynamics* 8, no. 2: 17–33.

Yourdon, Edward. 1995. "When Good Enough Software Is Best." *IEEE Software* 12, no. 3: 79–81.

Zelizer, Viviana A. 2005. *The Purchase of Intimacy*. Princeton, NJ: Princeton University Press.

Zuboff, Shoshana. 1988. *In the Age of the Smart Machine: The Future of Work and Power*. New York: Basic Books, Inc.

INDEX

Note: Page numbers followed by an 'f' refer to figures.
Page numbers followed by an 'n' refer to notes.

A NOTE ON THE TYPE

This book has been composed in Adobe Text and Gotham.
Adobe Text, designed by Robert Slimbach for Adobe,
bridges the gap between fifteenth- and sixteenth-century
calligraphic and eighteenth-century Modern styles.
Gotham, inspired by New York street signs, was designed
by Tobias Frere-Jones for Hoefler & Co.